HOW TO CREATE YOUR OWN REALITY
AND ALTER YOUR DNA

FRANK McKINNEY

Caring House
BOOKS
FLORIDA

For permissions requests, speaking inquiries, and bulk order purchase options, e-mail pamela@frank-mckinney.com.

Caring House Books
P.O. Box 388, Boynton Beach, Florida 33425

ISBN: 978-1-7362376-1-8

1st edition, November 2021
Printed in the United States of America

Cover design: Erik Hollander
Interior design: Robert Mott for RobertMottDesigns.com
Author photo: Nilsa McKinney

is dedicated to those who read all the way

to the final two words in this book: new life.

You now have the power, understanding, and knowledge

to create your own reality and alter your DNA.

Now, go do it!

CONTENTS

Introduction

"You gotta kill the person you were
born to be in order to become
the person you want to be."

FROM THE FILM *ROCKETMAN*

Despite all the usual naysayers and pundits telling me I was crazy to try to sell a multimillion-dollar mansion during a global pandemic, I did it: I sold my final masterpiece, a direct oceanfront home at 3492 South Ocean in South Palm Beach, Florida. The property boasts spectacular elements, including a spherical jellyfish tank in the living room, kitchen countertops made of eleven-thousand-year-old azure-blue lava from France, and stunning ocean views from the 110 linear feet of floor-to-twelve-foot-ceiling glass, and the cherry on top—a rooftop lounge perched forty-two feet above the sea. This one-of-a-kind estate sold for more than $12 million and at a record price per square foot for Palm Beach County.

In typical fashion (well, typical for me—after all, the *Wall Street Journal* called me the "Real Estate Rock Czar"), I'd unveiled the property at a drama-filled, Vegas-style event. I'd rappelled down from a helicopter while it struggled to hover precariously, one hundred feet above the Atlantic Ocean in near-gale-force winds, onto the third-story rooftop—and then ignited a choreographed pyrotechnic display that serpentined around all three levels of the most beautiful oceanfront creation of my career. Noting my nearly thirty years of building and selling multimillion-dollar homes on spec, the *Palm Beach Post* remarked in a cover feature about the unveiling, "The showman hasn't lost his touch."

Ten weeks after the sale, on September 9, 2020, I said goodbye for a while to my own, much more modest home in South Florida. I left my oceanfront treehouse office, kissed my wife, and climbed into my 1988 Yugo (115,000 miles on the odometer, a 61-horsepower engine, 0 to 60 in *never*) for a trip across the United States. Though I'd never loved what I did more, or been better at it than with the 3492 South Ocean property, I believe that a Renaissance man or woman shifts passion at the peak of his or her life. So it was time to redirect my passion into yet another new, exciting direction. That's why I left Delray Beach to spend twenty-three days in my thirty-three-year-old Yugo that has the dubious honor of being considered one of the worst cars ever made. There are less than two hundred of these beauties remaining, and they can rattle up to sixty miles per hour . . . downhill. But only with a good tailwind.

My plan? Wrap the car to look as if it had been rusting in a barn for thirty years. Point it west and keep driving until I hit Death Valley, California, stopping at twenty-two cities in between. Then turn around and drive back. Along the 6,288-mile odyssey that I called the "Yugo We-go Tour," I would interview people at churches, homeless shelters, cemeteries, soup kitchens, funerals, political rallies, schools, public parks, and hospitals, all with one intention: to see and come to deeply understand their challenges, and to discover the mindset they needed, not just to overcome whatever they were facing daily, but instead to *completely transform their reality.*

. . . .

I've been a lifelong believer in personal growth/development. (To tell the truth, leaving my fourth high school in four years with a 1.8 GPA and seven stints in juvenile detention left me no alternative but to grow.) Over the past thirty-plus years, I've focused on pushing the envelope professionally as well as personally. I've built forty-four mansions on spec (meaning I put up all the money and assumed all the financial risks) and sold them all with an average price of $14 million while setting ever-higher standards for luxury and artistry with each new oceanfront property. I became one of the best in the world at what I do, if not the best, and that success never would have occurred without proactively pursuing explosive growth.

Growth has been a driver in other areas, as well. I have run the Badwater® 135-mile ultramarathon in Death Valley, California ("the world's toughest footrace" according to *National Geographic*) twelve times and finished it seven times. I've written seven bestselling books in six different genres. Our Caring House Project Foundation has built twenty-nine self-sustaining villages in the poorest country in the Western Hemisphere, Haiti, providing over thirteen thousand children and their families with new concrete homes, clean water, schools, clinics, churches, community centers, and the means to grow renewable food and earn an above-average income. And, oh yes, I've managed to stay married to my guardian angel, Nilsa, for thirty-one years, and together we've raised our incredible daughter, Laura.

Sounds like I've got myself together, right? Not even close . . .

Unfortunately, over those same three decades, I've allowed my mono-maniacal focus to negatively affect my health, my mindset, my marriage, my friendships, and my business. I have a serious addiction to excitement and adrenaline (see the prior description of the house unveiling), along with a disdain for rules—almost all rules. For example, on one of my first dates with Nilsa thirty-four years ago I had to ask her to come to the local jail to bail me out: I'd been arrested for fleeing and attempting to elude a police officer while speeding in my Lotus Turbo Esprit, for driving with a suspended driver's license, and as a habitual traffic offender. Not proud of that.

Some of my past employees also said that I'm a difficult boss with little patience or tolerance for people with standards that I perceive are lower than mine. And don't get me started on what it's like to live with me. There's a reason I call Nilsa my guardian angel: she has to be an angel to put up with my love affair with extremes.

A few years ago, I *finally* started going to a therapist, Dr. Jan Ganesh, who diagnosed my adrenaline addiction and helped me understand myself a whole lot better. I think I wore her out! But in 2020, I pushed the envelope into a new, volatile phase of personal growth. It started with spending thirty days isolated from family, friends, and anything familiar, in what I called a "retreat, rehab, and separation." Nothing about it was traditional, but it was extremely challenging and, at times, exceedingly painful. It involved three forms of daily journaling, spiritual and psychological advisors, seclusion, and living somewhere unfamiliar yet keeping with my day-to-day involvements. I underwent immediate (not gradual) elimination of all forms of toxicity. Withdrawals? Yes. Success? You bet—because I believe that retreat (and the Yugo We-go Tour) presented yet another opportunity to alter the direction and trajectory of my life.

As philosopher Alan Watts wrote, "The moment you set your foot on the path of liberation, you are apt to find that all your karmic creditors will come to your door." That means as soon as you start pursuing growth intensely, anything that gets in the way will show up for you to deal with immediately. In March 2020, I came down with a life-threatening illness/condition (not COVID-19) that caused me to lose twenty pounds in one month and made me so weak that Nilsa had to help me walk the twenty feet from our bed to the bathroom. It was months before I had the strength to start running again, and even then it took me thirty-three minutes and twenty-seven seconds to go a half-mile. In many ways this near-fatal illness (yes, I really could have died) was a gift, however, because it proved that it was time for me to focus on rebuilding myself from the ground up. What had worked for thirty years and gotten me to the pinnacle of personal and professional success was no longer enough. Even reinvention, re-creation, and renewal were not going to cut it. Instead, it was time to transform myself (again) at the most fundamental level, even down to my DNA.

That's the reason I found myself in my 1988 Yugo in September 2020: I was driving away from my identity, what I'm known for and what had given me purpose my entire adult life. It was time to discover whether all the thoughts, theses, and ideas I'd been having about how human beings transform their lives were true. And to do this, I needed to put into practice one of my core beliefs: *When you spend time in the insurmountable, incom-*

prehensible, and impossible, the rational brain surrenders, giving birth to an entirely new reality; an intoxicating, irrational, and fantastical one beyond anything you could have planned. I firmly believed that a new reality—as insurmountable, incomprehensible, and impossible as it might be—was out there. And I was determined to experience it.

I know it's possible to create a new reality because I've done it on more than one occasion in my life, like when I left behind my family and friends in Indiana, with their expectations that I would follow in the footsteps of two generations of bankers. More important, I believe that *all of us have the capability of building the reality we want at any time.* No one's life path is fixed. We can change our path at any moment. In fact, we can change our very DNA at any moment in time, simply by choosing something new to *aspire* to.

And that, in short, is why I wrote this book.

The idea is simple. I believe anyone can make a change in the moment if they're motivated, but that's about as long as the change lasts: a moment. Some people may be inspired to do something new only to go back to the same old same old as soon as things get the least bit difficult or mundane (read attention span). But other people find within themselves the aspiration to become new and different at the cellular level—in other words, to transform their very DNA. When that happens, you can create your own reality no matter what's happening in the world outside.

Here's the good news: creating your own reality isn't complicated, and you don't have to be perfect to do it. In fact, I believe that our scars, failures, and shortcomings are the rocket fuel that propels transformation. My life is far from perfect, and I'm not an authority on mindset, God knows. Yet I've managed to accomplish quite a bit over the years by working harder *and* smarter, with healthy doses of hard knocks and failure, and always with the aspiration to be better today than I was the day before. Now after nearly forty years, it's time to share how aspiration has helped me—and others—to transform.

This book is divided into five sections representing the five areas I be-lieve are essential for anyone who wants to live a life of meaning and impact, to create their own reality and alter their DNA:

- How to focus your mind on the thoughts, beliefs, and aspirations that will exponentially expand your growth

- How to overcome the fear that everybody faces when they're taking a risk to pursue something significant

- How to transform your professional life by amplifying your essence and using it to create a personal brand

- How to appreciate, honor, and enjoy your relationships, especially with your significant other (and yes, this includes lots of mind-blowing sex)

- How to uplift others, and ultimately, the world, through the dovetailing of your professional and spiritual highest calling.

Each section and chapter are short, because not only do I believe in getting to the point, but also I want you to enjoy the process of transformation. While I am sure every word I've written will benefit you, don't feel you need to do everything in this book. Instead, grab on to the handful of things that you aspire to emulate or become, based on the legacy you want to leave, and put those things into practice—daily. Don't feel as if the only way to read this book is all at once, either. The chapters complement and build on one another, but there is also intentional repetition. That's both to reinforce key ideas and also to ensure that any time you come back to this book, a chapter can be useful to you on its own.

I hope you'll keep *Aspire!* handy so you can use some of its ideas whenever you need to renew or refresh again, whether it's by force (a global pandemic, an economic downturn, a breakup or divorce, etc.) or by choice, and whenever you're at the height of your profession or relationship. I know that some of the stories in this book may be perceived as pretty out there. ("Go big or go broke" is one of my own mantras.) But let me assure you that *anything* you do to take your life in a different direction can have a lasting impact. And anything you do to change your reality can have a lasting impact on others, too. I saw that every day during the twenty-two-city, 6,288-mile Yugo We-go Tour, where I met people across the United States who were happy to share the legacy they wanted to leave, help a complete stranger, and tell their stories of the "angels" they had met during their lives.

I called it the Yugo We-go Tour because I believe that as you go, we all go. I hope this book will help you not just transform your life but help you help others to do the same. After all, you have as many scars as I do, and if I was able to create my own reality, so can you. Let's do it! Let's change our DNA and leave a lasting impact on the world.

Aspire!

The DNA
Difference Between
Motivation,
Inspiration, and
Aspiration

The DNA Difference Between Motivation, Inspiration, and Aspiration

The world as we have created it is a process of our thinking. It cannot be changed without changing our thinking.

ALBERT EINSTEIN

've always been attracted to extremes (an adrenaline addiction will do that to you), so it shouldn't come as a surprise that for our family vacation in the summer of 2004, we chose (or really, I did) to go to Death Valley, California, the hottest place on the planet, with a recorded temperature of 134 degrees on July 10, 1913. Upon our arrival, I was fascinated, if not intoxicated, by the intense heat, so I decided to quickly put on my running clothes and head out for my regular six-mile run, only to find myself light-headed, delirious, and ready to pass out after only three miles. I slowed to a walk, then to a crawl, before luckily spotting a general store a few yards ahead in Furnace Creek (one of the few towns/hotels in Death Valley National Park).

Suffering from severe heat exhaustion and on the brink of heat stroke, I staggered through the doors, grabbed a banana and the biggest bottle of Gatorade they had, and went up to the counter to pay. The clerk, looking very much like an old 49er prospector with his scruffy grey beard and thin, round-rimmed spectacles, took one look at me in my running gear, sweating and dehydrated, and said, "You'd better get back out there, son. If you don't get going, you're never gonna make the time cutoff!"

He had mistaken me for a Badwater ultramarathon competitor, apparently in last place. Who else would be crazy enough to run in 120-degree-plus heat in Death Valley in July?

That was the first time I heard the word *Badwater* and learned of the annual 135-mile footrace that's known as the ultimate test of a runner's physical, mental, and emotional endurance. Since 1981, the race course has started at a point 282 feet below sea level (the lowest elevation in North America). It traverses three mountain ranges and finishes on Mount Whitney, the tallest mountain in the contiguous United States. Only one hundred qualified runners from around the world are invited to compete in any given year, and they must finish in 48 hours or less, running pretty much nonstop for the entire 135 miles. Temperatures at race time can exceed 130 degrees Fahrenheit, and heat on the race course's blacktop pavement has registered at over 200 degrees. Runners' shoes have been known to melt during the race; renal failure, heat stroke, muscle cramps, and hallucinations are commonplace. Each year, twenty to thirty percent of these elite runners drop out or fail to finish in the allotted time. It truly is the toughest footrace in the world.

Beginning on that fateful day in 2004, for me Badwater became more than a goal and more than an obsession. It became an *aspiration*, one that would drive me to compete in the race for the first time in 2005 and twelve times in fifteen years. It would mean training nearly year-round, running thousands of miles in every kind of weather, setting up a treadmill in my sauna and pushing myself to the point of passing out to acclimate to the dry heat of the desert. Five times I've had to drop out of the race due to heart problems (arrhythmia), severe dehydration, ruptured tendon, mental breakdown, or feet so covered with blood and blisters that I could no longer run. But I'm prouder of the seven Badwater buckles I've earned for finishing the race than I am of some of the multimillion-dollar properties I've created.

The intense effort required by Badwater has done far more than transform my physical body. It has radically altered my reality down to the cellular level of my DNA. Aspiration will do that for you. And that's why it's vastly different from motivation or inspiration.

Aspiration = Otherworldly Desire

There's an entire industry built around motivation—speakers, seminars, books, images that feature beautiful pictures and literary phrases, and so on. But how many of us are *motivated* to start exercising or saving or studying or building a business, only to see our motivation disappear, washing off like soap in the shower? And then we feel terrible that we failed to follow through . . . again.

Or maybe a good movie, book, or someone's example has *inspired* us to lose weight or get our finances in order or be an entrepreneur or pursue a romantic relationship. But after a week or two, we find ourselves back where we started, looking for another inspiration to get us going.

Face it: all of us have been caught in the motivation/inspiration cycle that ends up taking us nowhere. That's because motivation and inspiration just aren't deep enough. They don't tap into what *really* drives us. And as a result, they won't come close to keeping us going over the long term. For that, we must have the kind of desire and drive that's created only by *aspiration:* **an almost otherworldly desire to achieve something high or great.**

The bottom line is this: Motivation washes off and goes down the drain with the soap. Inspiration lasts about as long as a bad sunburn. But **aspiration will forever alter your DNA and allow you to create your own reality, forever changing your life and the lives of those you love.**

Let me use Badwater as an example. I know the commitment it takes to prepare to run the Badwater race. But am I *motivated* to get up nearly every morning at 3 A.M. when it's time to run twenty miles? No. Am I *inspired* to deny myself many of the foods that I enjoy and eat a special diet day after day? Heck no. Bake in a 150-degree sauna while running on a treadmill for hours on end? Nope. And rather than relaxing with my wife, Nilsa, spending my Friday nights hiding water bottles filled with a special caloric drink every five miles of my running route, so I can keep my energy up on the more than thirty-mile run that begins at 2 A.M. on Saturdays? Not in a million years. Only my *aspiration* to finish Badwater keeps me going.

And here's another example. For my project at 3492 South Ocean, am I *motivated* to visit the job site every day for eighteen months and hear the myriad problems encountered in the last twenty-four hours? No again. Am I *inspired* to continue to find new and never-before-seen finishes when almost everyone around me tells me it can't be done? Again: heck no. And finally, having to play glorified babysitter as I hear from subcontractor after subcontractor why they can't perform on time, within budget or to my standard of quality? Not really. Only my *aspiration* to express my real estate artistry by creating a magnum opus, with an intoxicating appeal and a sensory assault which has yet to be experienced, keeps me going. While I might lose motivation and inspiration, the aspiration is sacred.

By the way, I'm not saying you shouldn't be motivated or inspired. I use both of these qualities to *ignite* aspiration. But if you only feel motivated or inspired reading this book, I've failed. I want to call you to something higher.

Now, I hope you're beginning to think, "Whew! I'll never beat myself up again for not being able to stay motivated or inspired. There's nothing wrong with me—I'm just like every other human being." Sure, you can use motivation and inspiration to ignite your aspiration, but to create your own reality, only aspiration will do. So please, stop berating yourself for not being able to stay motivated. I've learned that, as a species, humans simply aren't wired for that.

Aspiration Reshapes Your DNA

Aspiration is a dream or desire so significant, so deeply embedded, that it will cause you to create your own reality as you pursue it. Aspirations are not resolutions or goals; they are far bigger and more meaningful. They are the inner drivers found deep in the soul that will take you into new levels of success, quality of life, and LOVE far beyond what you could've ever imagined.

Aspirations are not resolutions or goals; they are far bigger and more meaningful.

In the process of pursuing your aspirations, you transform on the cellular level, down to your very DNA. Every aspect of your being is stretched beyond what you might have thought possible. And like a rubber band pulled beyond its elasticity, you can never go back to your previous limits again.

If you think I'm exaggerating the ability of aspiration to transform your DNA, think again. Over the past twenty years, a whole new field of science, *epigenetics*, has focused on understanding how "environmental" factors (including our thoughts, beliefs, and actions) can influence the expression of our genes—not just when we're children[1] but throughout our lives.

Medical studies have proven the positive effects of mind-body techniques like meditation, mindfulness, and emotional support on the telomeres of cancer patients.[2] (Telomeres are bits of genetic material at the ends of DNA strands, and they indicate how long the cell will live.) Another study showed that cancer patients' immune responses were strengthened when they participated in an eight-week program of relaxation, meditation, and yoga.[3] In other words, the cells were healthier due to the influence of their thoughts and emotions.

While I'm no scientist, and I didn't even know the field of epigenetics existed before I experienced it, the bottom line is *what we think, what we believe, and how we feel can affect every cell in our bodies.* Having a strong aspiration to accomplish something great can dramatically shape our physical reality.

And perhaps something more . . .

Aspirations Create a New Reality

I thoroughly enjoyed the movie *Rocketman*, which is based on Elton John's life story. It shows how a young man, born Reginald Dwight, could aspire to make amazing music by transforming himself into Elton Hercules John (yes, that's really his middle name). If you read the introduction to this book, you saw my favorite quote from the film: "You gotta kill the person you were born to be in order to become the person you want to be." But you also have to *create* the person you want to be from scratch. You need to build a new reality for yourself, and then the world will shape itself to you.

You, too, can do what Elton John did. You must believe that the "life sentence" you've been given at birth—be it a good sentence, a privileged sentence, an underprivileged sentence, or a sentence where you're destined for mediocrity—is not final. You can "kill" the person you were supposed to be (as determined by your birth, your family, your circumstances, your past, your economics, your lack of education, or whatever has constrained you) and live a life of *your* choosing, the way *you* want it to be.

By the way, pursuing an aspiration with commitment, dedication, and resolve not only has the power to create a new reality but also to change the world. For example, Elon Musk's SpaceX company brought private enterprise into space exploration. Steve Jobs took the cumbersome "smartphones" of the 1990s with their keyboards and styluses, substituted a touchscreen interface, and launched the first iPhone in 2007, inaugurating a mobile revolution. Sara Blakely cut the feet off of her pantyhose and sold the resulting product, Spanx, to millions of women everywhere, making Blakely the world's youngest self-made female billionaire in 2012. Mahatma Gandhi's single-minded dedication to nonviolence and independence resulted in the founding of the nation of India in 1947. And Nelson Mandela's vision for a new South Africa led his country to grow beyond apartheid and create a new political reality.

These examples should prove that you don't have to suppress who you truly are because of the world in which you find yourself. You can—in fact, I believe you *must*—find within yourself the aspirations that will transform who you are into who you are *meant* to be. And in some cases, you'll change the world in the process.

My Five Aspirations

Because they are so important and take so much of your time, effort, and energy, you will have only a limited number of aspirations throughout your life. Believe it or not, to date, I've aspired to only five things in my life. Some of them took twenty-five years to accomplish, but all of them altered my DNA and created a new reality for me, my family, and those I know or influence.

#1: BE A BESTSELLING AUTHOR. I graduated from high school with a 1.8 GPA and never went to college, yet I have written seven bestselling books in six genres. This aspiration has caused me to study writing, to watch and listen to great speakers and authors, to spend nights with the dictionary looking up words so I could use them intelligently. Speak well, write well = well respected.

#2: RACE BADWATER. Within one year of arriving in Florida at age eighteen, I worked as a tennis pro. By 2004, I was a regular fast-twitch runner with a top distance of around six miles in forty minutes. I had never completed a marathon, much less an ultramarathon of 100 miles or longer. Yet hearing about Badwater awakened the aspiration in me to pursue the impossible, incomprehensible, and insurmountable (the three Is) and compete at the most elite level, in conditions that would terrify any sane athlete.

#3: BE A REAL ESTATE ARTIST. I can't carry a tune or play an instrument. I can't sculpt, and while I recently started painting, I'm not very good—yet. But I always knew that I had an artistic mind, and I aspired to use that talent in a significant way. So I became a three-dimensional artist who builds works of art for people to live in. As far back as the late 1990s, the *Wall Street Journal* and *New York Times* started calling me a "real estate artist" and the "Real Estate Rock Czar" because I created one-of-a-kind, multimillion-dollar masterpieces along the beaches of South Florida, and each property was a reflection of my unique artistic vision.

#4. RUN A CHARITY IN THE POOREST COUNTRY IN THE WESTERN HEMISPHERE. A few years after I designed, built, and sold my first big property, I started feeding the homeless once a week in Delray Beach. (There's a story behind that which I'll share in section 5.) That aspiration to help the poorest of the poor, those who have next to nothing, or who are struggling after a natural disaster, has produced twenty-nine self-sustaining villages in Haiti, providing a self-sufficient existence to thousands of children and their families, as well as multiple relief efforts in the United States.

#5: FAMILY. I came from something less than a perfect family, so being married to Nilsa for more than thirty years and having a beautiful daughter means everything to me. This aspiration meant that I walked my daughter to school every day from pre-K to eighth grade—1,652 times. It meant (as you'll see in section 4) that my relationship with Nilsa has been one of the most important parts of my life ever since I met her. I'm not perfect, God knows, but my wife and daughter know that my relationship with them is one of the central pillars of my life.

These are the five things that I aspired to on a big scale. Each one of them has changed my cellular composition and made me the man I am today. In the course of following these aspirations, I have blown past everyone's expectations but mine and done things that others wouldn't consider possible or even probable. Through the years, many people have alternated between calling me crazy or eccentric and asking me how I produce such extraordinary results time after time. I now know that it is due to aspiration—deep, deep aspiration.

Through pursuit of these aspirations, I have created my own reality.

And I know you can do the same.

What Are Your Aspirations?

I wrote this book not to motivate or inspire you, but to push you into discovering your own aspirations. What high or great things do you burn to achieve? What are the deepest desires of your soul? Where do your passions lie—the passions that, when you express them, make you feel most alive? What's something you've wanted to do or become that scares you a little, or a lot? If you were one hundred years old and looking back over your life, what would you be the proudest and happiest to have accomplished?

Make a list for yourself of anything and everything you can think of that might be one of your aspirations. Take your time and do this over the course of reading this book.

Remember, these desires don't have to be big and flashy; they just need to help you create a reality that is exactly right for *you*. To me, the aspiration to create an amazing family life for my wife and daughter is just as important as building a multimillion-dollar property or writing another bestselling book. You may aspire to create an extraordinary herb garden,

---

... motivation and inspiration don't work because they lack the deep conscious and subconscious feeling created when you aspire to something mighty.

---

or to be an incredible fifth grade teacher or school counselor, or to play the piano, or be best the LEGO® builder, or create a successful small business in your hometown. Whatever they may be, your aspirations must have three characteristics.

First, they must *excite and energize you, and fully engage your emotions.* I believe that motivation and inspiration don't work because they lack the deep conscious and subconscious feeling created when you aspire to something mighty. Because aspirations are designed to be high and great, they're going to take energy, commitment, and follow-through over the long run. You'll need a lot of positive emotions to keep moving forward.

Second, they must *feel sacred*. Imagine that your aspirations are nestled in a beautiful jeweled box, almost like a Fabergé egg. You show extreme care and reverence for that diamond-encrusted box and place it where you will see it constantly, where it will remind you daily of what is pulling you toward your new reality.

Third, *you will not stop until you achieve them*. Pursuing your aspirations will take guts. You may need to let go of everything you thought was important. But your aspirations must be so important to you that giving up is not a choice. In fact, if your aspirations are true, you simply won't give up on them. You'll have to be ready to use the power of what Mahatma Gandhi called "indomitable will" to shape reality to fit your aspirations.

The first section of this book covers five ideas that will help you achieve your aspirations. Who do you wish to emulate? What legacy do you want to leave behind? What do you aspire to execute that's beyond your current ability to comprehend? What mindset do you need to develop to accomplish those aspirations? And what do you need to leave behind, reinvent, or renew to make your aspirations a reality?

Remember, you don't need to aspire to run Badwater, or become the next Elton John or Nelson Mandela, or invent the iPhone, or found a company like SpaceX or Spanx. But I guarantee that when you use aspirations to drive your life forward, it will take you on a very different path, one that will put you in charge of the reality in which you live. And it's sure to be an exciting and exhilarating ride!

Emulation Is the Sincerest Form of Aspiration

Don't forget what happened to the man who suddenly got everything he always wanted: he lived happily ever after.

WILLY WONKA

Who were your heroes growing up? What were the bedtime stories you asked to hear again and again? What movies or cartoons did you love to watch? What books did you love to read? Maybe you acted out scenes from those movies, cartoons, books or bedtime stories, imagining yourself a superhero, a knight, a comic strip character, a magician, an inventor, a prince or princess . . . embodying the characters . . . feeling their emotions . . . experiencing their challenges and victories. I'll bet that as you "became" those characters, you felt a spark inside, something resonating with your own soul. You felt braver, or cleverer, or stronger, or more adventurous, or smarter, or more capable. And maybe, just maybe, if you dared, you found yourself taking on more of those traits in real life.

As adults, we can consciously choose who we wish to emulate based on the reality we want to create. I never did well in a classroom environment, so for me, the best way to "sample" someone's DNA, so to speak, was through emulating people I admired. I thought of it like walking down the beach, following these people, putting my feet in their footprints every four or five steps, getting a sense of who they are and what they represent.

Emulation is the sincerest form of aspiration. It is a short-cut to becoming a new and better version of yourself.

Emulating others allows you to dream bigger than your own circumstances and to step outside of the way you have defined yourself (or let yourself be defined by your environment). Far too many people get stuck in mindsets that are cut and dried—what psychologist Carol Dweck calls a "fixed mindset."[1] But as a kid you hadn't yet developed those constraints, so you could imagine yourself as an astronaut, an explorer, a treasure hunter, a pitcher, a cowboy (or girl), all in the same afternoon. Everything was possible. What if you could expand, or explode, your ideas of what is possible for you today, simply by choosing people to emulate that will transform your sense of who you are?

Choosing the Best Role Models for Your Aspirations

When you choose the people you want to emulate today, make sure to keep your aspirations at the forefront of your mind. It's important to know they *don't* have to be "real" people: if you feel that emulating Superman, Wonder Woman, or Black Panther will help you pursue your aspirations, do that. You can choose people you know (a teacher, a coach, a mentor, a parent or other relative) or people you don't know (Abraham Lincoln, Jesus, Beyoncé, Bruce Lee, Mother Teresa, or Michelle Obama, for example). Remember, however, never attempt to obsessively duplicate everything about your role models. Don't copy *anybody;* instead, sample small pieces from different role models depending on what you need.

The parts we emulate are usually things we feel we need more of, or need to bring to the forefront of our personalities. For example, maybe you admired Spiderman growing up because even when he's afraid, he steps up and faces danger head-on, and you wanted to be more like that yourself. For the purposes of this chapter, however, you should think of the characteristics that you believe will help you achieve your aspirations and choose role models that draw out and embody those qualities.

To show you what I mean, here are the people, fictional and real, I chose to emulate, based on the five aspirations I've had in my life so far.

#1: WILLY WONKA. I saw *Willy Wonka and the Chocolate Factory* for the first time two days after I turned eight years old, and I immediately aspired to be like Willy Wonka. Now, many years later when an interviewer asks, "What's the best business book you ever read?" I'll still say, *"Charlie and Chocolate Factory*, because of its marketing brilliance." For Willy Wonka, candy wasn't just a product: it was a passion. He took great pride in inventing sweets, like Everlasting Gobstoppers, that expanded people's ideas of what candy could be. Sure, he was different, even eccentric. But look at what he did with the Golden Ticket contest! He used eccentricity, exclusivity, theatricality, quality, mystique, and word of mouth to create enormous excitement and demand for what he had to offer, and he did all of this long before the advent of social media and the cell phone.

If you look at the unveiling events we've done for our properties throughout the years, you might see the Willy Wonka-esque elements of eccentricity, exclusivity, theatricality, and quality at play. No one gets to see the property prior to the unveiling, which is by invitation only. (Once I did a literal unveiling and covered the entire house in a special stitched silk fabric to keep it from view.) Our events typically feature stunts, pyrotechnics, costumes, spotlights, signature drinks, epicurean delights, and red carpets. We've included over-the-top elements like mermaids diving for pearls in a resort-style pool with its own waterfall, and waitstaff wearing fruit for a tropical vibe. I always make a memorable entrance. I zip-lined into one opening dressed as a good pirate who was battling Blackbeard. I magically disappeared from a property's rooftop only to reappear seconds later from beneath the trembling earth and emerge from a coffin (to do that, I studied under a renowned illusionist). I've zoomed up to the property's beach on a jet ski in a white wetsuit only to unzip it and reveal a jet-black tux like a superspy. I've jumped a motorcycle over a replica of the first house I ever did (an homage to one of my role models to follow); I converted a hovercraft into a pirate ship and shuttled guests via the ocean between two waterfront properties that were unveiled on the same night; and in one of my tamer entrances, I drove up in a hybrid automobile dressed as a cross between Robin Hood and the Green Giant. People would show up at our unveilings just to experience the experiential genius of Frank McKinney!

But like Willy Wonka, my exhibitionism has a purpose. First, every unveiling event raises money for our Caring House Project Foundation, and as Willy Wonka knew, the more spectacle, the more people will come, and the more people will contribute. Second, in a crowded industry like real estate, when you're building houses on spec and asking buyers to pay millions of dollars for a property, you need to "wow" everyone right from the start. Our unveilings certainly do that; and then, just like Willy Wonka did, we take the "wow factor" to a new level as potential buyers walk through every stunning room of the home. *Eccentricity, exclusivity, theatricality, quality, mystique*: these elements have distinguished my properties from every other developer in South Florida, and I believe we have done Willy Wonka proud.

#2: RICH DEVOS. The late Rich DeVos was the billionaire co-founder of Amway, and he believed that material success was not meant for our sole benefit, but should be used to assist others. His example and mentorship taught me how to be a responsible steward with the blessings God has given me. Rich was a devout Christian and major contributor to causes that he believed in, including our Caring House Project Foundation. He wrote books about personal development; in particular, he wrote about how to combine capitalism with philanthropy. He was also known as one of the best storyteller-speakers in the world, as he would often address audiences of 25,000-plus. I admired Rich and wanted to emulate his approach to life—while still keeping my long hair and rock-star demeanor, of course (see #4).

#3. ROBIN HOOD. When I was a kid back in Indiana, I loved going into the dense backwoods with my friends. We would play all kinds of games: cowboys and Indians, explorers, treasure hunters, adventurers. But the times I remember the most were the days that I'd carry with me the bow and arrow I'd gotten at Woolworth's (think Walmart, only smaller and out of business) and pretend I was Robin Hood. Sure, I had a great time shooting arrows at trees and other targets, including my friends, and having mock battles with the Sheriff of Nottingham's men. But what I really loved was Robin Hood's passion for stealing from the rich and giving to the poor. Today, I get to be a modern-day Robin Hood—except instead of stealing from the rich, I sell them very expensive homes for upwards of $3,000 per square foot, and then use the proceeds to provide shelter to tens of thousands of children and their families in Haiti. It's my way of emulating both Robin Hood and Rich DeVos in fulfilling my aspiration to make a significant difference with the blessings I have received.

#4: DAVID LEE ROTH. On February 10, 1978, I was fourteen years old, just beginning to acquire my tastes in music, and I was sitting in the back of a beat-up old Greyhound bus on my way to a school ski trip. That was the day Van Halen's first album dropped. That music penetrated through to my bone marrow and melted me into that torn vinyl seat like the witch melting on the floor in *The Wizard of Oz*. Over the years I watched and read about the antics of their lead singer, David Lee Roth. He was the epitome of a front man: bombastic, flamboyant, confident, athletic, a true performer and entertainer. He commanded the stage, was well-spoken in interviews, and had a unique appearance both in his good looks and clothing/costumes. He always seemed happy. "I get up! And nothin' gets meee down," go the lyrics to the song *Jump*. One of my favorite quotes of his is, "If all the world's a stage, then I want a brighter spotlight." He was larger than life to millions and, in 1984, was runner-up to President Ronald Reagan for *Time Magazine*'s Person of the Year. When you own a business, there's only one front man or woman, and I felt it would be beneficial to absorb parts of David Lee Roth into the businessman in me. (P.S. Since then my music tastes have expanded, and today I enjoy Vivaldi as much as Van Halen.)

#5: EVEL KNIEVEL. Back in the late 1960s, Evel Knievel was a daredevil motorcycle rider with a dream to jump over the fountain in front of Caesars Palace in Las Vegas. But he wasn't yet well known enough to simply call the hotel and set up the stunt. Instead, he called the hotel's owner and impersonated various attorneys, businesspeople, and reporters, asking when Knievel would be performing the stunt. He even called and threatened to sue because he said that Caesars Palace was using his name without his permission to promote his (non-existent) event![2] The calls got him a meeting with the owner, who soon agreed to let the stunt go ahead. Unfortunately, Knievel didn't make it over the fountain (and crushed his pelvis and other bones in the accident), but the publicity jump-started a career that lasted for decades and seventy-four additional death-defying jumps. He is now considered the last gladiator—the godfather—and in the vanguard of extreme sports daredevils.

Evel Knievel's skill at self-promotion, his risk-taking, his charm, and his ability to stare into a camera and make you believe Every Single Word he was saying, were all aspects of his character that I have used throughout my career. When I built my first big property, long before anyone knew who I was, I would call reporters as different people (neighbors, newspaper delivery boy, meter reader, etc.) with different accents and tell them they had to come check out what this Frank McKinney guy had built. And if you watched the "reveal" event for the cover, title, and premise of this book, you saw my inner Evel Knievel come out when I was lit on fire then rode a motorcycle through a huge banner of the book cover that was also a raging inferno. (You can see the stunt at TheAspireBook.com.)

Looking at the descriptions of the people I have emulated, you can see how their characteristics helped me define the new DNA required to kill the person I was and become the person I wanted to be. Willy Wonka: passionate, creative, eccentric, and a world-class marketer. Rich DeVos: capitalistic *and* philanthropic, and a great storyteller. Robin Hood: altruistic and a little outside the law. David Lee Roth: bombastic, flamboyant front man. Evel Knievel: daredevil and risk-taker. Sure, many of those qualities I already may have possessed, but my role models gave me examples of how to extract those qualities buried deep in my soul, bring them to the forefront of my DNA, and use them to achieve the lofty aspirations I chose to pursue. As you'll see in chapter 13, those qualities have allowed me to live my inside on the outside.

Who Do You Aspire to Emulate?

Now it's your turn. Look at your aspirations and ask yourself, "Who should I aspire to emulate? What role models would help me do what I want to do and be who I want to become?" Most of us can rattle off people from our childhood, for example, that we wanted to be like. Who was that hero you dreamed of being when you were young? What was it about him or her that excited you? What are the characteristics that made you want to be like this person? What would happen if you developed those same qualities in yourself? Resurrect this person, fictional or real!

Emotional freedom can come from going outside your own circumstances and thinking, *If I could, I'd be like that person. What is it about that person that excites me and gets me jazzed?* If something in a role model excites you, I believe it's because you share some characteristic with them, something buried deep inside you that is crying to be released, to come out and propel you forward. However, if other characteristics of a particular role model aren't a good fit, choose someone else. Perhaps you want to have the courage of an Evel Knievel, but you know you'd never be

---

. . . you share some characteristic with them, something buried deep inside you that is crying to be released, to come out and propel you forward.

---

that much of a risk-taker. What's another role model you could emulate to give you the kind of courage you need? Maybe it's someone like John Lewis, or Mahatma Gandhi, or Malala Yousafzai, the young Pakistani woman who was shot because she advocated for women's education. Maybe it's one of the firefighters who rushed into the burning towers on 9/11. Maybe it's someone you know in your family or community whose faith or courage you admire.

There are literally hundreds of possible role models for you to emulate. Choose the people you can imagine enjoying themselves as they achieved *your* aspirations. Imagine how it will feel when you recognize and nurture those same characteristics inside yourself. Then you too will become whatever version of yourself is needed for you to pursue your aspirations and create your own reality.

What Legacy Do You Aspire to Leave Behind?

The idea is not to live forever
but to create something that will.

ANDY WARHOL

All twenty-five chapters of *Aspire!* are meant to evoke deep thought and actionable learning, yet only one chapter is posed in the form of a question. I believe when you have successfully created your own reality, and in turn altered your DNA, you will have truly left a legacy.

Find a mirror or flip your phone's camera around and read the title to this chapter aloud: *What legacy do you aspire to leave behind?*

It's not a question that many of us think about until we are getting close to the end of our lives or something happens to make us ponder our mortality. But it's likely *the* most important question when it comes to altering your DNA and creating your own reality. And it's a question I believe we also should ask—and try to answer well—throughout our lives. You've heard of a reality check? Well, since we are creating our own reality, I suggest a periodic *legacy check.* Your legacy is a work in progress built upon choices that you make each day, and the sooner you identify what it is, the better.

On the Yugo We-go Tour, I often asked the legacy question, and I was deeply moved by the answers I received. One man, Vinnie (you'll meet him again in chapter 24), who had worked at a Veterans Administration hospital for twenty-three years, said that his legacy was "to take care of people who took care of our country." Beautiful, simple, purposeful, and profound. Another gentleman, Ben, the eighty-seven-year-old unofficial "Mayor of Badwater" who lives in the tiny desert town of Lone Pine, California, told me that his legacy was choosing to be a doctor in a rural community. Given his credentials, he could have practiced medicine anywhere in the world, he said, but he made a conscious choice to care for the people in this small town for more than fifty-five years.

You would think that younger people would have a tougher time thinking about legacy, and in many cases you'd be correct, but a few millennials I talked with on the Tour shared incredibly wise responses. While staying at the beautiful Los Poblanos Historic Inn and Organic Farm in Albuquerque, I asked my twenty-two-year-old waiter what he wanted his legacy to be. He stepped back from the table, put down his tray, and brought his index finger and thumb up to his chin as he went away to get some water to refill my glass. When he came back, he said, "I simply want to leave a wake of empathy." How profound is that? I told him to make a bumper sticker out of those last five words and I'd buy the first one hundred. Another young lady, in her mid-twenties and working at the St. Regis in Aspen, Colorado, told me she wanted her legacy to be helping people make beautiful memories. Her goal, she said, was to have a wedding planning business, because there's nothing more beautiful or memorable than a wedding.

These millennials were declaring what they want their legacy to be in the future. Vinnie and the mayor of Badwater were looking back and reflecting on a legacy lived. But no matter what stage of life you are currently in, I believe that spending some time focusing on your legacy will help to make your life richer and more fulfilling.

You Are Worthy of Leaving a Great Legacy

To me, legacy is simply a demonstration of how you are living your life, and how that life impacts others. For a lot of people, however, "legacy" is an intimidating word, and they don't think of themselves as being big enough, or worthy enough, to leave a legacy. As a bestselling author, I frequently get asked to write a foreword or an endorsement for a book. When I get such a request, someone in my office or I will do a little research on the person and their book. If it's something I want to do (which is almost always the case), I'll email or text the author and say, "Send me a draft of a few examples of exactly what you want me to say in the most flattering way you'd want me to say it. Extol your virtues, put humility and humbleness aside, then send it to me for review." Well, out of the one hundred times I've done this, ninety-five of the drafts authors send me are woefully inadequate, bordering on *pathetic*. Sadly, most responses are a reflection of deep-seated insecurities, with the extremely worthy author unwilling to sing their own praises and declare their aspirations!

Remember, you are *more* than worthy of leaving a legacy that you can be proud and happy to leave behind. You just need to be brave enough and bold enough not to leave your legacy to chance—or worse yet, not to leave one at all.

Tie Your Legacy to Your Aspirations

Just like your aspirations, your legacy doesn't need to be something big and bombastic. If you aspire to leave a legacy of a beautiful herb garden for you, your family, and your neighbors to enjoy, and that garden really lays itself on your heart, great! (Full disclosure: I once thought I was motivated to plant and care for a garden, but I found that I wasn't very good at gardening, and all the plants died, except for the few coconuts I stuck in the ground. Those trees are now ten feet tall!) The only requirement is that you should choose a legacy that you truly want to be remembered for.

Not long ago I visited a woman, Debbie, in Tallahassee, Florida, who answered the legacy question like this: "I want to set an example of what a good wife should be. A lot of the women I meet either talk down to their husbands or talk bad about them, but I enjoy doing things for Hunter. I enjoy making my husband's lunch every day. And even though we work together and I work as hard as or harder than him, I enjoy making dinner for him. These are the things that a good wife does."

Debbie is a high-powered, very successful real estate investor, and her answer was not at all what I expected. But it made me think of my wife, Nilsa. She is an incredibly talented interior designer who designed the interior elements of all of my oceanfront estates; she spearheaded fundraising drives for our Caring House Project Foundation and for a local hospital; she ran the support crew all twelve times that I ran Badwater; and if you asked Nilsa about her legacy, I'm sure being an amazing wife and mother would be part of it. (I'll talk a lot about Nilsa and relationships in section 4.) Whatever your aspiration—whether it is to create an amazing garden, raise a beautiful family, send your child to college for the first time in your family's history, build a small business that's a cornerstone of your community, become a bestselling author or top athlete, or to be a philanthropist and support causes that are important to you—if you are truly pursuing it with all your heart, mind, and soul, then in time, it will become your legacy.

Years ago I believed that my legacy would certainly be the oceanfront mansions I created, with their artistry, grandeur, opulence, and showmanship. But then I recognized that even the most magnificent house, either through physical, functional, or economic obsolescence, will turn to rubble. Especially in South Florida, where the value of the land eventually

---

If your aspirations create the road, legacy is the destination . . .

---

will exceed the value of the physical structure built on it, I know that the houses I built will be gone, and the memory of how I presented them to the market will fade, as well. But what *won't* be gone is the generational impact that the Caring House Project Foundation is having on the families in Haiti. I'm prouder of that legacy—a better life for the poorest of the poor in the poorest country in the Western hemisphere—than I am of any mansion I ever created, built, and sold.

Motivation and inspiration will fail, but aspiration tied to legacy will span generations. Am I always motivated to go to Haiti or do the fundraising to build another village? At times, no. But I *never* lose the aspiration to leave a generational legacy for those families and children. The combination of aspiration and legacy creates a vivid mental image, a clear path for you to follow as you journey through life. If your aspirations create the road, legacy is the destination at life's conscious and various end points. And you'll receive emotional satisfaction from taking the small steps that will keep you moving toward the realization of your aspiration, which ultimately *is* your legacy.

Create a Legacy of Service

Occasionally when I ask the legacy question, people will say things like, "I want to be remembered as a self-made billionaire!" or "I want to die the most famous (actor/musician/performer/writer/real estate investor) in the world!" That's fine, but I always want to ask, "Why? What's so important about being a billionaire or famous?" I believe that in order to be happy, all human beings want a sense of purpose and some appreciation for who we are and what we do, yet unfortunately, many people link money and fame to purpose and appreciation. But if money is your only measure of success, or fame is your only indication of how much others appreciate you, then you're going to be pretty unhappy. Money and fame will provide two things in abundance: relief and comfort—pretty much all the relief and comfort you want. And relief and comfort will make you very happy . . . for a little while. Then, like the rush from heroin, it's gone, leaving you craving more and more (relief and comfort). It is a vicious, never-ending, maddening cycle.

I have no issues with people having legacies that include doing well financially, being successful in their businesses, or being recognized for their talents. (If you go back to those I aspired to emulate in chapter 1, you'll see I admire those traits.) And if they want part of their legacy to be giving money to a hospital or university or other organization to get a wing or a building named after them, or using their fame to support causes that are important to them, great! As you'll see in chapter 23, I'm a big believer in philanthro-capitalism, using financial blessings to do good. But I also believe that it is just as important to leave a legacy of compassion and kindness for every human being, whether it's the homeless woman outside of the 7-Eleven or the city employee who picks up the garbage at my house twice a week.

The best way to leave a lasting legacy is to live so that you have a positive effect on others or the world. If you want immortality (and we all do), make it a practice to share your blessings in service to others and you're likely to have it—in heaven, if that's your belief, and on earth because people will remember what you did for them.

Other People Will Determine Your Legacy

I once read that all the big newspapers write obituaries for famous people in advance to be prepared to go to print just as soon as they hear that so-and-so has died. That, to me, is a great reminder of the fact that your obituary will be written and your legacy decided by people who know you, were affected by you, and who see the results of your aspirations. For example, while I aspire to leave a legacy in the poorest country in the Western hemisphere, I'll never know really truly if I've done that. But in pursuing that aspiration I *do* know that we have made an impact on the over thirteen thousand children we've saved.

Remember: it's never the destination; it's the journey. It's never the legacy; it's the actions you take along the way to fulfill your aspirations. Think of Martin Luther King, Jr., speaking in Memphis, Tennessee, in 1968, the night before he was assassinated. He said, "I've been to the mountaintop . . . And I've seen the promised land. I may not get there with you. But I want you to know tonight, that we, as a people, will get to the promised land."[1] King knew a thing or two about aspiration—not for himself, but for all African Americans. And while many feel that his aspirations for equality and justice have yet to be fulfilled, it's the legacy of his journey, and his unrelenting pursuit of those aspirations, that make him still an inspiration to millions.

Identify the Legacy You Want to Leave Behind

It's time for you to declare what you want your legacy to be. After reading the prior section you already should have been thinking about two questions and begun to make short lists: #1: *What are your aspirations?* And #2: *Who do you want to emulate?* Now it's time for #3: *What legacy do you aspire to leave behind?* To me, this list is just as enjoyable to compose as the other two, as it encourages you to dig deeper and face your own mortality to a degree. But if you want to really live your aspirations and create your own reality, choosing a legacy (or legacies) can help you design a roadmap to get there.

There are many different ways to go about answering the legacy question. There's the rocking-chair test, where you imagine yourself sitting in a rocking chair at the end of your life, looking back over what you've done. Or you can imagine people gathered at your memorial service, sharing their memories of your life and accomplishments. You could imagine friends, colleagues, and family posting their tributes on your social media page. Or you could write your own obituary as it might appear in the local newspaper. On two occasions in my life I have attended funerals of people I didn't know and imagined it was me in the coffin. As I sat there in the pew in church, I visualized what I'd hope my eulogy would sound like.

In writing *Aspire!* I suggest a slightly different version of the exercise:

1. Look at the list of aspirations you created at the beginning of this section, as well as the list of people you wanted to emulate.

2. Imagine yourself at a certain point in the future—one, five, ten, or twenty years, or longer (you pick the length). Visualize that you've been pursing your aspiration with dedication and commitment the entire time between now and then.

3. Looking back over those years, vividly yet succinctly describe the legacy created by your aspirations. What have you accomplished? Who have you helped or affected in some way? How have you grown? What are you proud of?

4. Reviewing what you wrote, what do you think your most important legacy will be? How can you set things in motion *today* to make that legacy a reality?

One of the great advantages of choosing your legacy today is that it can provide a crystal ball reflecting the actions you need to take in the near term. I'll equate it to the oceanfront properties I built: I had to have a vision of what the mansion would look like when it was finished in order to create weekly plans to make that vision a reality. It's the same way with building self-sustaining villages in Haiti. I'm driven by the vision of leaving a legacy in Haiti represented by these villages that allow tens of thousands of children, and their children, to live better lives, now and in the future. But when I first aspired to build those villages, I knew nothing about running a nonprofit or raising money. So my first step was to find someone to talk to about charities and how to run them. After that, I devised plans for fundraising, connecting with donors, finding the right partners in Haiti, working with the local authorities, and so on.

Whether today you're in your seventies, or only twenty years old and hoping to be around for another seventy or eighty years, deciding upon a legacy and tying it to your aspirations is one of the most important life exercises you'll ever do. So go ahead give yourself that legacy check. Then pursue it with commitment and watch your DNA start to change as you begin to believe in the power of creating your own reality.

Be an Executioner

A really great talent finds its happiness in execution.

JOHANN WOLFGANG VON GOETHE

Most idea people bore me. *Doers* intrigue me. There's no shortage of dreamers out there, yet true executioners are rare indeed. Dreams are something we have when we sleep. I have aspirations that violently wake me that I make come true.

A few years ago, I led a series of seminars called the "Make it BIG! Event" based on content from my first book, and I even came up with an image of a hooded executioner, axe in hand, for the 114-page workbook. It was pretty grim, but it also made a graphic point: the only way to create your own reality is to *do* not just learn; *act* not just theorize. While it's great to identify your aspirations and legacy, the only way to make them a reality is to *execute*—day in, day out. Execution is the daily application of aspiration. It's how you close the loop on anything in your life, and it's essential for turning vision and aspiration into results-driven reality.

Remember, your aspirations are sacred, so you should never give up on making them real. Daily you must put down the book, journal, podcast, or seminar, and implement what's in your head. It won't be easy, and all the motivation and inspiration in the world won't be enough. You're going to have to dig deep and keep going. You may not know how to produce the

---

Execution is the daily application of aspiration.

---

result, but as long as you pack that lunch pail (Part Three of *Make it BIG!*—more later in this chapter) and show up every day, you must trust that the results will come.

The Cycle of Execution

I excel at ruthlessly executing my vision and aspiration, and while most people will beat me in a debate contest, I'll win a *do* contest. After writing seven bestsellers, finishing the toughest footrace on the planet seven times, creating and selling dozens of multimillion-dollar mansions on spec, and building twenty-nine self-sustaining villages in Haiti, I've found there is a predictable process when it comes to execution—and predictable roadblocks along the way.

We can use the image of a clock to describe the habits of people attempting to execute their goals. The stages of execution are represented by twelve, three, six, nine, and twelve o'clock again.

Twelve O'Clock— Running on Excitement

At twelve you get an idea you're super *excited* about. Excitement is that flash-bang titillation in the moment. It's the feeling created by news soundbites, social media, and waves of information that are specifically designed to trigger our emotions, making us excited or angry or fearful or happy or all of the above. Many of us love that feeling of excitement and seek it out again and again. (It's one of my lifelong addictions.)

You should be glad when you encounter something that triggers excitement at the twelve o'clock stage because it can point you toward *passion*. Passion speaks to you at a deeper level. It ignites the soul. It touches a part of you that excitement can't come close to reaching. Feeling the deep drive of passion is a clear signal that this endeavor is one of your aspirations and thus worthy of pursuing. However, passion is never enough and should never be mistaken for simple excitement. It's only the start.

Three O'Clock—Don't Be a Flea

Excitement is like lighter fluid that starts a fire and burns off very quickly. It's quick, it's superficial, and it won't keep you going for long. That's why at three, a lot of ideas that made it through the excitement filter start to lose momentum. And as the excitement starts to wane, you are compelled by various outside influences to jump to something new, looking for another hit of the excitement you once felt. I call people in the three o'clock stage *fleas*, because they hop from one thing to the next without ever working long enough to get results. For example, have you ever followed a diet or a particular eating regimen only to quit because you aren't losing weight fast enough? Then you start another diet, and then you follow yet another weight-loss fad that you're *sure* will work better? That's classic flea behavior, and it's exactly the opposite of what's needed when it comes to execution.

Because of my reputation, I meet a lot of people of all ages who are just getting started in real estate, and they are truly excited about the opportunity. They become short sellers, for example, but when that doesn't produce results fast enough they try wholesaling properties. Then they start selling retail, then bank REOs, then tax deed sales, then mobile home investments, then storage units . . . but they never stick with anything long enough to get good at it, much less become an expert. They wake up in twenty years never having seen anything through to the end. Where's the legacy in that?

Maybe our modern world is to blame for what I see as a massive growth in flea behavior. We're constantly bombarded with information from social media, blogs, articles, podcasts, videos. Research shows that this increasing content volume "exhausts our attention" while increasing our desire for something new to pique our interest.[1] Unfortunately, while the brain gets a zap from the neurochemical dopamine whenever we learn something new and interesting,[2] there are a lot fewer neurochemical rewards for putting in the work to master a task. At three, then, you must avoid the tendency to keep looking for something new to give you that next dopamine hit of excitement. Instead, you need to identify whether this endeavor is linked to your passion and therefore worthy of pursuing.

Here are a few of the signs that can help you distinguish excitement from passion.

#1: *You've only known about this particular endeavor for a month or less.* Passion requires that you really sink your teeth into something. You need to develop a relationship with an endeavor before you can feel real passion for it.

#2: *You can't tie this endeavor to one of your aspirations.* Remember, an aspiration is an almost otherworldly desire to achieve something high and great. Is this endeavor something that will help you achieve your high and great aspirations and thus be worth your time and energy over months or years?

#3: *You find your excitement or energy dropping off quickly.* Have you ever started a new kind of exercise or hobby, only to find your enthusiasm for it waning within the first few tries? That's a sure sign of excitement rather than passion. While excitement will fade, passion lays itself on your heart and won't let go.

Excitement is available to everyone. True passion takes discipline and introspection—and it's what you will need to be an executioner. Passion will help you start to dig deep at three o'clock and keep pushing until you reach the halfway point of six and beyond.

Six O'Clock— No Half-Assers Allowed

Six represents the drudgery of putting in the work, day in and day out. This stage of execution is never glamorous, and it's rarely fun. It's making your hundredth cold call of the week . . . going out for yet another twenty-mile training run when it's sleeting or snowing (or 100 degrees outside) . . . eating what seems like the millionth piece of celery instead of the hot fudge sundae you are craving . . . or doing the accounting for your business at 2 A.M. when everyone else went home yesterday. For me, it might be showing up at a job site at the earlier stages of building a multimillion-dollar home, when there's no electricity and no water yet, and one of the workers decided to make use of a nonfunctioning toilet the day before—and I have to use the Shop Vac to clean out the stinking mess (and then clean *it* out of the Shop Vac). Hold that image in your mind for a moment. Yes, after thirty years this *still* occasionally happens to me, even in a $15 million oceanfront home!

In my book, *Make It BIG!,* I called this "taking the lunch pail approach," in honor of all the hardworking guys and women I worked with every day at the job sites of my properties. To make it through the six o'clock stage of execution and reach our aspirations, we all need to take the lunch pail approach of getting the job done every day—as long as we fuel it with the passion created when we are pursuing something tied to our aspiration.

Sad to say, at this point in the cycle of execution, a lot of people give up even though they're halfway to their goal. "It's too hard," they say. Or "This business sucks." Or "I don't want to do this anymore." Or "There must be an easier way" to make money, lose weight, train for a race, be married—fill in the blank. Or "I quit." I call people like this *half-assers* because they give up when things get tough. They forget that ninety-seven percent of life is filled with ordinary, everyday moments, and only three percent of life gives us extraordinarily golden moments—that we reach only by working hard ninety-seven percent of the time! But it's up to us to figure out how to enjoy the six o'clock stage in all its ordinariness, because we won't reach the three percent without it.

If you're thinking about quitting at six, try looking at how far you've come instead. Many times when I was running Badwater, there would come a point where I was ready to give up due to physical and mental exhaustion. God bless Nilsa, my support team captain, who would say to me, "Francisco, you've made it to Panamint (seventy-two miles in). Do you really want to get on that plane and go home a quitter? You've put in all this time and all this training, and now you have two choices: you can put your running shoes and sunglasses back on and quit crying, or you can give up. You can either walk back to the van and we'll drive back to the airport, or you can walk toward the finish line. Choose a direction: either way you're going to have to put one foot in front of the other. You don't have to run—just keep walking, a little bit at a time." (For more on how to get through the six o'clock stage, see chapter 9, "Relentless Forward Motion.")

Don't be a half-asser. Look at the image of the clock on the earlier page. Do you really want to see yourself stopping at six? I don't think so. Keep going. You'll be at nine before you know it.*

Nine O'Clock— You Tied Your Own Shoes Together???

Congratulations! You've made it past three and six, and you're on the execution upswing at nine o'clock. Now be aware: while this doesn't happen to many people, at this point about twenty percent find themselves stuck. Even though they can almost see the finish line, they've become so embroiled in the process that they refuse to move ahead. Someone got divorced five years ago but hasn't dated again because of that "horrible marriage." A perpetual student is three credits away from getting that degree. An entrepreneur is offered a ton of money to sell the company but just can't let go of their "baby." These people tie their *own* shoes together and stop in their tracks even though they're seventy-five percent of the way to their goal. These "shoe-lacers" are prime examples of a passage from the New Testament: ". . . always learning but never able to come to a knowledge of the truth" (2 Timothy 3:7, NIV). The process has become so much a part of their identity that they panic when they see the end of the endeavor coming.

I always enjoyed the process of designing and marketing a new oceanfront masterpiece, and while the brand may read "Real Estate Artist," I'm a businessman first and a real estate artist a distant second—which means the process isn't complete until the sale is done. I never once got attached to a property, no matter how beautiful it was. I'd say, "This was great, loved it, let me just sell it and start the process all over again." Remember, at some point process must give way to purpose. It's a conscious molting, a shedding, a jettisoning of the solid fuel launchers from your rocket ship. No more process. It's showtime. It's purpose time!

Back to Twelve O'Clock— Redirect Your Passion to Something New

At twelve the cycle of execution is complete. You're officially in rarified air: you're an executioner. You've run the race, finished the degree, started or sold the business, reached the goal that was driven by your aspiration and fueled by your passion. It's the culmination of all your efforts. This is one of those extraordinarily golden moments when you should celebrate your accomplishments!

Two things typically happen when you reach twelve o'clock again. First, getting to that beautiful finish line gives you absolute certainty about your ability to execute. You've done it once, so you know you can do it again and again. Your confidence is built by celebrating every execution (even the small ones) as a triumphant achievement. It starts what I call "the upward spiral of confidence" that can carry over into your aspirations in other areas of life. Finishing that 5K race, for example, may give you the confidence to start a business. Getting your degree might give you the certainty to pursue a relationship with that special someone.

The second thing that often happens when you reach the finish line in one endeavor is a desire to pursue something even bigger, loftier, and grander in the same field. When I built my very first oceanfront property back in 1992, I didn't make a lot of money on the sale—but boy, did it ever send my confidence into the stratosphere! And every property afterwards was yet another step on the upward spiral of confidence. That's why I believe that it's always a good idea to have another, even bigger or more creative goal in mind when the finish line is clearly in sight, but not before. Yes, you should enjoy that golden moment and congratulate yourself on what you have accomplished. But don't let your momentum die. Let the lessons and the good feelings engendered by your success fuel the next endeavor linked to one of your aspirations.

Where Did You Execute—and Where Did You Fail to Close the Loop?

I designed the cycle of execution as a series of checkpoints for people to evaluate their own efforts toward their goals. Have there been times where you were a flea, easily bored, jumping from one endeavor to the next? Have you gotten halfway to a goal only to become lazy or intimidated by the hard work ahead and flat-out quit? Have you gotten close to the finish line on a goal only to metaphorically tie your own shoelaces together because you're either afraid or so in love with the process you can't stand to let go? And where in your life have you closed the loop on an important goal and seen your confidence soar as a result?

Look, I'm not an unequivocal executioner; I've fallen short at three, six, and nine myself. But I've learned that reaching that twelve o'clock mark consistently creates a habit that will improve every area of your life. Once an executioner, always an executioner.

Before you look at your goals and create a plan to execute them, here are a few things to remember. First, the cycle of execution is not a process that literally takes three, six, nine, twelve months (although in certain cases, that's a perfect template). Depending on your goal, the stages of execution could take days, weeks, months, or years. And contrary to what you might

---

Once an executioner, always an executioner.

---

have thought, you shouldn't set a hard time limit on the accomplishment of your goal. But you *do* need to make sure you are continually moving forward.

Second, if you haven't seen significant progress after a year of executing on one particular endeavor, then it might be time to try a different approach. Ask yourself, "Okay, I've been working on this, I've still got the aspiration— is it possible this application isn't for me?" Say you have an aspiration to be a long-distance competitive cyclist. You put in a solid year of riding the bike for thirty to fifty miles a day, several times a week, in many different conditions. But toward the end of a year you realize riding the bike in traffic is affecting your passion and purpose of becoming a competitive racer. So maybe you start riding in a velodrome (a cycle racing track) rather than on the roads, or you switch to a mountain bike and train for off-road racing. Your aspiration is the same, but the approach is now different, and your passion is rekindled. For any goal where you find yourself stuck, you should ask, "How far have I come? Am I reaching my aspiration through this goal? And do I need to find a different application or approach that will gain me what I want?"

However, as in #1, if you are still passionate about a goal after a year of executing, don't let a lack of results hold you back from continuing to pursue it with all your heart and soul. There are hundreds of examples of people with big aspirations whose success took years to achieve. Inventor James Dyson took fifteen years and 5,126 prototypes to create the bagless vacuum cleaner.[3] Thelonious Monk played piano with all the jazz greats for decades, but he didn't have a solo hit record until he was forty-six.[4] Elon Musk's company, Tesla, took ten years to have its first profitable quarter.[5] Jamie Kern Lima founded IT Cosmetics in 2008 and mailed her products to QVC for two straight years before they gave her a ten-minute spot in their lineup.[6] (Within five years IT Cosmetics was QVC's number-one beauty brand and the company had $182 million in sales.)[7] And as for me, after six consecutive finishes at Badwater, it took four consecutive failed attempts (and all the training in between) until I saw my seventh finish. It took two years and twenty-two different publisher rejections of the manuscript for my first book, *Make it BIG!*, before Wiley bought it. As long as your goal is fueled with aspiration and passion, then it's worthy of being pursued even if you don't get quick results. Just make sure you are *executing* and not just dreaming.

Third, when you have completed several cycles of execution in a particular field or area, there may come a time when you are ready to move on to something new. This should *not* be when you are burnt out. In fact, I believe the best time to leave the field of play is when you're at the top of your game. In 2020 I decided that 3492 South Ocean would be my final masterpiece, and when it sold I would retire from creating and selling real estate artistry. People thought I was crazy: the "Real Estate Rock Czar" voluntarily taking the adrenaline "needle" out of his arm? I'll admit that it was scary (and sometimes it still is), because I'd never been better at what I did and never loved my art more than with that property. But to me its completion signaled that it was time for me to reinvent, recreate, and renew. You'll read more about that in chapter 5.

What's Your Execution Plan?

Many mindset books talk about the importance of creating concrete plans to help you get from where you are to the point where your goals become real. But what I believe sets *Aspire!* apart from all the rest is the fact that you are going to tie those plans to your sacred aspirations, and thus fuel the cycle of execution with your now-altered DNA.

Answer these questions:

1. Looking back at your aspirations and the legacy you wish to leave behind, what is a single project you need to take on, starting *today*, to make those aspirations a reality? Why are you passionate about this project? How will it help you create a legacy you will be proud of? Remember, becoming an executioner takes laser-like focus and consistent effort, so keep your list short. If you've successfully executed before, you can choose more than one project, but if you haven't built the habit of executing yet, it's better to take one project through to its conclusion and then create a plan for the next one— always being cognizant of the minefields at three, six, and nine.

2. If your undertaking will take longer than a year, what do you need to do in the next twelve months to move it forward? I'm not a big fan of long-term planning; I don't go out more than a year for anything that I plan. While your cycle of execution may extend past a year, you should create a plan for the next twelve months, adjusting as necessary along the way, and then do a big reevaluation and decide what you need to do differently at that point.

3. Once you've gotten some momentum on this project—in other words, you're past three and six—and you're feeling like you're getting the hang of being an executioner (pun intended), you can then consider starting an additional project tied to your aspirations and legacy. But you need to have the experience of making it well past halfway through the cycle of execution before you start to multitask.

Finally, get started *today*. If you don't start, you'll never finish. When you start and make it a priority to do something on your project *each day*, you'll discover how quickly you can make significant progress while you're building the habit of executing. And then nothing will get in the way of you reaching those sacred aspirations that bring meaning to your life and the lives of those you love.

Get the Mind Right and the Money Will Follow

Don't make money your goal.
Instead, pursue the things you love doing,
and then do them so well that people
can't take their eyes off you.

MAYA ANGELOU

Mindset precedes *everything*. In fact, the title of this chapter could just as well be "First Things First," because you have to get your mindset right before you can achieve any worthwhile endeavor. If the literary gods allowed only nine words per chapter, the title alone would suffice.

Take a look at the execution plan you created in chapter 3. What did you put for your first step? If it wasn't to create the mindset needed to get this result, go back and change it now. Whatever your aspiration, you should think, *Get my mind right and the miles will follow . . . Get my mind right and the relationship will follow . . .* or fill in the blank with "the new business will follow" or "the degree" or "the garden" or whatever aspiration is driving you. If your mindset is off, you'll be fighting an uphill battle that will keep you from transforming your DNA and creating your own reality.

Too many people make the mistake of leading with the result rather than the mindset and find themselves crashing and burning before they've executed and closed the loop. For example, three of the five times I didn't complete the Badwater Ultramarathon were due to mindset issues that I couldn't recover from. I let the miles blow up in my mind, didn't run the race I planned, and dropped out. There's no sugarcoating it nor solace found in making it "92 miles": I flat-out failed. The seven times I *did* finish the race, my team and I worked incredibly hard to keep my mind focused, with a calm yet laser-like intensity, on whatever was required of my next step. Instead of thinking of the race as 135 miles, for example, we broke the course into six different segments, signified by the six checkpoints in the race, each needing a different strategy to make it through.

At one point in the race, when I was completely exhausted and sleep-deprived after twenty hours of continuous running, I even had my team rent a room in this scary, rundown, fourteen-room motel in the middle of the desert (seriously, it looked like the motel in a horror film like *The Hills Have Eyes*). When I reached the hotel in the hottest part of the race, feeling completely beaten, I took a shower, put on my pajamas, laid on the bed and closed my eyes. The alarm went off twenty minutes later, and, like the dawning of a new day, I got up, took off my pajamas, took a shower, put my running clothes on, got back on the course, and started running again, tricking my mind into thinking I'd gotten a lot more sleep than I actually had. That's just one case of using mindset to keep you going one mile at a time, one section at a time, to get to that prized finish line.

To reach your aspirations, you must develop the mindset of someone who has been massively successful in that area. If you want to grow that beautiful garden, for instance, you need to change your mindset to that of a master gardener so you will do what's needed to cultivate your flowers. If you want to start a business or make your relationship magnificent or transform your body, you must get your mind aligned with people who are the best in those fields and absorb that mindset. And yes, developing a master's mindset will also help you make the money you can use to benefit yourself, your family, and (hopefully) others.

As I look back at the other four nonfiction books I've written (one business, one spiritual, and two real estate books), I remember that each one started with some reference to preparing the mind for what was to follow. Initial sections or chapters like "Why a Ph.D. in Paradoxicology Is Required," "Have Vision for Your Passion," "Tap Into Eternal Success," and "Figure Yourself Out: Spend Time in Introspection" are but a few.

Remember, mindset must come first, no matter what you are aspiring to achieve.

What Do You Want Money For?

The reason I included money in the chapter title is that whenever people list their goals, inevitably one of them will be linked to having or making more money. When I ask money-related questions of the audience when keynoting business or real estate events, for example, they'll answer by saying things like, "Frank, I don't mind flipping little houses, but eventually I want to be selling multimillion-dollar houses on the ocean like you." So I'll ask, "Why do you want to do that?" "Because I want to make more money," they'll reply. "Why do you want to make more money?" "Well, I want a better house." "Why do you want a better house?" "I need a bigger garage for the cars I want to buy." "Why do you want more cars in your garage?" And on and on. If I keep digging, eventually they'll either tell me to ask the next person or they'll say, "Frank, I just want to be happy." *That's* the true "why" for money: happiness. It's not that you want money, per se. You want what you perceive money will do for you.

Let me be clear. Money provides two things in absolute abundance, as much as you can dream of or imagine: *relief* and *comfort*—relief from financial pressure, fear of the future, or arguments with a spouse, for example, and greater comfort in the form of material things to satisfy your wildest desires. Of course there's nothing wrong with wanting greater relief and comfort, but that's not what you said you wanted. You said you wanted happiness, right? When your desire for money becomes a need just to have *more*—in other words, when desire becomes unabated greed—a maddening cycle ensues.

I'm a philanthro-capitalist; therefore, I have no problem with a goal to make money, especially when it's used to benefit others (and some studies show that spending money on others makes you happier anyway).[1] But in my observation, human beings weren't wired for, and struggle with, any form of excess (except for love). Research backs this up: a 2018 survey of 1.7 million people from 164 countries established there was a certain amount of income per year that produced optimal emotional well-being,[2] and earning too much beyond that amount led to "unhealthy social comparisons and unfulfilling material pursuits."[3] As a species, we don't do well with too much food, too much alcohol, too much time, too much money. How many high-profile individuals can you name where the love of money took over and their lives spun out of control? And today the drive for *more* is exacerbated by the consumerism and materialism we see every day on our screens (phone, computer, television). Bottom line: people who are ensnared by a bottomless hunger for "more" will never feel a deep sense of relief, comfort, or happiness. "The more things you get, the more you want, just tradin' one for the other": so goes the lyrics to Van Halen's song, "Right Now."

I'll be honest: I went through the phase where the things and toys that money can buy were of paramount importance to me. Coming from a small town in Indiana to Palm Beach at eighteen years old will have that effect on

---

. . . material things never return the energy that we put into them.

---

you, and in my early years as a successful entrepreneur, like a kid in a candy store, I had Ferraris, a Mercedes Gullwing, a Lotus Turbo Esprit, a Hummer H1; I wore custom suits (yes, I wore suits); and for a decade I had to buy the fastest production motorcycle every year one was made. But then I realized that the amount of happy energy I put into desiring then attaining those things never lasted for very long, and I went back to basics—nice basics, but basics nonetheless. I've lived in the same eighty-seven-year-old historic oceanfront home (a 5,490-square-foot vintage South Florida property, much simpler than the mansions I build) for twenty-five years. That 1988 Yugo that took me cross-country? My hairdresser has a pair of scissors that cost more than that car did when I bought it!

Problems or impediments to your aspirations don't really exist; what exists is an artificially inflated evaluation of the importance of things. I'm fortunate to have discovered years ago that material things never return the energy that we put into them. I enjoy the things I have, sure, but I've left behind the need to pursue a lot of things I don't need. It seems the simpler the things, the deeper the appreciation. Remember, money is just one byproduct of pursuing our sacred aspirations with the right mindset. Nothing wrong with money at all, but our aspirations should be so much bigger and better than a certain amount in the bank.

Combine Passion and Practicality to Fulfill Your Aspirations

That's not to say you should leave considerations like money out of your aspirations—I'm not saying that at all. Your aspirations must be fueled with passion, yes; but if you let your passions overcome your common sense or lead you to make bad decisions, they will derail that cycle of execution you planned out in the last chapter. That's why the best mindset to support your aspirations always contains a healthy dose of the *practical*. The first time I made money on real estate, I was so happy that I had taken and validated the concept of buying an undervalued piece of property—creating value in it like nobody else, marketing it like nobody else, and making a $7,000 profit on that first house—they could have paid me in Monopoly® money and it wouldn't have mattered. The combination of aspiration, purpose, and mindset had been proved right, and I was over the moon. But I quickly realized that passion alone wouldn't get me access to the resources I needed to create the beautiful oceanfront masterpieces I envisioned. I couldn't let the "real estate artist" have free rein; I had to bring the practical side to the party as well.

Now, you may have heard different versions of the right brain/left brain theory, that people whose right brains are more developed tend to be more artistic and creative, and people who are left-brain dominant tend to be more analytical and detail-oriented.[4] While that is an oversimplification of very complicated scientific research, certainly some people are more spatially and visually oriented and are better at the visual arts, and others tend to focus more on words and are good at following step-by-step directions.[5] But far too many parents and teachers make the mistake of identifying their children or students from a very early age as either right-brained or left-brained. So we end up saying either, "I am not creative," or "I have no business sense whatsoever."

You might be surprised to learn that my background was a lot more attuned to the practical "left brain" side than the artistic "right brain" side. If it wasn't for my A's in math, my 1.8 GPA in high school would have been *far* lower. My father and grandfather were bankers, and I was conditioned to think that I would follow in their footsteps because I had a banker's DNA. I believed it for decades—until I realized, "No, I want to change my DNA. I will be creative." So I left Indiana and came to Florida. Even though I assumed that I didn't have a creative bone in my body, I was determined to awaken that side of my brain. While it took some years to develop, I eventually became what the *Wall Street Journal*, *The New York Times*, and *USA Today* call a "real estate artist." So, I was able to transform from what I was born to be—a spreadsheet/number cruncher/bean counter—to become what I wanted to be: an extremely creative individual.

How did I wake up the creative side of my brain? Simply put, it was *aspiration.* Having that otherworldly desire to achieve something high or great requires that you use more of yourself—you have to be "all in." You must date destiny before marrying her, and part of that courtship is trying things that rapidly fire in the left brain and right brain. Logic, then imagination. Facts, then intuition. Analysis, then art. Creativity, then practicality. Big picture, then detail. You must awaken the side that you've been taught is not your strength. Even if you were told your entire life that you're not creative, your synapses weren't turned off to make you a non-creative individual; you can awaken your creativity at any time, like I did. And if you've always favored the creative side and said to yourself, "I'm not good at numbers," you can develop that side of your brain with training and focus too.

I find trying new things without a script, lesson plan, rules, or boundaries ignites the process. To me, the ability to toggle in nanoseconds between right brain and left brain is the ultimate definition of getting the mind right, and one of the developed gifts of the uber-successful. And as the title of this chapter says, when the mind is right, the money will follow.

We need the creative drive and energy to keep us passionate about our aspirations, but we also need the practical voice of reason in our heads to make those aspirations real. And your aspirations will suffer if you overuse one side at the expense of the other. A decade ago, with a $30 million ocean-to-Intracoastal property known as Acqua Liana, I let the artist overcome my practical side. I put things into that house that cost way too much money—like the first-ever glass "water floor" that covered the entire 500-square-foot foyer, with hand-painted Monet-inspired tiles brilliantly illuminated from below the shimmering surface, a two-thousand-gallon arched aquarium wet bar that you could walk underneath and see over one hundred exotic fish swimming above, and twenty-four-foot oceanfront sheeting water walls. My margins were severely compressed because I became enamored with the artist and disregarded the businessman. It made for a great museum but not a great profit center. Ever since, I have been disciplined in leading with creativity and passion and then immediately following up with practicality. Practicality allows you to activate then execute what your creativity and aspirations create.

The Other Mindset Trap: "Often Happy, Seldom Satisfied"

A word of caution when it comes to your mindset: please avoid a trap that I have found myself in all too often during my career. It's a different version of the "more" that I talked about earlier, the "more" that keeps you from being happy with what you have achieved thus far, and instead makes you focus on reaching the next mile, the next milestone, the next level. I call it the "next" syndrome, and it can keep you from recognizing the value of what you have and the magnificence of what you've accomplished.

For years when I finished Badwater every July, I was already preparing for the following year's race. Just as soon as I put an oceanfront property on the market, I was scouting for yet another prime piece of real estate and envisioning my next masterpiece.

Certainly, I believe you can always better your previous best, and I've lived most of my life never letting myself rest on my previous accomplishments. But I've found that this kind of thinking can burn people out, including me, including you. I've lost some good employees because I believed that if you work for me, you should always be trying to better your previous best. And for overachievers, this "next" thinking also

---

. . . balance the drive to better your previous best with the ability to enjoy your accomplishments as you go.

---

creates a lot of anxiety and stress. They will say to themselves, "It just took everything I had to raise the bar to this level, and now I gotta do it again because that's what I believe?" Failing to acknowledge the greatness of what you've managed to do because you're so focused on finding what's next can create an emptiness inside and a very lonely life.

Just like you need to balance the creative and practical sides of your brain, you need to balance the drive to better your previous best with the ability to enjoy your accomplishments as you go. When you complete the cycle of execution on a project or an endeavor, celebrate it. When you cross the finish line of a race, revel in it for a week, not just for the moment you raise your hands over your head in victory. That's the kind of mindset that will help keep you on the upward spiral of confidence and lead you to the results you are capable of creating.

Creative, Practical, or Both?

Let's make this discussion of mindset practical, precise, and personal. Take a look at the plan you created in chapter 3 from the perspective of using both sides of yourself. Where are you exercising the creative side? Where did you bring in the practical side? Does your plan have too much of one and too little of the other? Is it clear that you need to develop greater strength in your creative or practical sides? If you want to grow that beautiful garden, for example, have you dedicated most of your time to designing it while you failed to consider things like growing season, site and soil characteristics, and the amount of time it will take you to tend it?

As you pursue your aspirations, how can you toggle between both sides of the brain to produce a mindset with both passion *and* practicality, a creative process *and* tangible results? Equally important, does your plan help you avoid the "next" syndrome? Does it build in acknowledgment of your accomplishments even as you look forward to your next adventure or challenge?

Mindset precedes results every time. Producing results will reinforce the mindset that will put you on the path of realizing those aspirations that make you feel happy and give your life meaning and purpose. Ultimately, mindset is a critical part of reshaping your DNA and recreating your reality.

Re-Invent and Re-Create

*In order to do great things, you must be
unafraid to recreate yourself.
You can't do that holding on to
a glory from yesterday.*

PHARRELL WILLIAMS

Back in September 2020, when I hopped into my 1988 Yugo and set off across the country, I wasn't just driving away from South Florida: I was watching my identity voluntarily disappear in the rearview mirror. The OBJECTS ARE CLOSER THAN THEY APPEAR warning seemingly held no truth. I had officially retired from creating real estate artistry, and with every mile I was recreating myself. I was driving away from everything that had given me purpose for the past thirty years, as I sought to validate my beliefs and ideas around the topic of aspiration so that when I wrote this book, it would be the best it could be. The Yugo We-go Tour was a chance to let go of everything I was used to doing and being and to become someone new, away from all the people who knew me or knew of me. That moment was a perfect example of the *reinvention and recreation* that I've applied in the past and that are certainly in the center of my life's windshield right now—a whole new form of aspiration and rebirth.

Granted, for those whose lives were turned upside down by the events of 2020, mine may seem like a very minor form of reinvention. It was a year when many people felt as if the world went from turning on its axis at one thousand miles per hour to zero in less than a week. Everyone's life was disrupted, some more than others. But it was also a great time to assess what is truly meaningful and shape our days accordingly. When Florida went into lockdown, for example, I re-read some of my old journals to examine my thought processes of past years, to see what had led me to where I was in 2020, and to look for thoughts and actions I was still doing that no longer served me and that I should abandon or redirect. The assessment stage is important when it comes to reinvention. When you look back on those days of 2020, and even into 2021, what was your response to having your life turned upside down? Did you dog-paddle just to keep yourself afloat? Did you feel as if you were going backward? Or did you use the time to look at where you were, what you were doing, how you were living your life, and then ask yourself, *How can I reinvent or recreate moving forward?*

No matter whether 2020/2021 were great or difficult years for you, all of us will have COVID-like situations in our lives at some point. Whether it's a divorce, illness, death of a loved one, a failing business, bankruptcy, or other challenges, inevitably events will sweep the legs out from under everything we consider important. In my experience, that's the best time to reassess your life and aspirations and reinvent or recreate. To paraphrase the movie *Rocketman* again, you must be willing to kill the person you were born to be in order to become the person you want to be. Be warned,

---

. . . each one of us has a bright star inside, just waiting for that supernova event . . .

---

however: peeling away the things that tie you to your past can make you feel extraordinarily vulnerable and raw. It's like being in my 1988 Yugo: no creature comforts, a frayed seatbelt, no windshield washer reservoir, a gas tank that holds only seven gallons, no radio; not even able to go the speed limit on back roads, running clothes drying on a tiny shelf beneath the rear window where they'll get the most sun. It's old-school, minimalist, stripped raw—and beautiful.

In these circumstances it may take a while for you to see what a great thing reinvention is. It's a chance to rewrite your DNA and create your own reality. You must recognize that the sentence you were supposedly given at birth—be it a good sentence, a privileged sentence, or a death sentence—isn't fixed in stone. Like Elton John or Freddie Mercury, at any moment you can reinvent yourself with a single choice. Instead of following in his dad's footsteps and joining the Royal Air Force, Reginald Dwight went to the London School of Music, and then he left two weeks before graduation to follow his passion for rock music, renaming himself Elton John.[1] Freddie Mercury, born as Farrokh Bulsara, came to London to study art, then formed the rock group Queen when he was twenty-five years old.[2] Sure, Elton and Freddie are mega-stars, but I believe each one of us has a bright star inside, just waiting for that supernova event, ready to break out of the idea of who we are "supposed" to be so we can reinvent and recreate into who we truly want to be.

Regrets = Time to Reinvent

One of the clearest signals that it's time to reinvent yourself is a feeling of regret, and in my live seminars, I've done an exercise designed to bring this home. I would ask for a volunteer to come to the front of the room, where there was a beautiful bronze metal and mahogany wooden casket. Two assistants dressed as angels would take that person's hands and help them to climb in and lie down. Then, closing the bottom half of the casket so just their chest and head where showing, and holding the volunteer's hand, I'd look deep into their eyes and say, "One day you'll be lying in something like this for real. And moments or days before then, you will likely have been thinking about things you should have done, or wish you had pursued. I want you to articulate and share one regret that you have right now, knowing that when you get out of this casket, the only thing to die will be that regret." It's a powerful purging exercise for everyone in the room, and it brings home an important point: we all have only a limited time here on earth, and we need to be ready at any point to reinvent ourselves—if for no other reason than to escape from the regrets that can stagnate and then poison our lives.

One of the first places I stopped on the Yugo We-go Tour was the largest cemetery in Tallahassee, Florida. While there, I came across two very different men doing maintenance on the grounds and headstones. Robert is in his seventies, lacking formal education beyond eighth grade, homeless and living in a shelter. Darnell, twenty-four years old, is on a work-release program from prison. I asked them both the same question: "Being in a cemetery all day must make you think about your own mortality. Tell me: do you have any regrets?"

Robert told me, "Yes, but at my age I can't do anything about them. I'm just happy to have a job, a warm place to stay, and I'm not underneath the ground just yet!" But Darnell's perspective was completely different. When he saw headstones with dates that showed people who had died when they were younger than he was, it made him think about his past—especially when he saw a headstone with his last name on it, which happened more frequently than he liked. "I'm not goin' back to the kind of life that was gettin' me here earlier than I should be," he said. "I've taken a few wrong turns in my life, but, man, now every day is a clean slate."

I appreciate cemeteries and funerals because there's a depth of reflection in those environments that you really can't get anywhere else. Whenever I look at a casket or headstone, I wonder what that person would say if they could come back to life for just an hour. Throughout the nineteenth century, there were coffins that incorporated a system for someone who was still alive and buried by mistake to signal the living by ringing a bell above the ground, hence the origin of the saying "saved by the bell."[3] Even today there are stories of people being declared dead, only for them to wake up in the morgue or mortuary.[4] What if, after your death, you had the chance to "ring the bell" and get a second crack at life? What would you have regretted? What would you do differently? When you're at the end of your life, which do you think will weigh more heavily on your mind and heart: what you did, or what you failed to do? And what if you could use your regrets as an incentive to make amends for things you did or to take action on the things you didn't dare to do?

Let's face it, we all have regrets. That's just the way life is. But there's a reason the good Lord gives us the sensation of regret, and we can choose to see it as a signal to reinvent and recreate. And maybe we should add *rebirth* to that list.

Recognizing Pivot Points

How do you know when it's time to reinvent and recreate? Regret is a key signal, and so are failure and (as in Darnell's case) destructive behavior. But most of us experience pivot points in our lives simply when our old ways and paths no longer take us where we want to go and we feel either a push or pull toward reinvention. For instance, some people find themselves staring in the bathroom mirror, not liking who they see in the reflection. Or it may be a come-to-Jesus moment, when someone no longer can stand to continue with the habit, the job, the relationship, the way of life, and somehow he or she finds the courage and will to reinvent or recreate. For others, the impulse to reinvent feels like a steady buildup of pressure, like movement of tectonic plates in the earth's crust. Regardless, you avoid or bury such pivot points at your peril. Rather than waiting for the "earthquake" of a divorce, an illness, or a business failure to occur, it's better to proactively choose to reinvent yourself and discover new aspirations and new realities.

Pivot points don't happen all that often, thank goodness—otherwise it would be difficult to complete those cycles of execution we talked about in chapter 3, or to pursue our aspirations to their ultimate fulfillment. For example, my path has been quite linear: I've been in the real estate artistry business for thirty years, married to Nilsa for thirty-one years, competing at Badwater for fifteen years, writing seven bestselling books in six genres for twenty years, and running the Caring House Project Foundation for twenty-three years. Yet I've had seminal moments of reinvention and re-creation: the seventh and last time I walked out of juvenile detention and said "no more" . . . when I left Indiana for Florida at eighteen with a duffle bag and $50 . . . when I changed from the tennis pro "Mick" to Frank the businessman . . . pivoting from flipping $50,000 crack houses to become an oceanfront real estate artist . . . recreating by pioneering micro-mansions instead of continuing to build mega-mansions . . . deciding to write books not just about real estate, but philosophy, spirituality, young reader fantasy, Christian romance, and mindset . . . and finally, the reinvention point I'm pursuing at this very moment. All of these pivot points were big opportunities where I chose to create a new reality and, in turn, alter my DNA.

Along the way there also have been small recreations and renewals in my career and life, but this past year has definitely been a pivot point, when I sold my final oceanfront mansion and hopped in my Yugo to drive cross-country to do research for this book. At the time of this writing, I'm not quite sure what I'm being drawn to yet, but I do know that wherever I land, I'm not looking for a new normal; instead, I want a more frequent extraordinary. And that doesn't just happen with a new hair color or the change of a profile picture.

Reinvention comes in as many forms as there are people. Yours may be physical, through diet or exercise. It may be leaving one profession behind and embarking on another, or perhaps taking a different approach to your career (going out on your own, moving your business online, or

---

**I'm not looking for a new normal; instead,
I want a more frequent extraordinary.**

---

turning a hobby into a profit center, and so on). It may be proposing to a significant other, or separating from a spouse, or going on a marriage retreat together, or renewing your vows. It may be starting an advanced degree, or moving to another state or country, or sailing around the world, seeing the Northern Lights, or taking a sabbatical on a tropical island somewhere. Whatever way you choose to reinvent or recreate, recognize this process as being joyful and fun. You've been on the same, comfortable path for a while, and it took time to clear that path through the jungle of life. But comfort is overrated, and we aren't wired to reside there for long lest we dull our radiant senses. Now you get to take out your machete, sharpen it, go back into the jungle, and clear a new path! Yes, it'll take time and effort. Yes, the idea of picking up that machete again may be daunting. But there's enormous freeing energy created when you set your sights on a new destination and put your entire heart, mind, and will to reaching it.

Reinvention Doesn't Have to Be a 180-Degree Turn

Do you remember the story from the New Testament of how Saul was transformed, from persecuting Christians into Paul who spread Christianity, in one blinding moment on the road to Damascus (Acts 9:1–19)? That's an example of a 180-degree reinvention, a complete transformation by God of everything that Saul had done and believed in prior to that instant. There are situations where a 180-degree reinvention is appropriate: substance abuse issues or destructive behavior, for example. I've experienced the 180-degree variety when I walked out of juvenile detention and left Indiana. However, reinvention is usually a lot less head-spinning and more subtle—a 45-degree rather than 180-degree shift. Killing the person you were born to be to become the person you want to be often occurs in stages; it's not waking up one morning and deciding that you are a different person. Instead, it's a series of small, internal shifts that, when accumulated, change your DNA and create a new reality.

Most people would consider me a go-big-or-go-home kind of guy, and therefore they would assume my reinventions would be of the Saul-to-Paul type. But the degree of reinvention is really determined by the person doing it, by the core of their essence. You don't have to turn your back on everything in your life in order to reinvent. If your life is working—if you're pursuing your aspirations happily and successfully and mastering the cycle of execution—then you may not need to reinvent; you can simply recreate a means of reaching your aspiration. Throughout my real estate career my aspiration remained the same while I was constantly reinventing and re-creating my art through the evolution of the style of the properties, the location, the price, the size, the features, and so on.

Like him or not, Elon Musk is another example of reinvention within the same aspiration. He's a brilliant entrepreneurial inventor/capitalist who has poured his energy into companies from PayPal to Tesla to SpaceX to The Boring Company.[5] His core essence and aspiration remain, while he continues to recreate the vehicles he chooses to manifest that aspiration in the world. Take a look at your own aspirations to see if they would benefit from a little reinvention and recreation. Even a 20- or 30-degree shift often creates greater energy and passion in the short term, and significantly greater results in the long term as you attain your goals.

Prepare to Reinvent and Recreate in Advance

Pivot points can occur at the end of a particular phase in your life, or when you've completed a huge goal or aspiration. The last kid leaves home, for instance, or you sell the business or retire from a twenty- or thirty-year career, or you reach the summit of Mount Everest, and you find yourself thinking, "Now what?" Unless you anticipate such moments and proactively choose a new aspiration or goal to pursue, you will lose an important opportunity for reinvention. Remember the cycle of execution? When you hit twelve o'clock, you should have another aspiration or goal ready to go, to inspire you and keep you moving forward. And when one aspiration is fulfilled, it's a critical time to examine where you are, who you've become, and how you need to recreate or reinvent a new, exciting reality.

It's also wise to anticipate the pivot point when you must let go of a particular aspiration. For me, the Badwater Ultramarathon is approaching such a pivot point. There will come a time (sooner rather than later) when I can no longer run Badwater, due to my age and the toll the sport has taken on my body. I get very emotional thinking about it, but to prepare for that moment I need to dig deep *now* and find something that can take its place. Whenever you have accomplished an aspiration or you can no longer pursue it, that is the time to go back to the source of that aspiration and ask yourself, "What feelings did this aspiration give me? And what should I do now to create those same feelings in my life?"

Because I am an athlete and come from a family of athletes, Badwater gave me the feeling of being completely alive as I pursued something insurmountable, incomprehensible, and impossible. I loved competing in an extreme environment, in the toughest footrace in the world, one that pushed me to the very edge of raw survival and endurance. Such accomplishments are hard to come by as we get older. When that is gone, it's my hope I will be able to find a new aspiration that can fulfill the same drive and provide the same emotional elation.

Remember, all things, including your aspirations, come to an end. To continue creating a new reality you must always be ready to reinvent and recreate. You must plan for what's next while enjoying thoroughly the race you're running in the moment.

Pick One Thing to Reinvent

In this book, I hope you've noticed by now that I'm not interested in giving you a bunch of tasks to accomplish. You shouldn't feel like you're reading yet another meaningless to-do list that makes you feel bad when you fail to complete each item. Simply put, I encourage you to prioritize. By the time you finish *Aspire!,* pick a handful of reinvention or recreation ideas that speak to you in this moment of your life, and take action on *one* of them at a time. Do you want to reinvent your business, your look, your brand, your love life, your faith, your health, etc.? Pick one, execute on it, and when the time is right, you can come back to the book and see what applies to your then-current circumstances.

Reinvention isn't something you have to take on every day. It's a valuable tool for those pivot points when you get hit with an illness, or a pandemic, or a business disruption, or when things are great and you feel it's time to machete a new path through the jungle of your life. Just remember, whenever you reinvent or recreate, you are reshaping the DNA you were born with and transforming yourself on the deepest cellular level possible. Don't let over-Googling, over-pondering, over-spreadsheeting, or overthinking get in the way of killing the person you are today to become the person you aspire to be. Be willing to give up one part of your identity to be reborn as a new, better version of yourself. I guarantee that you'll end up with a lot fewer regrets when you're finally in that casket for real.

Aspire!

SECTION TWO

Risk = Fear = Big Change or Challenge

Risk = Fear = Big Change or Challenge

If you're going to try, go all the way.
There is no other feeling like that.
You will be alone with the gods,
and the nights will flame with fire.
CHARLES BUKOWSKI

A few years ago I participated in a well-known demolition derby in Durango, Colorado. In case you've never seen one, let me explain. A demolition derby looks like complete chaos: in a colosseum-like corral, dozens of drivers in older-model cars (a.k.a. junkers) crash into each other intentionally at top speed. These modern-day gladiators are some real badasses. They don't like outsiders, they wear old-school helmets (some wear leather football helmets), and seat belts consist of a few pieces of strategically placed rebar and welds for protection. The goal of the event is to do the most damage possible to the competitors' cars, as the winner of the derby is the last car still moving. Even though I had absolutely no experience in this kind of event, the guys who wanted to enter the contest and were going to build the car believed in me and asked me to drive for them a few weeks before the carnage.

I came to find out after they extended the invitation to me that Nilsa was the only wife who would allow her husband to participate, which is a testament to how well she knows me. (It's also something like the old Life cereal commercial: "I'm not gonna try it—*you* try it. No? I know. Let's get Mikey to try it. Hey, Mikey!") Now, I've been watching auto racing my entire life; we make an annual pilgrimage to attend the Indianapolis 500 every Memorial Day weekend. And in a past life I've been known to enjoy driving fast cars and motorcycles—crashed a couple of them, too. But I'd never deliberately rammed another car, nor had dozens of four-thousand-pound steel monsters slam into me for an hour on an enclosed battlefield. And, because I was an outsider, I had a big red bullseye emblazoned on my car, figuratively of course.

Before the flag dropped to start the event, my vision went foggy and I nearly passed out as the blood drained from my brain because my heart was pounding out of my chest. Not much scares me. This did. Yet what I remember best from that day are the sounds of metal being crushed, the heat of scalding car fluids hissing out with each crash, the impact of my helmet hitting the welded steel driver's window frame or whiplashing into the steering wheel covered in old couch filling, and the sheer force of adrenaline of each voluntary head-on collision. I also remember thinking, "Holy shit, this is fun!"

Although I sustained a concussion and didn't remember Nilsa the next day, I won third place. Better yet, I won over my fears. To my mind, we all need to take risks on an almost daily basis—I take Sundays off—so we can learn to overcome our fears on an almost daily basis. It's one of the most effective ways I've found to rewire our DNA and alter our reality.

When I say *rewire your DNA*, I mean it. Since prehistoric times, the link between risk and fear has been part of our genetic makeup. After all, when our distant ancestors left the cave to forage or hunt, they never knew whether they would end up *with* food or *as* food, so naturally they were afraid. But they also knew that if they *didn't* overcome their fear and take the risk of leaving the cave, their family or tribe would starve to death. That risk-fear-reward calculation has been baked into our human genome *forever*.

Today we human beings rarely find ourselves in a literal eat-or-be-eaten survival mode, thank goodness. But unfortunately we've also become so risk- and fear-*averse* that we stop ourselves from going after our goals and dreams. We need to re-activate the prehistoric coding built into our DNA that allows us to feel the fear yet take the risks that will bring the rewards we seek. This isn't a new microchip that we're embedding into our brain: it's in there already. It's just a matter of re-awakening the courage we need to pursue our sacred aspirations.

Fear Comes from the Thought of Risk, Not the Risk Itself

The Merriam-Webster dictionary defines fear as "an unpleasant, often strong emotion caused by anticipation or awareness of danger."[1] Now, re-read the description of the demolition derby at the beginning of this section, and notice when I felt afraid. It wasn't during the event but *before*, as I was anticipating what it would be like to be in the car as it was violently slammed again and again. Even after the green flag dropped to

> It's the *thought* that creates fear—
> not the risk or challenge itself.

start the derby and I watched a 1982 black Cadillac hearse with a skull and crossbones painted on its tail, spewing thick smoke from its exhaust, kicking up mud as it barreled straight for my front end, it was the thought, "Holy crap, that guy's a lot bigger and more experienced than me!" that created the fear, not the actual collision. (Once he hit me, I was too busy keeping control of the car to be afraid anymore.) The point is, typically we experience fear when we start *thinking* about the risk or *contemplating* taking on a big change or challenge. It's the *thought* that creates fear—not the risk or challenge itself.

Here's another example. Imagine you're in line to ride the world's biggest, baddest roller coaster. As you inch along toward the front of the line, even before you get on the ride, your heart's already beating a little faster, isn't it? When you climb into your seat and the metal bar locks down tightly on top of your lap, your heart starts to race. As the train leaves the station and you start to clickety-clack up the first hill, your heart's racing even faster. Why is that? You're already on the ride, nothing scary has happened . . . yet. It's not the actual risk itself that creates fear; it's just the *thought* of what's in store that creates the sensation of fear as you move up, up, up to the top of the first big drop.

Now imagine getting to the top of that first hill, with your heart ready to explode out of your chest. The car hesitates for just a second and then WHOOSH! You're slammed back in your seat as you plummet almost straight down—and in that moment, fear is replaced with excitement and jubilation. Maybe you throw your arms in the air and scream, not because you're terrified, but because it's so much *fun*! You may enjoy the ride so much that once it's done you jump out of the car and race to the back of the line so you can do it all over again. Remember, fear is a result of the *thought* of risk, and it will dissipate and be replaced with excitement and joy once you're actually pursuing your aspiration.

But what if you let the fear you felt at the beginning of the ride hold you back, and instead of getting into the roller coaster car you panicked and ran out of the station? You weren't in any danger, yet you let the fear created by your thoughts keep you from even making the attempt to get on the ride. Have you ever stopped yourself from pursuing something you really wanted because you were afraid? All too often people let their fears become overblown and hold them back from going after the success, joy, and enlightenment they seek. And every time they let fear get in the way of pursuing something that they really want, it creates a pattern of risk avoidance that shrinks their comfort zone and keeps them playing small. We've all had moments when we let fear hold us back. But after reading *Aspire!*—or maybe after reading this section—I'll bet that you won't allow it to happen again.

What's worse is to let the opinions of others discourage you from pursuing your dreams. Have you ever gotten discouraging comments from friends, family, or even strangers on social media when you talked about your goal or aspiration? Things like, "Are you sure you want to go into that business? It's very risky." Or "He or she isn't really your type." Or "Do you know enough about (stock market investing, cryptocurrency, real estate, etc.) not to lose your shirt?" Or "I think you're crazy to buy a motorcycle." Or "You signed up for a half-marathon when you've never run a mile? What were you thinking?" Your friends and family may think they're helping you be realistic—but if I had listened to such naysayers, I would have stayed in Indiana, become a banker, and died of a heart attack at fifty because I hated my life.

Luckily, the same adrenaline-craving drive that caused enormous challenges and even self-inflicted problems in some areas of my life made me view the risk-fear dynamic in a completely different way than most people. I've always loved taking risks and facing my fears because it makes me feel alive. Yes, I did some stupid things along the way, and I'll reveal a few of them in this section, but those risks also helped me grow exponentially. If you have a desire for a better life, you're not going to get it without taking risks, and those who enjoy success at higher levels take bigger risks. That's why I am so passionate about the need to do what I described in my first book, *Make It BIG!:* "You must exercise your risk tolerance like a muscle, so that over time it becomes stronger and able to withstand greater pressure." Exercising your risk tolerance must be a consistent practice—maybe not daily, but frequently.

Take a look at your aspirations and ask, "What risks am I going to *have* to take while pursuing them and making them real?" If a risk you're facing seems insurmountable, then start with something smaller and work your way up to the big risk. The first property I renovated wasn't a multimillion-dollar oceanfront spec home; it was a former crack house in a marginal neighborhood, and I made a grand total of $7,000 on the deal. But when that risk paid off, I was just as excited as if the deal had been worth a million dollars, simply because I then had the confidence to pursue my real aspiration of being a real estate artist whose canvas would be some of the most spectacular oceanfront properties ever built.

Remember, the reason you're facing your fears is to reap the potential rewards represented by the changes and challenges you face. But I believe that your *greatest* reward will come from the process of building your risk tolerance. Every time I overcame a fear, took a risk, and did something people said was impossible, I swear I could actually feel it altering my DNA. I became better, more confident, more certain that I was ready to create my own reality and take on the next big change or challenge.

Granted, everyone's fear threshold and risk tolerance are different, and most people don't need the extreme risks I take to practice pushing past their fears. For you, exercising your risk tolerance might mean putting in an offer on your first $200,000 investment property, or signing up for that course or exercise program or dating app, or posting your first book or song or artwork online. Just remember: every mile of training you put in when you're running builds your stamina and gets you ready for the marathon you aspire to run. Every weight you lift in the gym today makes it possible for you to bench press a heavier weight next week. In the same way, every time you exercise your risk tolerance like a muscle, you are building a habit of pushing past your fears and staying focused on the aspiration or goal you desire to reach. The key is to keep pushing yourself a little farther, and to challenge yourself to take a bigger risk time and time again.

The Critical Relationship Between Risk, Fear, and Change/Challenge

The title of this section, "Risk = Fear = Big Change or Challenge," describes an important relationship that you need to understand in order to pursue your aspirations. The formula is simple. Whenever you consider taking a risk, it will produce fear unless you've faced the same risk in the past, or you've strengthened your risk tolerance over the years. Whenever you feel that fear, it's probably due to the contemplation of a risk you perceive to be imminent in your present or near future. And the feelings of fear associated with risk are a clear signal that you are wanting to make a big change or take on a big challenge in your life.

Feeling fear is never the problem—letting fear stop you is. But what if fear is the emotion you are *supposed* to feel when you are on the right track? What if the only way to rewire your DNA and create your own reality is to accept the risk, face the fear, and pursue big changes or challenges on a regular basis? Every time you push through your fears, you are building up your risk tolerance while telling fear that you welcome it and respect it, yet you will control it. Eventually you'll realize those little thrills of fear

> ... what if fear is the emotion you are *supposed* to feel when you are on the right track?

are simply signs that you've got your sights on a big change or challenge, and you're on the right track. I'm not saying that the risks, changes or challenges you face will be easier. But when you use fear as a signal to move forward rather than retreat, making the decision to take them on *will* be easier. When you can say to fear, "Great! This means there's a big change or challenge ahead of me that might produce a great reward," then life is very different.

Look, I'm wired the same way you are. I still feel fear every day, but I refuse to let it stop me. Sure, fear can signal that it might be prudent not to take this particular risk. But because I've exercised my risk tolerance so consistently, I can evaluate most risks very quickly and make the decision whether they're worth taking. Regardless, I'm not going to let those initial feelings of fear get in my way, because I know that anything great that I ever aspire to become, emulate, or achieve will always bring risk and require boldness.

This upcoming section of *Aspire!* will guide you through the process of facing your fear, exercising your risk tolerance, and taking on the big changes or challenges necessary for you to create a new reality. You'll learn what I believe has been the biggest differentiator in achieving my success. You'll see how your thoughts can either lead to disaster or triumph. You'll discover why intense self-knowledge is required in facing your fears and pursuing your aspirations. You'll breathe a sigh of relief when you understand that you don't have to change to reach your sacred aspirations—you simply can redirect the energies you already possess. Finally, you'll master the unglamorous yet critical skill that has allowed me to create the world's most spectacular oceanfront mansions and finish the world's toughest footrace seven times.

It takes guts to create your own reality, but *you can do this*. Whether your aspirations are physical, financial, spiritual, entrepreneurial, relational, emotional, dietary, or professional, you must boldly face your fears and take risks, even when it scares you. Overcoming fear, strengthening your risk tolerance, and taking on bigger and bigger challenges is the *only* way to alter your DNA. Better yet, it will lead you to a new, more fulfilling reality, one demolition derby at a time.

The Differentiator

I am always doing that which I cannot do,
in order that I may learn how to do it.
PABLO PICASSO

I f ever someone came up to me and said, "I'll pay you a million dollars for one statement that would give me the best chance of success," my answer would be simple. *The biggest differentiator in my life—and in the lives of the people (real and fictional) I admire most—has been the level of risk that I've been able to take, withstand, embrace, and endure throughout my career.* When I first moved to Florida and started in real estate, I didn't have the connections, the network, the finances, or even the education that any of my rivals did. To some degree, I still don't, but I've always been willing to take risks that few other people would entertain. My biggest wins have never been about the money. They've been about accepting risk, getting over the fear, putting an idea into practice and knowing that I did it, I took the risk, and I succeeded. Where would the world, my world, your world, be if no one took risks?

One of the hallmarks of my real estate career has been to build these magnificent oceanfront properties in areas where I was setting new benchmarks for creativity, luxury, and price. When I first started out, however, no one built multimillion-dollar spec homes in places like Delray Beach, Manalapan, Ocean Ridge, and Gulf Stream; the prevailing "wisdom" was that buyers for such homes only wanted to be in Palm Beach or Boca Raton. But time and time again, the risk paid off. The same pattern held with my last property at 3492 South Ocean Boulevard, in South Palm Beach, a tiny city only six-tenths of a mile long. It had seceded from Palm Beach in the 1950s because the community didn't want developers to build high rises there, and today the only residences in South Palm Beach are low-rise condos and four single-family houses (three of them directly on the ocean) along a quirky little private road. You read that right: only four homes in the entire town. So when I bought one of those oceanfront houses with the goal of building a larger version of the micro-mansion I had just sold in Ocean Ridge, the naysayers came out of the woodwork. "A multimillion-dollar house, on a secluded marginal street, in this tiny downscale community surrounded by a bunch of condos? This isn't Palm Beach! Are you crazy?" Of course it was a big risk, but once again, it paid off, and we quickly sold the property at the height of a global pandemic and with an asking price of $14 million.

Forgive me, ladies, but guys say to me with some frequency, "You build these multimillion-dollar homes on spec, you must have brass balls." (I've had this said to me in close quarters while standing at the urinal, which is a little weird.) But I still feel fear every day that I'm faced with a big change or challenge. I wasn't born wired differently from you, and I'm not immune to doubt. I can take it to heart when I hear others talk about my latest risk being (expletive deleted) crazy. Yet fear of risk rarely stops me because I've conditioned myself to endure and then quickly move past the worry and anxiety. Instead, I keep coming back to the statement: *Risk equals fear equals a big change or challenge.* When I feel fear, I think, *Here we go on the roller coaster again!* and I quickly move into action.

Yes, You'll Fail Sometimes

I can hear some of you saying, "Yeah, Frank, I took a big risk once. I started the business, I invested in the property, I asked out the person of my dreams, I took the class—and I failed. Why should I try again?" Look, no one succeeds all the time; we just don't hear as much about the failures as we do the glamorous successes. The best hitters in baseball strike out seven out of ten at-bats, and the best quarterbacks in football miss more than thirty percent of their throws. In business, Mark Cuban might be a billionaire today, but early in his career he was fired from three jobs, his first business failed, and his second almost went under when a receptionist embezzled everything but the company's last $2,000.[1] Beauty mogul Mary Kay Ash started Mary Kay Cosmetics when she was passed over for a sales promotion at World Gift Company and the man she had trained got the job instead.[2] At age thirty, Steve Jobs was fired from Apple, the company he had founded ten years earlier, when the board sided with the CEO whom Jobs himself had hired to run the business.[3]

Successful people like Mark Cuban, Mary Kay Ash, Steve Jobs, and hundreds of others don't let failure stop them from taking another risk. When Spanx founder Sara Blakely was young, her father would ask her, "What did you fail at this week?" and then high-five her for every failure she reported. Blakely said that experience taught her that failure is an essential step on the path to success.[4] (I always told my daughter, Laura, that if she

> ... you'll never break free from that which constrains you unless you're willing to risk failure to test the strength of your perceived bondage.

brought home a C, it meant "See, I'm smart!") To create your own reality and succeed at the level of Sara Blakely, Steve Jobs, Mark Cuban, and Mary Kay Ash, you've got to be willing to accept failure as the price for taking on big risks. If past failures are keeping you from taking a risk, do everything in your power and imagination to find someone (therapist, mentor, coach, clergy, parent, et al.) to help you work through your feelings, because you'll never break free from that which constrains you unless you're willing to risk failure to test the strength of your perceived bondage.

Five Keys to Taking on Risk

Here are the five keys that I believe differentiate my approach to risk. These allow me to handle a lot of risk and still have a full head of hair and sleep eight hours a night.

#1. If there's no reward for you or humanity, don't bother to take the risk.

I used to take some stupid risks when I was younger—sometimes just for the pleasure of upending other people's expectations and lives. At the time I was young and naive and unafraid of consequences, and I also took risks that were destructive to my health, my finances, and my relationships. But eventually I came to the realization that *the whole purpose of taking a risk should be to gain a reward*—ideally, a sizeable one.

As you can imagine, I get proposals all the time for real estate opportunities from owners or realtors who want to sell me land or properties in South Florida or want me to come to their part of the state (or other states) to build my real estate masterpieces there. While I'm happy to listen to the offers, if it doesn't fit my "acquisition basis plus improvement basis should never equal more than sixty-five percent of retail" formula, then I dismiss it immediately. Why? To me it's a simple risk/reward calculation. If the reward doesn't outweigh the risk, what's the sense in taking it?

Even though you need to exercise your risk tolerance like a muscle so it will continue to grow stronger over time, make sure the risks you take are connected to a meaningful reward. If there's no reward for you or humanity, or it's not big enough, find a different risk to take.

#2. In any field of endeavor, it's better to make your first risk small.

When people come to me for advice on real estate, I tell them to be hyper-focused on making money on the first deal. Once you have at least one success and some cash in the bank from it, it won't be so traumatic if the next deal doesn't go as well. But if you go big the first time and fail, you've lost almost all your money and confidence, and you're not going to want to come back. That career may be over before it even starts. Instead, start with taking a series of small risks. It will give you increased confidence as those risks pay off and you accumulate rewards and knowledge for the next opportunity. Then you'll be more than ready when it's time to take on the really big change or challenge that can alter your DNA and create your new reality.

#3. Look for reasons to say yes.

Human beings subconsciously look for reasons to say no, especially to risk. We let over-Googling, over-pondering, over-spreadsheeting, or overthinking get in the way of taking on a risk, or we'll listen to our family, friends, and neighbors until we finally think we hear something validating and we say, "Ah, *that's* why I shouldn't do it." We use every subliminal message possible as an excuse not to take the risks that are essential for our growth.

To create a new reality, we need to flip that around and look for reasons to say yes rather than no. For example, when considering coming out of retirement, or running Badwater for the thirteenth time, of course I'm going to scan my soul and run it through the deeper purpose filter (see section 5). I'll calculate the upside and downside and assess whether the reward will be worth the creativity, time, energy, pain, and resources I'll need to commit to the comeback or the race. But I'll give a lot more weight to the reasons to say yes than I do to the reasons to decline. And ultimately, as long as I feel the benefits outweigh the risk, I'm in. When faced with a risk, do your research, sure, but look for reasons to say yes.

#4. It's okay to say no if the risk is too great or the reward too insignificant.

Even if the reward could be huge, if the likelihood of success is very small I believe it's okay to pull out or not to take on the risk in the first place. When Evel Knievel attempted to jump the Snake River Canyon in 1974 in a specially constructed "Sky Rocket," the parachute deployed prematurely and he drifted safely (somewhat) to the bottom of the canyon.[5] A lot of people who were watching said that they thought Knievel knew he wasn't going to make it across, and that's why he pulled the parachute right out of the gate. To his death he denied that he had aborted the jump, but he never attempted it again.

I can totally relate to that. Remember I said that fear rarely stops me from taking a risk? Well, life conditions, financial conditions, and family conditions need to play into the risk/reward assessment, and it's not always prudent to take on every risk you're contemplating. Fifteen years ago I aborted plans for a $135 million oceanfront spec home. I spent a year in Italy designing and developing what would have been the world's first nine-figure spec home, complete with 67,672 square feet, fourteen bedrooms, twenty-four bathrooms, an eighteen-car garage, and a 6,140-square-foot master bedroom suite. There were a couple of years that I chose not to run Badwater after rigorously training for the race for six months. I'm not going to go into the reasons why I chose not to pursue these monumental endeavors after spending so much time preparing for them, other than to say that, in the end, I judged that the risk was greater than the reward.

It's okay not to take on a risk. It's even okay to abort in the middle of a race, as I did a couple of times at Badwater. (I've DNF'd when I experienced heart arrhythmia, and another time when the bottoms of my feet were blistering and peeling off. By the way, the officials say DNF stands for *did not finish,* but some Badwater insiders say it's *did nothing fatal,* acknowledging that the decision to stop is often life-preserving.) There's no failure in deciding that at this moment in your life or career, the risk just isn't worth the price you will need to pay for the reward you seek. Just make sure that you quickly find a new risk to take, one that will provide a sizable reward, and go after it will all your might.

#5. If the only thing that's stopping you is fear, then take the risk.

As I said in the introduction to this section, it's often just the thought of taking a risk that stops you from pursuing it. But you'll find that every time you let fear get in your way, you're dying a slow, painful death inside. When fear stands in your way—*which it will*—go around it, over it, under it, or shove it to the ground: don't ever let it stop you. Once you've looked at your reasons for taking the risk and you believe that the reward is worth it, then take the risk. At the very least, it'll strengthen your risk tolerance. At best, you'll be breaking out of a comfort zone that may have been holding you back for far too long, and you'll experience the crystalline-pure joy of succeeding at something you thought was too hard or too far out of reach. When you recognize that feeling fear means you're on the right track, your fear will dissipate and be replaced with excitement and intrigue.

Remember, if you have a desire for a better life, I can guarantee you won't create it without taking quite a few risks. Don't just handle or overcome risk: *embrace* it, as it is sending a clear signal to every cell in your body that you are altering your DNA and creating a new reality. And that's the biggest differentiator for us all.

What Were You Thinking!

One hour of life, crowded to the full with glorious action and filled with noble risks, is worth whole years of those mean observances of paltry decorum.

SIR WALTER SCOTT

Were you one of those teenagers who toed the line, got good grades, and never came home after curfew or upset your parents or teachers? Or were you more like me—seemingly in a gravitational pull, always breaking the rules every chance you got, hauled in front of the law, your principal or teacher, or your mom or dad every other day to hear them exclaim, "What in God's name were you *thinking* when you (crashed the car, failed the test, smoked the dope, stole the booze, got arrested, stayed out all night, had unprotected sex, etc.)!?" While I may have been an example of such risky behaviors, even an *extreme* example of some of them, I do believe that we all need to push the risk-taking envelope frequently, beyond what some people would consider smart or prudent. In other words, you are playing way too small if during your lifetime at least a few people aren't shaking their heads and wondering what in the world you were thinking.

Think about a baby taking its first few steps, or a toddler trying a new food, or a child riding without training wheels for the first time, or any of the other firsts that are part and parcel of growing up. Every one of these represents a certain degree of risk. But if we don't take risks as babies and children, our bodies and brains won't develop normally. What if the baby stopped trying to walk after it fell down once? Or the toddler refused to try anything new and reverted to eating baby food again? Or after crashing the bicycle too many times, the child went back to riding a tricycle? *Any* kind of growth requires us to push beyond our current capabilities—in other words, to take risks.

When we hit adolescence, the risk-taking curve accelerates exponentially, exactly as nature intends it to. Because the teenage brain needs even more new, diverse information and stimuli in order to mature from childhood to adulthood, *we are biologically wired to push the risk envelope when we are teenagers.* The limbic system, the various areas of the brain that produce our emotions, including the immediate pleasure of short-term risk-taking, is very active. At the same time, the prefrontal cortex, the area that inhibits impulses and understands the pain of long-term consequences, is much slower to fire. To put it far less technically, the teenage brain is wired to take risks without taking into account any possible negative consequences.[1] It's always looking at the sweet, short-term rewards while forgetting about the sour, long-term penalties that might be waiting down the road.

During adolescence, we're biologically wired to take risks because we need to do so in order to grow. As we enter adulthood, however, the logical, decision-making, consequence-recognizing prefrontal cortex gets stronger while the connection to the emotional, short-term pleasure-seeking part of the brain gets weaker. So we're less likely to be swayed by our emotions and more likely to let the more logical part of the brain be the final arbiter.[2] Here's the problem: whether we are teenagers or adults, if we let the prefrontal cortex shut down too much of our risk-taking, we won't grow.

A lot of us have let the "risk" pendulum swing way too far toward caution and consequences, and away from excitement, anticipation, and action. We've forgotten the necessity of risk-taking to keep expanding who we are and what we can accomplish. We've allowed the cautious, rational mind to run the show, and we no longer listen to the urgings of the heart and soul to "Go for it!" We've forgotten the thrill of speed, of pushing way

---

A lot of us have let the "risk" pendulum swing way too far toward caution and consequences . . .

---

past what we've ever done before and trying something new, of feeling fully alive! Is it any wonder that most teenagers look at the older generation with pity and not a little scorn?

Greatness is never attained through over-thinking. Over-acting, yes, but never by overly cautious thinking that keeps us from pushing through our self-imposed boundaries. As adults, too many of us are channeling our parents when it comes to taking on risk and (as I said in chapter 6) looking for the reasons to say no instead of yes. We need to bring back a little more of that teenage focus on the emotional rewards of risk, and to tell the prefrontal cortex (the part of the brain that is acting parental) to shut the eff up. No matter what our chronological age, we all must embrace the thrill of risk again, and take a defibrillator or jumper cables to the emotional limbic system that will kick-start us and allow us to embrace the kind of challenges that will lead to exponential rewards.

Risk Can Make You Feel Alive

There is a subset of people who take risk to the extreme because it makes them feel alive. Neurological studies have shown that such people have exceptionally strong activity in the area of the brain that produces feelings of emotional reward when they take big risks.[3] It's the risk-taking, *not* the success, that produces the emotional reward. We're more likely to be the big-time drinkers, hard partiers, fast drivers, extreme sports junkies— and to take risks that others may say are crazy.

When I was a teenager in boarding school run by Benedictine monks in Cañon City, Colorado, my roommate and I sprinted alongside a moving freight train and hopped into an open car. We had hoped to get off in a few blocks so we could be back in time for the monks to check to be sure we were in our dorm room doing homework, but by then the train was moving way too fast for us to jump off. We rode that train at fifty miles per hour for two hours as it serpentined through the narrow gorges of the Rocky Mountains. It was thrilling!

Finally, the train slowed enough as it crossed through a rail yard for us to leap out of the boxcar. Back then, conductors carried shotguns with salt pellets to keep people from doing what we had just done. We sprinted into the underbrush as we dodged the conductor's pellets, but we both knew there would be no evading the consequences that awaited us back

---

You must purposely smash into the guardrails of life to see if they're real or illusion.

---

at school—if and when we ever got there. After roaming the rail yard for a bit, wondering how the heck we were going to get back, we found a railroad maintenance worker and talked him into putting us inside his small maintenance train. The cab was meant for one person, but we jammed into the cramped space and made it back to school.

Yes, we got into big trouble, as the monks had already called the police. Yes, there were some painful consequences. But boy, did we feel alive when we jumped that train, as it swayed and tilted, winding its way through the Rocky Mountains! That feeling of being alive is one of the perks of taking the big risks and accepting those big changes and challenges.

If you want a bigger life, if you want to alter your DNA and create your reality, you must decide to take on the bigger risks that take you off of the usual roads and onto roads less traveled. Riches, excitement, and enlightenment are rarely found by following the marked exits on the highway of life. As the bumper sticker says, "Well-behaved women rarely make history." Same goes for the rest of us. Instead, we all need to seek for the obscure, dark, scary, and remote paths that few people dare to follow. To create the reality you want faster and reach your aspirations sooner, you must be willing to push way beyond what most people would consider the limits of safety. *You must purposely smash into the guardrails of life to see if they're real or illusion.* If they're real, you'll find out quickly. But if they're illusion, breaking through them will be easy, and you'll never be confined by the illusion again.

Use Consequences to Take Better Risks the Next Time

Today, as a man of five-plus decades, I view risk differently than when I was younger. When I left Indiana and came to Florida, I did a lot of stupid things and got away with them. I would drive extremely fast, even recklessly, fleeing and attempting to elude the police for the thrill of it, get caught, and then get out of dozens of tickets or summonses. I took some pretty significant financial risks, too, when I started building my oceanfront properties here in Florida. It didn't help my sense of immunity to risk when articles would appear in the local papers saying things like, "His middle name is Midas, as everything he touches turns to gold." We all know that doesn't always happen, but I started to believe it. And that proved to be very unwise.

My therapist says that for most of my life I have skillfully avoided the consequences of my extreme risk-taking. I don't remember the pain of a bad business decision or a bad personal decision; I'm like a woman who has fifteen children because she forgets the pain of childbirth each time, or a gambler who puts last night's losses behind him and eagerly heads back to the tables again. Through the years I've come to realize that it's wiser to remember the pain associated with certain decisions so I don't make them again. Unfortunately, this does not come naturally for me, and I really have to work at it, but remembering the pain of bad choices can help me figure out a way to make a better choice the next time. Let me be clear, however: you should *never* let the pain of a bad decision stop you from taking a risk. Too many people use the excuse of a failed business, a failed relationship, a failed exercise program, or even a failed diet to stop them from moving forward, saying to themselves, "That was too painful. Why should I go through that again?" To let the pain of failure stop you is, in my opinion, a colossal waste, because it negates any potential benefit you could gain from the experience.

While I'm not that great at anticipating the pain of consequences, and even though I have thick skin and a well-developed risk tolerance, you may be surprised to learn that I still find failure very painful. And I don't just brush myself off and get right back on the proverbial horse. It can be months before I'm ready to go again, and I always do a post-mortem to analyze why the risk didn't pay off this time. But I'd rather make the attempt than be held back by fear, because I know that with every failure I'm getting closer to the reward that risk represents.

Try an Unconventional Approach

Some of the greatest risks you'll take will lead to places you cannot anticipate, but those are the risks that can produce legacy-leaving results. When Tony Hsieh became CEO of Zappos in 1999, he upended the business's success model. Instead of focusing on profits, Hsieh put company culture front and center, declaring his priority was to do whatever it takes to keep his employees, customers, and vendors happy. Zappos was famous for offering employees a cash payment to voluntarily quit during their first few months on the job. Those who refused stayed because they believed in the company and its way of doing business. Hsieh's unorthodox belief that putting happiness first would lead to higher profits paid off: in a little less than ten years Zappos went from $1.6 million to $2 billion in gross sales, and it was acquired by Amazon for $1.2 billion in 2009.[4]

Often it's the uncalculated, unconventional risks that return the greatest rewards, and sometimes the best way to handle risk is to try an unorthodox approach that no one else has used before. In real estate, going against the conventional wisdom of "location, location, location" and creating my own market time and again has been an extremely profitable, albeit unorthodox, approach. Fifteen years ago I put a treadmill in my sauna to help me train for my many Badwater ultramarathons. I'd never heard of anyone doing something like that, and over the years I've burned up four treadmills (and who knows how many brain cells). But I can assure you, getting to the finish line of a 135-mile nonstop footrace in 130-degree heat in the Death Valley desert has involved many instances where there was no choice but to take uncalculated risks. And it's worked; I've finished seven times.

You and I know that there's no guarantee that any risk is going to work out. That's why it's called risk, and that's why it makes me feel alive. And while some of the risks I've taken might have shaved a few years off my final total, when it comes time to permanently visit that big mansion in the sky, you won't find me regretting the risks I didn't take. I'll go happily because the years I have spent on this earth will have been full of life—and I want the same for you.

R.I.S.K. =
Requires Intense
Self-Knowledge

Make it thy business to know thyself,
which is the most difficult lesson
in the world.

MIGUEL DE CERVANTES

I have made a good living and lived a full life by taking all kinds of extreme risks, but it was only after I started seeing a therapist in the last six years that I understood the biggest risk anyone can take. It's getting to know yourself on a deep level, which is an epic odyssey that no one should take lightly. I don't care who you are, how happy or successful you've been, how many people praise you to the skies, how many businesses you've built, charities you've helped, or lives you've transformed. There always will be parts of your inner life, places found only in the deep dark caverns of your soul, that will make you want to run screaming into the night.

But it doesn't matter if you find out that the "real" you isn't the face that you've presented to the world. As Socrates famously wrote, "The unexamined life is not worth living." I would add that the only way to create a new reality for yourself is to understand what's real *right now*. Growth always requires R.I.S.K.—which is an acronym for *Requires Intense Self-Knowledge*. You've got to dig in and do the work of self-examination and deep introspection, which can cause raw wounds to surface from a subconscious place you never knew existed. But it's only when you take on the challenge of uncovering every aspect of who you are at your core—

good and bad, saint and sinner—that you can understand what makes you unique.

Where Self-Knowledge Comes From

As a practicing Catholic, from a young age I was taught to review my thoughts, words, and deeds, see where I had failed to live up to the church's teachings, and then to confess my sins to the priest, receive penance, and be absolved. Believe me, I've always had a long list of shortcomings to share. While confession is not the best process for creating self-esteem, it did show me the value of ongoing self-examination, introspection, and reflection to gain self-knowledge.

During the 2020-21 COVID pandemic, we all were given a nightly reminder of our own mortality as the case numbers grew and many people found their lives and livelihoods turned upside down. And during those many months, those who were not on the front lines or under extreme duress had an unusual opportunity to use that time to turn their focus inward. For some, it was a chance to think about what they wanted in life and maybe they got a little clearer on what was important to them and what their aspirations should be. To keep growing, you have to take the time to stop, slow down, reflect, and sit with the truth of who you are and what you've done with your life.

In most cases it can be very helpful to have another person—a therapist or a life coach—to guide you on the journey. Now, I'm not naturally super-self-reflective: I tend to be more of an "act first and *maybe* think about it later" guy. But about six years ago I found myself doing some truly stupid things that threatened my health, my business, and my marriage. Those things painfully persisted for years. The best thing about this self-inflicted crisis was that it finally pushed me into therapy, so I could understand what my self-destructive and self-sabotaging behavior was really doing. In our sessions, my therapist was able to drill down into the reasons for my actions and show me how I'd been living with these physical, mental, and emotional patterns all my life.

Along with childhood gifts like attention deficit hyperactivity disorder (ADHD), impulsive control disorder (ICD), narcissistic tendencies, and a few other gems, she diagnosed me as being addicted to the thrill of excitement and danger. Although she couldn't pinpoint when it occurred or how long it took to become a part of me, I am wired biochemically to have my pleasure center stimulated by intense physical, mental, and emotional risks. Events that would upset and horrify other people—for example, as a teenager, precariously climbing to the top of a 1,132-foot TV tower to tie my shirt at the top to prove (through binoculars) to my high school buddies I did it; stealing neighbors' cars; jumping a motorcycle over a replica of the first crack house I ever renovated; rappelling out of a helicopter onto a roof of my $15-million spec home; lighting myself and my motorcycle on fire for the reveal of the book cover for *Aspire!;* and continually risking millions on spec deals—for me were terrifyingly beautiful.

Therapy helped me see that, while it was a good thing to build up my risk tolerance from a young age, at some point my need for risk could very well cross over into self-destructive behavior. My pleasure center was triggered not just by the intensity of the risk but the compounded thrill of the possibility of getting caught. When I stole the car and went joyriding, for example, there was limited emotional pleasure if the threat of the cops showing up and hauling me in was not present. I would put everything on the line financially to build a multimillion-dollar property on spec, and artistically to include over-the-top opulent design elements that broke new ground for luxury. Then, when the property sold at a new record price per square foot in Palm Beach, my reward sensor would be triggered briefly by the financial and reputational rewards—yet somehow in short order I'd feel emotionally flat. So I would seek out a new, exciting activity or project.

Now, most of the time these projects were constructive: a new mansion, a new race, a new book genre, a new grand unveiling, or another new endeavor. But if for some reason the constructive outlet didn't work out, my unconscious need for the next hit of excitement and risk could, if not for self-awareness, potentially push me into self-destructive behavior. I was like a rat in one of those behavior-modification experiments, pushing a lever again and again, sometimes getting food and other times getting zapped. In some ways I liked that feeling of getting "zapped" (or caught) almost as much as I did the "food" because it made me feel alive. (This chapter is a good example of what I call "ATV": Authenticity, Transparency, and Vulnerability. I'll talk more about this in chapter 13, "Live Your Inside on the Outside.")

Like most people, I found that having a professional therapist to help me figure out the tendencies and triggers that caused me to go off the rails was huge. The biggest gift that my therapist gave me, however, was to show me how I could love myself, even with all my faults. I tend to be very judgmental in a lingering kind of way, and hard on myself for what I consider my flaws and failings, and I'm sensitive to criticism from others. But through therapy I learned to love *all* of myself, good and bad, virtues and vices, strengths and flaws. In short, my therapist taught me to love the human that is Frank. Look, we've all had experiences in our lives that have lifted us up or brought us to our knees. We all have parts of ourselves we dislike and may be ashamed of. But pursuing intense self-knowledge isn't a process of looking for what's wrong or right. It's just about seeing what's *real.*

The Hard Yet Direct Road to Self-Knowledge

Processes like the examination of conscience, introspection, journaling, drawing, doodling, meditating, and therapy cause you to take an honest look at who you are at your core and how you are showing up in the world. But there's another uncomfortable yet direct route to intense self-knowledge: facing enormous odds or great hardships. For his entire life, Nelson Mandela was involved in the struggle against apartheid in South Africa. He had been convicted of lesser offenses and sentenced to up to five years in jail, but then in 1964 he was charged with sabotage and treason, sentenced to life in prison, and transferred to Robben Island. He spent the next eighteen years confined to a small cell with no bed and a bucket for a toilet, and doing hard labor daily in a quarry. He was forbidden visitors except for thirty minutes once a year, and allowed to send just one letter to family every six months. But while in prison Mandela could read, write—and think. He wrote letters, anti-apartheid statements, and even a five-hundred-page autobiography that was smuggled out of Robben Island. He became a leader of his fellow prisoners and advocated for their rights. He also taught himself Afrikaans so he could converse with his jailers and understand them better.[1]

Most important, Mandela worked constantly to understand and master himself throughout his incarceration. Not long ago I read a story that Bill Clinton told of Mandela's release from prison in 1990. As Mandela walked out of the cellblock toward the bank of cameras waiting for him, a look of anger and hatred flashed across his face. But in the next second the anger vanished, and he was once again in control. Years later, when Clinton asked about it, Mandela admitted that in that moment he was thinking, *These people have robbed me of twenty-seven years.* But then, he told Clinton, "The Spirit of Jesus said to me, 'Nelson, while you were in prison you were free. Now that you are free, don't become a prisoner.' "[2] That is a man who has spent years in self-reflection and inner work.

Another example of intense self-knowledge coming from hardship is Mother Teresa. Mother Teresa had been a nun for fifteen years when she felt the call to establish an order of nuns to minister to the poorest of the poor in Calcutta. It took her two years of consistently petitioning the Vatican before her request to found the Missionaries of Charity was granted. But that wasn't the greatest hardship Mother Teresa faced. In 2007, ten years after her death, a book containing excerpts from her journals and letters revealed that for almost fifty years Mother Teresa had served the poor tirelessly while feeling no connection to God whatsoever.[3] She felt abandoned by God and separated from his love. Eventually, however, she came to believe that her "dark night of the soul" offered an opportunity to identify with the darkness experienced by Christ on the cross and with the poor whom she served and who had been abandoned by society.[4] Such self-knowledge and understanding are exemplary and were hard-won.

Some people buckle under hardship. Others use it to know themselves on a deeper level and to become better than they were before. Whenever you encounter hardship, see it as a blessing and use it to take a hard look at who you are and how you think, feel, and act.

Strengths and Weaknesses: Which Is Which?

Part of your intense self-knowledge should be a frank assessment of your strengths and weaknesses. You would think this would be an easy task, but we're often wrong about which is which: something you feel is a weakness may actually be a strength, and vice versa. For example, in her 2012 book *Quiet: The Power of Introverts in a World That Can't Stop Talking*, Susan Cain showed how introverts, who make up one-third of the U.S. population, and are often misperceived as shy, socially awkward, and less successful, can use their introversion to be better leaders and team members than their more extroverted peers.[5] Some people even call introversion their superpower.[6]

Remember my addiction to excitement and extreme levels of risk? Well, those same traits have made me very successful. (Plus, as I later share, these tendencies may very well be part of my genetic make-up;[7] and even though this book is all about altering your DNA, I don't want to get rid of *all* of this particular genetic sequence.) I wouldn't be who I am today without that wiring—either pre-coded or rewired—to seek out risk, to take on the biggest challenges, and to overcome the greatest obstacles. What some would consider a weakness, I have found to be a strength most of the time.

Strengths and weaknesses often depend on context. Take running, for example. Runners tend to divide into two categories: sprinters and distance. And it turns out that the types of muscles required to excel in each category are different. Sprinters need *fast-twitch* muscles that give them explosive power at the start of a race. They use those same muscles to provide the final burst of energy to propel them across the finish line. However, fast-twitch muscles are fueled by glycogen, which lasts for only about fifteen minutes. That's why these muscles get tired quickly and are good only for short bursts. Distance runners, on the other hand, use *slow-twitch* muscles, which are fueled by oxygen and can keep going for much longer periods of time.[8] A sprinter trying to run a distance race might pull out in front of the pack in a race but will fade as his energy runs out. A distance runner competing in a sprint will be slow off the block and would not be able to accelerate enough to beat the rest of the field to the finish line. What is a strength in one context is a weakness in another.

Sometimes your strength and weakness can be the exact same thing. A trait Mother Teresa and I share is monomaniacal focus. When I get an idea in my head—as I did in 2010 right after a devastating earthquake in Haiti: to assemble a search and rescue team, commandeer two private planes, load them with supplies, fly into a country that had just lost 300,000 lives, and then land on a runway that was still belching with aftershocks—I will decide to do it on impulse, in the moment. And once I decide, nothing's going to get in my way. That focus and decisiveness is a big part of the extraordinary results I've been able to achieve, but being impulsive also has gotten me into a *lot* of trouble through the years. It's both a strength and a weakness, and I have to be careful to assess which it is in a particular context. I call it putting the initial thought through the impulse filter to quickly learn if it's constructive or destructive. I know, you would think being able to tell the two apart would be easy, yet for me, the lines can become blurred.

A strength *overused* can quickly turn into a weakness also. Have you ever had someone on your team or in your business who was incredibly good with details, able to spot any mistake, error, or typo no matter how small? You want that kind of person as your tax accountant, for example, or your quality control (QC) manager. But what if your accountant becomes so obsessed with the details that he or she failed to file your returns on time? Or the QC manager refused to release the latest groundbreaking product because he/she needed to check it one more time, and your competitor beat your company to market? I'm all for attention to detail, but at some point you have to file the returns, release the product, or hold the grand unveiling for the next oceanfront mansion. Any strength that's overused and unchecked becomes an obstacle rather than an asset.

Sometimes a perceived weakness can be of benefit as long as you keep it under control. I once said to my therapist, "I've been told by a few haters that I'm a narcissist, and I looked up the definition[9] and it startled me. Am I *really* a narcissist?" And she answered, "Frank, there's no way in hell you would have succeeded at the level that you did if you didn't display what's known as healthy narcissistic behavior.[10] For you, it's a gift because you keep it well under control. And I can tell you that while you are very

---

Any strength that's overused and unchecked becomes an obstacle rather than an asset.

---

bombastic outside, inside you're a very humble and kind person. What's more, a narcissist has no empathy. Look at the love you've shown to so very many children in Haiti over the years."

You, too, have strengths and weaknesses that are great in some contexts and unhelpful in others. The best thing you can do is to identify them and see how *both* can help you in the most important areas of your life.

Nature Versus Nurture

Understanding yourself begins by understanding where you came from and what you're made of—and that takes some digging. You've probably heard about the concepts of nature and nurture: how human beings are shaped by genetics and environment. For much of the twentieth century, scientists focused heavily on genetics and DNA as the most important influences. Researchers cited studies on identical twins separated at birth as demonstrating the power of genetics: many such pairs exhibited similarities in characteristics (like choice of cigarettes and religiosity[11]) that were not previously considered to be genetically linked. But in the twenty-first century, it's becoming clearer that who we are as individuals is a result of an intricate interplay between the DNA that we are born with and the effects of our environment throughout childhood and beyond.[12] Most studies seem to indicate that it's about fifty-fifty: who we are and how we behave is half determined by genetic predispositions, and half by the environment in which we are raised and in which we live today.

We've talked a lot about how it's possible to alter your DNA—well, your environment has been doing just that for your entire life. That's why intense self-knowledge begins by understanding where you came from, both genetically and environmentally. You need to explore the way that you were wired within your own family, what you were destined to be and do—and how you can choose to reshape that destiny *right now*.

If you had to write an autobiography describing why you are who you are today, what would it say? Who were your parents and grandparents? Do you have siblings? Are you the oldest, youngest, or a middle child? What was your home life like when you were growing up? Did you experience any significant emotional or physical trauma? Did you grow up in a close-knit family? Did your parents divorce? Were you part of a blended family? Was your family religious? Did you come from money, or was your family middle class, or did they struggle to get by? What did your family consider most important for their children—good grades, athletics, independence, looks? How did people describe you as a child and teenager? What characteristics would they say were significant parts of your personality? And how would they describe you as an adult? All of these questions are designed to help paint a portrait of what makes you uniquely you. But it's not until we examine those experiences that we can see the gifts in our failures or the lessons in our successes.

Remember: while your biological and psychological wiring is shaped significantly during childhood, you can bend the wiring, or even throw all the wiring out the window and choose to become someone else starting today. Maybe you've already done so. Like Sir Elton John, maybe you were brave enough to kill the person you were supposed to be so you could become the person you truly wanted to be. Or perhaps circumstances *forced* you to leave behind the person you were supposedly meant to be, and as a result you became the person you should have been all along.

Here's the good news: R.I.S.K is about *knowing* yourself, not *changing* yourself. As you'll learn in chapter 9, creating a new reality doesn't require you to change at all. Instead, you can rewire and redirect any tendency that you or society feels is a liability and turn it into an asset.

Don't Change: Redirect

Even if our core impulses can't be banished, they can be tempered and redirected.

ROBERT WRIGHT

Over the years I've been asked to give several commencement speeches. Some took place outside of mainstream education, like those that I've given at rehab and drug treatment centers. (I consider myself somewhat fortunate that I've never had to go through a program like that, although I probably could have used one at certain points early in my life.) I'm always surprised that they ask me back, because I tell the graduates something that goes against what most treatment programs espouse. *I tell graduates they don't have to change.*

"If you were addicted to drugs or alcohol, you have a gift in the form of a different kind of wiring, a special type of synapse in your brain," I tell them. "You and I have what's called an addictive personality, and you are here because you chose a self-destructive outlet to fill that need. But here's good news: you don't have to change that wiring. All you have to do is *redirect* what's landed you in here into something constructive. Find a constructive outlet for your addictive tendency and you can set the world on fire. And you'll be more likely to stay out of rehab for good."

Look for self-help books on change, and you'll come up with more than fifty thousand choices. But even though I've been around personal development for close to three decades, I don't think it's possible for us to change who we are. Yes, that's a bold statement and a scary thought, but stay with me. Social scientists and psychologists including Sigmund Freud have said that the personality is pretty well set by the time we are five years old.[1] And over the past fifty years, different longitudinal studies (where social scientists track the behaviors of large groups of people from early childhood through adulthood) have demonstrated conclusively that the personality traits we demonstrate as preschoolers—like aggression, verbal fluency, impulsiveness, and shyness—continue to appear as we go from childhood to adolescence to adulthood.[2] One study even showed that men who engaged in risky behaviors like alcohol dependence, violent crime, unsafe sex, and dangerous driving habits as teenagers and adults demonstrated aggressive and troublemaking tendencies as young as three years old![3] It's pretty clear that while the environment we're raised in and the stresses we experience may intensify certain traits in our personalities and diminish others,[4] they still only accentuate who we already are.

Now, you'd think that someone like me, who might have acronyms like ADHD, ODD, and OCD behind his name instead of Ph.D., not to mention narcissistic and impulsive tendencies and an addiction to risk and excitement, would be depressed by the idea that you can't change. Not in the least! In fact, I believe that everything we are, good and bad and everything in between, can fuel our aspirations and give us the drive to accomplish them. **We don't *have* to change. We can simply take what's already inside and *redirect* it to help us to create our own reality.**

Here's what I mean by redirecting. I'd been told my whole life that I had faults, which we all do. However, I believe that what others may call shortcomings, defects, disorders, or even addictions have energy that can be redirected into constructive channels. And growing up, I never wanted to change the parts of myself that other people said were getting in my way. I loved the risk-taking, the excitement, the adrenaline, and so on. But not long after I moved to Florida when I was eighteen, I decided that I no longer wanted to deal with the consequences of what I'd been doing to get those feelings. So I redirected that energy into constructive avenues: designing, building, and marketing stunning multimillion-dollar oceanfront mansions on spec; running 135-mile ultramarathons; writing three books in three genres at the same time and releasing them on the same day; creating luxury real estate markets in towns where no one thought it was possible; and so on. However, I never changed my core personality or my style. Even my sense of style today was born back in high school: I can trace a direct line from my favorite jeans riddled with holes to the white leather pants I might have worn to class, and I keep my hair as long or

> ## Redirecting essentially rewires your DNA, and it will let you re-ignite your power . . .

longer than I did back then. Clearly, I never gave up the addiction to risk and excitement; instead, I used that energy to get the same rewards from different, better sources. All it took was a little rewiring, a slight deviation in my DNA to point me toward constructive risk-taking.

If you're one of the lucky few who have managed to "change" yourself, congratulations! For most people, change is a hard, long slog that takes enormous effort and willpower. And if it's true that most Americans abandon their New Year's resolutions by the first of February,[5] it's pretty clear that most of us aren't very good at the whole change thing. But redirecting is another matter. Redirecting essentially rewires your DNA, and it will let you re-ignite your power, re-awaken your drive, and renew all of the wonderful bits and pieces of you.

I hope you're breathing a sigh of relief right about now. How many of us have tried to change ourselves with a diet, or a budget, or an exercise program, or a meditation regimen, or a million other things recommended in those *fifty thousand* books—and how many have failed? And how many of us have then beaten ourselves up, calling ourselves "losers" or "quitters" or said to ourselves, *I give up. I'm never going to make progress on (fill in the blank)*. What's worse, how many people with serious issues like addiction have given up on themselves because they've tried and failed to change?

But when you understand that you don't have to change, it takes a lot of the guilt and stress out of your life. It's actually a very simple formula:

1) Redirect the energy you may have spent on destructive or stagnating life practices into something constructive.

2) Amplify what's working for you: do more of it at a higher frequency.

And as a result, what was uncomfortable can become more comfortable, and what you might never have thought was possible becomes possible.

You Are Perfect and Whole at Your Core

Now, whenever you aspire to accomplish something that is beyond what you've done in the past, of course you may need to do things in a different way. But making a 180-degree turn from who you are and how you do things is rarely going to work out. An introvert isn't going to turn into Frank McKinney and jump motorcycles over buildings. I'm not going to become a computer-coding detail expert who can set up killer websites and design next-gen user interfaces. Redirecting what's already inside is more surgical, like taking a laser to cut or connect a few synapses here and there. Your essence stays the way it is; you're just redirecting it into something constructive, profitable, worthy, and enjoyable.

Underlying this chapter is an important point: You don't need to change, because *who you are at your core was molded by God and is perfect and whole.* Some people think that to live the lives they want, they need to give up certain core personality traits they've had from childhood, especially if those traits have caused trouble. Yet in a real sense, such traits make these people who they are, and deep down, they don't want to give up their "troublesome" traits. But why should anyone have to give up who they are? Why should you have to "white-knuckle" trying to change, when everything you need God has already put inside of you?

By the way, this also goes for those who see themselves as missing something inside. Maybe you're not like me, with a bunch of personality traits that so many people always told you to suppress. Instead, you feel you need to be more *something*—assertive, outgoing, brave, extroverted, organized, whatever—but you're terrified at the prospect of changing. I say the same thing to you: God made you perfect and whole, just as you are. You don't have to add anything to your personality. And you certainly don't have to become like me, or like your parents/teachers/bosses/mentors, or whoever you admire or who is telling you to change. Instead, simply go back to chapter 8 and do some self-analysis to discover who you are at your core, so you can redirect what's already inside to help you reach your aspirations.

Your Flaws Are Your Gifts

It seems today everybody's being diagnosed with something: it's like there is no normal. So I think that there's a tendency for people to feel that if they have a condition, tendency, or history that can be labeled in some negative way, it's a reason to give up or not to try to achieve their dreams. But what if our flaws were actually gifts? If we're all perfect and whole, if we're exactly who we're supposed to be, turning out exactly as we should, maybe the stuff that people have said is wrong with us is actually put there for us to use for good. What if all you really need to do is to ask, "How can I redirect or rewire this so that it's more constructive, productive, or profitable—both financially and spiritually?"

It wasn't all that long ago that I understood for the first time that what I had been told were problems were actually gifts that I had used throughout my career. So when my therapist kept layering on diagnoses of my "alphabet soup" of conditions, syndromes, tendencies, and addictions, I

. . . "rocket fuel for good" . . .

---

didn't freak out. In fact, I celebrated—first, because it explained so much of my self-destructive behavior through my early years, and second, because it gave me a clear sense of how these conditions were my "rocket fuel for good," to so speak.

I had used oppositional defiance disorder (ODD) to defy the common wisdom to create brand-new luxury real estate markets where they hadn't existed before, and to prove naysayers wrong when they told me I couldn't fly a search-and-rescue team to Haiti while aftershocks were still rumbling from the earthquake, or uplift tens of thousands of children and their families through our Caring House Project Foundation. I had used narcissistic and impulsive tendencies and extreme risk-taking behavior to devise and execute outrageous and theatrical stunts that made our grand unveilings and book launches into epic, can't-miss events. Obsessive compulsive disorder (OCD) had made me monomaniacal about creating every oceanfront masterpiece and laser-focused on *every* luxurious and

---

My "disorders" have been some of the biggest differentiators in my life, and I'm glad I never was forced to give any of them up . . .

---

minute detail of our properties, like folding the toilet paper to a perfect diamond tip point, or not having a single blade of grass or leaf blocking a landscape light, or making sure our mechanical rooms were as beautiful as our master bedrooms. (This list could go on forever. Pick up a copy of *Burst This!* if you want more.) Attention deficit hyperactivity disorder (ADHD) had moved me never to build the same property twice and led me to write bestselling books in six different categories. And my addictive personality had fueled each of the twelve times I ran the Badwater 135-mile ultramarathon in Death Valley. (By the way, many ultrarunners have addictive personalities, which they have channeled into their sport.) My "disorders" have been some of the biggest differentiators in my life, and I'm glad I never was forced to give any of them up by some treatment program or misguided therapist.

If you've been diagnosed with a condition, whether it's physical, mental, or emotional, or even if you've been told that you're slightly outside of the norm, never consider that a barrier to your aspirations. Sure, the condition may be real, and it may currently have a negative effect on you. But what if you're exactly who you're supposed to be, and you're acting exactly the way that you're supposed to? And what if everything you think is holding you back is actually designed to help you fulfill your aspirations? If something is a challenge for you, how can you rewire it, redirect it, deal with it in a way that's more constructive?

Billionaire entrepreneur Sir Richard Branson has built hundreds of businesses, including eight companies that are worth more than a billion dollars each, he has written eight books, and he's one of the first civilians to rocket into space. Yet Branson actually flunked out of school because he is dyslexic. His teachers thought he was lazy and rather stupid, but Branson says dyslexia has been key to his success. "My dyslexia has shaped Virgin right from the very beginning," he wrote.[6]

Here are two great examples of how Branson has used his "flaw" as a gift. Because he has trouble reading printed material, he has his team read Virgin's marketing materials aloud to him, and he insists that all marketing messages are clear, direct, and simple.[7] He also has created an inclusive culture at Virgin, one that appreciates differences and the uniqueness of individuals.[8] Dyslexics tend to be more intuitive and excel at problem-solving, creativity, and imagination, he says[9]—skills that are needed in business today more than ever.

Of course, anything overused or misdirected can become a curse, and I've had that happen, too. Such tendencies can end up ruling your life if you're not careful. But through the years I've learned the power of redirecting the energy created by all these tendencies into the right outlets. You can do the same. Whatever you feel has been holding you back or you haven't been able to change, you can accept them as gifts and use them to propel you forward. You don't have to follow twenty different steps to change who you were born to be. Instead, you can dig deep inside, take what others have considered the worst parts of your personality, see them as gifts, modify them, then redirect that incredible energy into who you want to be.

Redirection Is a Process

It's taken me a lifetime of mistakes to learn how to redirect my energy effectively. I'm constantly saying to myself, "I aspire to redirect a destructive tendency into something constructive without losing my identity." Or, "Is this impulse I'm ready to act upon *right now* constructive or destructive?" I don't want to lose who I truly am to conform and compromise and co-opt myself to society. I want my own reality. And I'm willing to redirect any self-destructive energy into constructive avenues while never losing the core of my identity.

When you first start out redirecting your energy and rewiring your synapses, it's like training to run a half-marathon. If you're not a regular runner, the first day of training you're probably breathless and walking before you get to the end of your first mile. The second day is the same. By the third or fourth day you might notice a tiny difference, but it still doesn't feel like you're making much progress. But by the end of the week you've shaved fifteen seconds off the time it took to run that mile; it's so gradual you don't see the improvement. And if you keep at it, very soon you're running multiple miles at a pace that would have impressed the old non-running you.

I hope that you find this idea of redirection and rewiring inspiring. If you're faced with a flaw, a condition, or a past that you believe has been holding you back, or others have told you that you can't succeed because of whatever, you now know that you can make a different choice. There's nothing you are, nothing you have endured, no supposed defect that can't become an asset through rewiring some synapses and redirecting some energy into constructive paths. Yes, it'll be a journey. It's never "one and done"; actually, it's never done. Redirection is not a door you pass through but a path you walk, day by day. You must take action consistently. As the Bible says, "Faith without deeds is dead" (James 2:26, NIV). And as you'll learn in the next chapter, it's relentless forward motion that will get you where you want to go.

In late 2021, I wrote a social media post that to me summarizes this concept. I am including it below in its entirety because thousands of people responded positively to its message.

So, as you wake and make your health shake on this Monday, if it includes a dash of ADD, a splash of ADHD, a pinch of ODD (Oppositional Defiant Disorder—my fave), a dusting of OCD, a little Narcissism, a sprinkle of Mania, and a measure of Addiction, so be it, you beautiful human being.

As you push "emulsify" and watch it all blend together, be sure the ingested ingredients find a constructive outlet, not a destructive one.

What others, especially the "professionals," have always seen as defects or disorders, I see as hidden blessings. That beautiful new reality through your altered DNA is there for the taking. Embrace your beautifully perfect imperfections, your neuro-diversity, every day.

Relentless Forward Motion

If you can't fly then run. If you can't run then walk. If you can't walk then crawl. But whatever you do, you have to keep moving forward.

MARTIN LUTHER KING, JR.

You run in the middle of the Mojave Desert, over a scorched landscape that resembles the surface of the moon. The heat mirages shimmer above the asphalt, and temperatures are hot enough to melt the soles of the shoes on your feet. There are few or no other runners in sight as you cover mile upon mile toward a horizon that never comes. After the first twenty-four hours, even with your crew leapfrogging you in the support van, you feel beautifully isolated and raw. Nothing else matters but your breath and relentless forward motion, putting one foot in front of the other along the white line from hell to heaven: from Badwater Basin, 282 feet below sea level, to the finish line at Whitney Portal, 8,360 feet elevation.

At mile 122, as you start the final thirteen-mile ascent up the brutal fourteen percent grades of the Mount Whitney Portal Road, forward motion becomes a battle of will against the indomitable force of gravity and the hallucination-filled fatigue caused by extreme sleep deprivation. It becomes eyes-rolling-back-in-your-head agony just to put one blister-covered foot in front of the other. But you can't stop. You *won't* stop. ("I'd rather die than not finish," you say in your single-minded delusion.) You have an obsessive, unshakeable drive to keep moving forward until you execute on something you started and cross the finish line of the Badwater 135 Ultramarathon.

At least that's what it's like for me.

To succeed in life, in sports, in business, in art, and in relationships, you must have a burning commitment, an otherworldly desire to make continual progress, to do the work and move forward no matter what. I call this *relentless forward motion*, and I equate it to following the white line of that highway in Death Valley. When I'm struggling with anything, whether it's running the miles at Badwater, completing a new multimillion-dollar project, writing a new book, recovering from illness or injury, or even driving the endless miles across the country during the Yugo We-go Tour in 2020, *relentless forward motion* is my mantra that I draw upon until I reach my aspiration.

Relentless forward motion will help you tap into your drive when you first get started, and, more important, it will keep you going when the excitement fades and your emotions will no longer carry you through the hard work of making your aspiration real. It requires you to pull from deep inside whatever feeling you need—whether it's unshakable will or steely-eyed resolve or just a dogged determination to prove others wrong—to keep executing on your aspirations. After your DNA rewires and you've redirected your energy (as you heard about in chapter 9), relentless forward motion will make that new direction a permanent part of who you are. Relentless forward motion will ultimately allow you to create a new reality.

Keep Moving Toward Your Aspirations

The idea of relentless forward motion combines a few ideas I've talked about in my earlier books. It borrows a little from the "lunch pail approach" described in chapter 3, "Be an Executioner," and in my book *Make It BIG!* I believe the lunch pail approach—the importance of doing the work every single day—is critical to success. I dislike it when I hear someone say, "Work smarter, not harder," because I think that belittles the importance of old-fashioned hard work that relentlessly moves forward until the job is done. Imagine if you worked both hard *and* smart. During the Yugo We-go Tour, I interviewed dozens of people who follow the lunch pail approach: servers at restaurants, cemetery workers, volunteers at food pantries, car mechanics, and so on. Their work may not be glamorous, but it's essential, and I sought them out because I honor and respect their dedication and humility. We all need that same level of hard work and dedication when it comes to pursuing our aspirations.

Unfortunately, some people can lose sight of their aspirations, especially if they don't believe hard work will get them there anytime soon. And sure, going through the motions is a kind of forward motion—but remember, the goal is to keep moving forward *while* you pursue the aspirations that will pull you higher. No hard work, no reaching your aspirations. Without aspirations, your hard work will seem dry as dust, and you're more likely to quit before you reach your goal.

In my book *The Tap*, there's a chapter titled, "Get Off Your Knees and Start Walking." I wrote it because too many people are on their knees in church on Sunday or by their bedside at night praying for God's blessings, but then the other six days of the week they do nothing to put their prayers to work! I absolutely believe in praying, but I also believe in getting up and starting to walk. We are meant to be God's junior partner in our aspirations. He creates the plan, but He relies on us to put it into action. Aspiration, faith, pretty much anything is worthless unless you get up off your knees, start walking, and keep walking until you reach your goal.

Always Seek to Better Your Previous Best

In chapter 3 I introduced the idea of execution ideally following an upward spiral pathway. Relentless forward motion often requires us to break through old cycles and leave old paths so we can find new ways of progressing toward our aspirations. The goal is not to do the same thing over and over again but to get *better* with each passing mile—learning lessons, applying them consistently, becoming more efficient and effective. Relentless forward motion will lead you higher and higher. Even when you circle back to a similar place (another business, another race, another project, another relationship), you're always one level higher than you were before.

We have done this in Haiti with the villages our Caring House Project Foundation builds. We recently built our twenty-ninth self-sufficient village, and each successive one has been different and, I believe, better. We've added micro-flush toilets and solar panels to each of the fifty homes and to the community centers, and we now build a school in each community. With each new village, we've tried to better our previous best—and you should strive to do the same with your aspirations.

One of the best ways to keep yourself moving forward is to do a post-mortem after every endeavor. Whether you failed or succeeded, you should review your efforts with a focus on getting better the next time. For example, if you got the date with that special someone, what worked? If you didn't, what do you think made him or her turn you down? If you didn't make the sports team, or the orchestra, or didn't get the job, where was the gap, and what can you do to get better so you will succeed in the future? How can you change what you did so the outcome will be different next time? And if you succeeded, what made the difference, and how can you improve upon your best as you pursue this aspiration, or one that's even loftier or more impactful?

But remember always to do your post-mortem while walking. Nothing should get in the way of your relentless forward motion.

Failure Is Part of the Process

I'm not someone who thinks that relentless forward motion guarantees success. Failure is always going to be part of pursuing your aspirations, particularly if you're taking risks and going after big goals, as I hope you are. For example, I mentioned earlier in this book that only twenty-two people in the world have finished the Badwater ultramarathon more times than I have, but I have DNF'd (did not finish) five times out of twelve races. (I'm tied with Marshall Ulrich for the number of DNFs, and he is probably the top extreme endurance athlete in the world. He's finished Badwater twenty times, won it four, and DNF'd five.) When you take big risks, you will fail upon occasion. Pursuing your aspirations is not going to be an unimpeded path to the top. It ain't all gonna be fun and games. But you've got to have something that just keeps you going, regardless of failure and setback.

This is especially true when you're redirecting energy and moving forward with the rewired DNA we talked about in the last chapter. When you're trying new ways of going after your aspirations, you're far more likely to make a mess of things. But the only way to make those new ways and rewired DNA a permanent part of your reality is with hard work and

---

Every day we have a chance to better our previous best, a chance to change the mind of fate itself.

---

relentless forward motion. Keep pursuing the aspiration, keep taking the constructive risk, and recognize that failure is part of the process because sometimes you're going to fail no matter how much preparation and hard work you've put in. As an ultrarunner in my fifties, my body has taken a beating over the years. I've had three knee operations in as many years. In November 2018, I had cadaver cartilage surgically implanted into my knee and a couple of stem cell procedures so I could keep training for Badwater. After the last knee operation, I was so happy when the doctor cleared me to run again that I swear cars could see their headlights reflected on my teeth as I grinned from ear to ear while I ran at 4 A.M. on Ocean Boulevard by my house in Florida! But then at Badwater in July 2019, I ran only 135 meters (yes, you read that right: meters not miles) before I freakishly tore a tendon in my foot right after the start gun sounded. After all the surgeries, recovery, rehab/PT, hundreds of miles of training, and travel to the starting line with my crew, my race was over before it ever started.

But I believe that *every setback is just an opportunity for a comeback.* Every day we have a chance to better our previous best, a chance to change the mind of fate itself. Every day we get a chance to *really* feel alive. Every day we have a chance to feel the rush associated with taking a life-advancing risk, and this setback only fueled my resolve to keep moving forward no matter what. Do I do so every day? Of course not. But I know I want to do the things that make me feel most alive, even while doing so with a dead person's cartilage in my knee.

If you experience significant setbacks, focusing on relentless forward motion will keep you on the path to your aspiration. One setback isn't necessarily going to derail you as long as you keep your eyes both on the final reward and your daily progress. I assure you, eventually your efforts will pay off.

Four Lessons of Running Badwater

Running Badwater has given me four significant life lessons tied to the power of relentless forward motion. The first is to *recognize that any aspiration is achievable if you simply make a start and then keep moving*. Whenever I deliver a keynote about Badwater, invariably someone in the audience will come up to me afterward and say, "I'd love to take on something like that, but I could never run 135 miles."

I smile and say, "Maybe not. But do you think you could run a mile?"

They'll look at me, confused. "Sure," they admit.

"Well, just do that 135 times and the finish line will eventually present itself," I tell them. Pursuing even the biggest aspiration begins by taking the first action—in this case, running one mile—and then committing to take that same action habitually, with relentless forward motion.

The second lesson is to *divide your aspiration into sections*. My running coach taught me to break up the 135 miles of Badwater into seven separate "races," tied to the seven checkpoints at mile 17, mile 42, mile 72, mile 90, mile 122, mile 131, and the finish line. Each segment required different strategies and support, but breaking 135 miles into seven segments turned a race that is insurmountable, incomprehensible, and impossible into something difficult but doable.

It can seem daunting when you're pursuing an aspiration that's going to take you a long time and a lot of effort. You can find yourself working day after day after day and not seeing much progress. However, breaking that aspiration into smaller pieces allows you to celebrate victories as you complete each section, and it will increase your motivation to keep moving forward. It also allows you to adapt your strategies to suit changing circumstances as you pursue your aspiration. For example, when creating my oceanfront mansions, I also divide the process into sections. One of them—marketing—I can adjust on the fly to anticipate the evolving preferences of the ultra-wealthy buyer.

The third lesson is to *run the mile you're in*. You can't think about all the miles you've already covered, nor about all the miles you still have to run. For example, during one of my more successful Badwater races, I refused

---

. . . concentrate on moving ahead right now, adapting to today's conditions, dealing with today's obstacles and opportunities, keeping your mind on the finish line even when it's out of sight, and never allowing yourself to quit.

---

to allow myself to look backward at any point on the course to see what I'd covered—not even once. Each step along the way you should focus both on the mile you're in while still remembering the reason you're there: to finish the race. You must concentrate on moving ahead right now, adapting to today's conditions, dealing with today's obstacles and opportunities, keeping your mind on the finish line even when it's out of sight, and never allowing yourself to quit.

As I mentioned in this book's introduction, in March of 2020, I got really sick (not from COVID) and came close to dying. I couldn't even go the twenty feet from my bed to the bathroom without help. During the thirty days or so that I was at death's doorstep, my thoughts and aspirations would often drift to Badwater. I was determined to build up my strength and stamina again so that I could go back. The first time I went out for a "run" (really a *very* slow walk) I could only go six blocks, and it took me thirty-three minutes to cover a little over a half-mile. If I had looked at how far I was from being ready to run Badwater, I might have given up. Instead, I ran (actually, I shuffled) the mile I was in. I did what I could and then pushed myself a little more each day. By that September during the Yugo We-go Tour, I stopped in Death Valley and ran twenty miles, from Stovepipe Wells up to Towne Pass and then back down. You probably could see the smile on my face from outer space! To go from six blocks to twenty miles is a testament to the power of running the mile you're in, of conditioning your mind to do one mile at a time, one section at a time, until you reach whatever aspiration you are pursuing.

The final lesson is to *keep going no matter what.* No matter whether it's hard or easy, no matter whether you've had to start over again and again, no matter how many setbacks you've faced or how daunting is the path before you, you *just keep going* until you reach your goal.

In 2011 I was having one of the best races I'd ever had at Badwater; I was on pace to set my personal best time and finish in thirty-nine hours or so. Then without warning, at mile 131, I passed out. I'd never fainted before in my life, but there I was, face down on the pavement, unconscious, lying in a pool of my own blood mixed with vomit. It turned out that dehydration, combined with the seven-thousand-foot altitude, had caused my blood to become so thick that it wasn't being pumped to my brain. With just four miles to go in the race, my support team had to drive me back down Mount Whitney to a lower altitude so I could rehydrate, try to thin my blood, balance out my fluids, and clean the dried concoction of bodily fluids from my face.

After I recovered a little at 2 A.M., back I went on the course. But within a few miles, I could feel myself getting dizzy again and close to fainting. Luckily, this time I caught myself before I crumpled down onto the road like one of those inflatables that had just been turned off in front of a used car lot. Lying flat on my back, I looked over my shoulder, uphill, and I could see the glow from the lights at the finish line less than a mile away. I thought, *I'm going to be known as the guy who ran 134 miles and DNF'd with a mile to go!* That simply wasn't an option—so I started crawling.

Now, typically when you crawl your head is down, but I knew that if I put my head below the level of my body, I would risk draining the little blood that was making its way to my brain, and I'd faint again. So I did what's called a "crab crawl," with my body facing upwards, moving oh-so-slowly on hands and feet, with my head elevated. But I kept moving forward no matter what. And yes, I made it past the finish line.

In life, sometimes you sprint, and sometimes you run like a marathoner. Sometimes you speed walk, sometimes you regular walk, sometimes you shuffle, sometimes you crawl—and sometimes you have to crab crawl. Ultimately, it's the forward motion that matters, not the speed. When you're committed to your aspiration, you envision it bright and beautiful in front of you, and you keep moving forward relentlessly despite failures or setbacks. Nothing will keep you from creating your own beautiful reality.

Aspire!

SECTION THREE

The Art of
Personal Branding

The Art of
Personal Branding

*No one ever made a difference by
being like everyone else.*

P. T. BARNUM,
THE GREATEST SHOWMAN

A t 3 A.M. ET on Saturday, October 24, 2020, six police cars closed the main street in Delray Beach so we could film the thrilling but dangerous stunt associated with revealing the title, cover, and premise for this book. Securing the streets with hands resting on their gun belts were six Delray cops, along with five stunt experts, ten Caring House donors, four volunteers, two event planners, one filmmaker, my wife and daughter, and a few lucky bystanders. (Well, at least I thought they were lucky.) I put on three layers of clothing, each treated with the kind of flame retardant gel they use on movie sets. The stunt crew then used the Vaseline-like slurry to cover my extremities and my hair. All of this was done to protect me from being incinerated in the two-thousand-plus-degree infernos that we would create for the stunt.

Feeling like a countdown to a hanging or going in front of a firing squad, the time finally came for me to straddle the back of a custom-made, red Harley Davidson Iron 883™ motorcycle as stunt crews painted the back of my jean jacket with a fire accelerant. I faced the camera and announced, "Are you ready for the big reveal of my seventh book? I know I am. This is for you! Let's FIRE UP this reality and aspire to break through it together!" As I delivered my last line to the camera, behind me the crew unfurled a massive twelve-foot-tall-by-eight-foot-wide banner from a custom frame. The banner showed the *Aspire!* book cover in all its glory—a fusion between Monet's "Water Lilies," Van Gogh's "Starry Night," and an Andy Warhol painting.

I put on my helmet and revved the motorcycle as the stunt crew took a blowtorch to the back of my jacket and the Harley, and both burst into flames. I smoked the rear tire and raced up the street as two other stunt crew lit the banner, turning it into a solid wall of fire. I sped around a patrol car flashing its lights and sirens and, with the back of my jacket in flames, went full throttle until I burst through the banner inferno, with parts of flaming fabric attached to me, my helmet facemask, and the bike.

I skidded to a halt as the stunt crew rushed toward me with fire extinguishers to put out the flames still burning on my back. I took off my helmet, looked at the camera and said, "Well, that was hot!" Bystanders cheered in the background as I closed with, "You think this was exciting? Wait until you read *Aspire!*" (Visit TheAspireBook.com to see the full video and stunt.)

I've always gravitated toward this kind of big, bombastic, and elaborate "reveal" event for all of my projects. I made a conscious decision early on to separate myself from other real estate professionals and authors and to garner the attention from the kind of buyers who would be interested in my oceanfront masterpieces or my newest book. From a real estate perspective, I build houses on spec, without a buyer in mind, so I needed to put on a thrilling show to get people to the front door. These have been grand unveilings tied into the size, luxury, and price tag of my oceanfront properties. They also served to establish and amplify something that I consider the most important part of my success: my personal brand in the marketplace I choose.

I define personal branding in a very specific way:

> **Personal branding is the art of amplifying your essence
> to the point where your customers (current or future)
> become subliminally intoxicated—with you first,
> then your product or service.**

Everyone, and every business, has a personal brand. Many people refer to a personal brand as your *reputation*, but it means somewhat the same thing: your identity in the world and in the marketplace. Every time you meet someone new, or every time a potential customer meets you, or sees some form of marketing for your business, you demonstrate your personal brand and create a reputation that's either positive, negative, or forgettable. This section is about identifying, designing, and then implementing a personal brand that will make you proud of who you are and the impact you intend to have.

Not too long ago there were articles online declaring that the human attention span had dropped below that of a goldfish.[1] While that's been debunked,[2] it is estimated that the average individual is exposed to between six thousand and ten thousand brand impressions per day.[3] We're inundated by people and companies fighting for a small piece of our attention. It used to be your elevator pitch was a quick, snappy description of who you are, what you do, or what you have to offer—something that you could deliver in the time it took an elevator to deliver you to your floor. Today, though, imagine that you and someone you want to impress enter an elevator together on the twentieth floor, only to find that, once you push the button for the first floor, the elevator cables release and you freefall from the twentieth floor to the first. Due to shortened attention spans, that's about all the time you have these days to make an impression. That's why the need to create, nurture, and expand our personal brand/reputation is greater than ever.

The idea of a personal brand is difficult for some people to embrace because they don't want to set themselves apart from the crowd. Remember our Neanderthal ancestors? Back then, separating yourself from the tribe was a great way to get killed. And that drive to conform is still as strong as ever: in the mid-twentieth century, psychological studies demonstrated that people will do the wrong thing and give the wrong answer just to conform with their social group.[4] People may call it "not being egotistical" or "staying humble," but most of the time I think they're simply terrified to stand out because they might be ridiculed and cut down. (In Australia it's known as the "tall poppy syndrome."[5]) Yet there is an equally strong drive to be seen as an individual and to be recognized for our uniqueness and special qualities.[6] It's a key part of developing healthy self-esteem. And I believe deliberately creating your own personal brand is a great opportunity to become more of the person you are at your best.

Some people I've coached started out thinking that the idea of having a personal brand is egotistical. But let's be honest: whether you have constructed it consciously or not, you have a personal brand as a parent, as a friend, as a part of an organization, as a volunteer. So rather than letting other people decide what your brand is, why not put in the time and effort to create a personal brand you love? To me, creating a personal brand is an art form, and should be approached with an artist's eye. It's not academic or something that's learned from a book or in school. As mentioned in chapter 4, it is right brain/creative activity and should be approached like a van Gogh or Monet painting, a canvas that represents the truth of how you see the world, not just how you'd like the world to see you. Like a true artist, your personal brand should be unique, shaped then amplified by your experiences and designed to fully express who you are at your core.

In business especially, a strong personal brand is essential for success. Your personal brand is your own version of Apple, or Whole Foods, or Coca-Cola, or Tesla: you want it to tell people at a glance exactly what it is they're getting when they come to you. I would not have been able to build the same kind of career in real estate had I not worked incredibly hard to build the Frank McKinney brand from the start. I always tell the people

I'm coaching that they should put all of their business decisions through their personal brand-building filter. In other words, is this choice going to amplify my personal brand or dampen it?

If you've seen me deliver a keynote in person, you've probably heard me say, "Build your reputation before building your bottom line" or "Sacrifice bottom line for reputation." When I moved to Florida and decided to go into real estate, I knew that I would have to set myself apart from everyone in order to stand a chance of selling my properties. So, from that very first

---

. . . rather than letting other people decide what your brand is, why not put in the time and effort to create a personal brand you love?

---

crack house that I renovated, I chose consciously to make that $50,000 house much nicer than anything else on the block. Yes, I made less money, but people really loved the finished product, and my business reputation for quality and "wow" appeal was born. Eventually it led to our "103 factor": consistently selling our properties for 103 percent of asking price.

Nowadays people look at the lavish kitchen countertops made of eleven-thousand-year-old lava from France and say, "Oh, that's just what Frank does." And Frank was doing the same thing (minus the lava countertops) thirty years ago in that crack house in a bad part of town, before anyone had ever heard of the "Frank McKinney brand." And if I hadn't started my career with that focus on artistry, care, and concern even in the $50,000 house, I wouldn't have the reputation I have today for meticulous craftsmanship and unparalleled artistry.

In this section I'm going to pull back the curtain so you can watch the Wizard of Oz work the levers that create the magic of a strong personal brand. As I defined it earlier, that brand contains three elements: 1) it amplifies who you are, 2) it intoxicates your customers, and 3) it is tied to you, not just your product or service.

Your Personal Brand Must Amplify Your Essence

When I ask businesspeople, "What's your personal brand?" I can't tell you how many say something like, "I give great customer service," or "I'm very attentive to detail." Well, that says absolutely nothing about who *you* are or what sets you apart from your competitors. That's a throwaway line; please, never use it. And unless you describe what is unique and valuable about you and your brand, no one is going to notice you, much less buy from you.

I believe ***you need to aspire to create a powerful, dynamic, authentic personal brand that amplifies your true essence—the core of who you are—and allows you to bring more of that person outside***. To amplify your essence, your personal brand should have the following characteristics.

#1. It should be original, unique, and memorable.

If you remember from the first chapter, one of the people I wanted to emulate was Willy Wonka. Willy Wonka made chocolate, but he was remembered for being original and unique. No one dressed like him or spoke like him; no one could match his unconventional wisdom or his creativity as a confectioner. He designed his personal brand to stand out from everyone else. But Willy Wonka's brand was simply an extension and amplification of his own innate traits and qualities. In the same way, your brand should be unique to you.

Early in my life, I developed the foundation of a personal brand that lingers to this day. The young adult who dressed unconventionally, dreamed big, took bigger risks, and defied authority became the man who sets himself on fire and rides a motorcycle through a flaming banner to reveal the cover of this book. As far as outward appearances go, my personal brand could never be mistaken for a stereotypical businessman. In a misguided attempt at best, and a synapse failure at worst, I once tried to adopt the look: Brooks Brothers suit, perfectly folded pocket square, a matching tie, Shiller shoes, and a slicked-back haircut. It was a miserable failure. You'll read about that in chapter 13. But your brand should be unique to you as well.

Never try to copy someone else thinking you can duplicate their success. Your personal brand should be such an original, unique, and memorable creation that trying to find the pieces of the mold from which you chose to be formed would be like trying to find the spark that started the universe.

#2. It should be authentically you, flaws and all.

In 2010 Jamie Kern Lima first appeared on QVC to sell her beauty line, IT Cosmetics. She faced the camera, looking flawless, and then proceeded to wipe off foundation on the right side of her face, to reveal bright red patches of rosacea on her cheek. "Being authentically you is the only way to connect with your customers," she says.[7] That willingness to be authentic and show her flaws on national television helped Jamie to create a strong personal brand and helped turn IT Cosmetics into a billion-dollar beauty company.

Once you've done the work and unearthed the vulnerability from your core, your personal brand must be true to who you are, not something that's put on or fake. And I believe it's only made stronger when you share who you are, your flaws and your gifts. I'm a big fan of *The Greatest Showman*— not just because I've had a few people compare me with the movie's main character, P. T. Barnum, but because of its message of accepting people for who they are, with all their unique traits and originality. In the movie

---

. . . design a personal brand that amplifies your essence while bringing what is best in you into the world.

---

there's a song all about being beautiful despite your bruises and scars. It brings home that we all have our stories and our struggles, and it's okay to share them with others. I call this being ATV, *authentic, transparent, and vulnerable.*

Today, the best way to influence people is to stop trying so hard to conceal your scars and faults. People are tired of scrolling through the perfect images and stories on their social media feeds. They want to know who you *really* are, deep down inside, and they're often understanding and empathetic when you express your fears, your flaws, and your foibles. As long as they feel you're being authentic, they will connect with you and be more likely to believe what you say.

#3. At the same time, it should be you at your best.

Ideally, before you design a personal brand, you've done the interior work included in sections 1 and 2: you've set your aspirations, decided upon your legacy, faced fear, and embraced risk. You've identified who you want to be, flaws and all; you've redirected anything that has gotten in the way in the past; and you've taken the action to become who you truly are at your best. Once you've done that, you can design a personal brand that amplifies your essence while bringing what is best in you into the world.

Think of going on a date, or meeting a new customer or investor, or getting a new job. In any situation where people don't know you, you want to have a personal brand that amplifies the best parts of you, right? Yes, you must be authentic; you can be vulnerable and even admit your flaws as part of your personal brand. But no one is going to date you, buy from you, invest in you, or relate to you based solely on your weaknesses. That's why we work on ourselves: so we have more to offer than our injuries and failures, and we can give of our abundance and strength to others.

You want to be proud of your personal brand because it represents who you are at your best. You're still a work in progress, certainly, but always moving upwards. The great news is that every time you aspire to do something greater, to stretch beyond your current limits, or to create a new reality and modify your DNA, you expand and augment your personal brand at the same time. In this section we'll devote an entire chapter on how to amplify your essence.

It Must Intoxicate Your Customers.

In the brochure for my last $15 million oceanfront masterpiece, I described the experience of the property like this: "When you spend time in the inconceivable, incomprehensible, and impossible, the rational brain surrenders, giving birth to an entirely new reality, an intoxicating, irrational, and fantastical one." That's what I mean when I say that your personal brand must "intoxicate" your customers. Any time you walk into any oceanfront masterpiece that I've created, the experience is designed to titillate and arouse your five senses (and maybe even your sixth) with uniqueness, luxury, and beauty. As you proceed throughout the grounds and each of the rooms, you're inundated by one unique sensory delight after another: a swirl of color and light; the sounds of wind, water, and ocean; the smooth coolness of glass, stainless steel, and marble contrasting with the warmth of tropical wood and the softness of greenery and opulent fabrics; and unique touches that produce gasps of pleasure and astonishment. Intoxication occurs when you have the heightened attention of every single one of the other person's senses, to the point where there is a momentary lapse of concentration in the mind and breath in the lungs. I've seen it happen countless times: the color of someone's face changes slightly as they walk into one of my oceanfront properties. Their pupils dart and dilate, and I've even seen them stop breathing for a split-second. It's in these moments of intoxication that your personal brand becomes fixed in people's minds and elevated beyond that of any competitor.

This intoxication is involuntary and usually subliminal, meaning that it isn't something they went in looking for or expecting. It's more like an evening where you are enjoying a great bottle of wine. As you savor one glass after another, there's a slow buildup of sensual overwhelm and you aren't aware of how intoxicated you really are. That's the kind of experience you want to create for your customers. You want them gradually to fall so in love with your brand that they cannot imagine doing business with anyone else.

You may be thinking, "Great for you, Frank, you have millions of dollars to create that kind of impression. How am I supposed to intoxicate my customers or the people I meet?" Simple: while my product may not be for everybody, the approach works for *every single personal brand*. Intoxication comes from generating surprise and delight in the other person so they are off-guard and receptive to the impression you wish to create. If you've ever gasped at the daredevil acts you've witnessed at the circus, or Cirque du Soleil, or Las Vegas, you've experienced the effects of intoxication. But I also remember the surprise and overwhelming delight on Nilsa's face when I pulled up for our first date in my 1987 Mercedes 450 SL with the rumble seat filled with custom speakers turned up to eleven, blasting Mötley Crüe. At least I believed it was surprise and delight at the time. Since she married me, I have to assume my personal brand made a decent impression. (By the way, when I read this part to Nilsa before *Aspire!* was released, she couldn't stop laughing!)

When I was selling my very first properties, "surprise and delight" took another form. Like my oceanfront mansions of today, I also sold these early houses with the help of brokers, but I was always there for the showings. I could see the looks on people's faces when they came in the door, wondering who this person with the long hair and rock musician clothing was, and whether they were at the wrong house. Then they'd hear my voice, and it was the same voice they'd heard on the phone. Because their psychological defenses were lowered in that moment of confusion, I could grab their attention and take charge of the interaction. I got to be the first to make substantial points about the house and to take control of the dialogue.

Ultimately, the best way to create intoxication is with your own enthusiasm about what you are offering. You need to be so excited about what you've produced and why you produced it that others become influenced by your love for your brand. But always remember: the "sizzle" that creates intoxication must be backed up with a great "steak." My projects will dazzle you with flash, but they contain far more substance.

It Must Lead with *You*, Not Your Product or Service.

When I got into high-end real estate, I realized that to reach the buyers for my properties not only did the properties need to stand out, but *I* needed to stand out. I needed to be willing to be the public face of the Frank McKinney brand, to be the P. T. Barnum or Willy Wonka or Jamie Kern Lima for my properties. Personal branding means your customers

---

Somebody's got to be the carnival barker that entices people into the show.

---

are enticed and subliminally intoxicated by you first, and *then* by your product or service. It's not your team, and it's not your product. It's on you to amplify your essence and create your brand. When you do that, the rest will fall naturally into place.

I know this runs counter to a lot of business school advice that you should center your business around your customers, or your team, or your product or service. I'm sorry, but in today's teeming marketplace, products or services just can't speak for themselves. Somebody's got to be P. T. Barnum. Somebody's got to be the carnival barker that entices people into the show. Somebody's got to be the one who is so in love with the product or service that other people are intoxicated by their purpose and enthusiasm. Somebody's got to be the one to downplay the naysayers and refute the negative comments that will show up no matter how good you are. Somebody's got to speak for the product, and you've got to have the courage to be that spokesperson.

Remember that you are the artist who has created this product or service, and people always want to get a glimpse of the creative process. Imagine if you could ask van Gogh, Renoir, or Monet what they were thinking when they were painting waterlilies, or sunflowers, or any of their famous paintings. Wouldn't it increase your appreciation of their art? I've been asked, "Tell me the story behind the 250-year-old reclaimed wood from that barn in Iowa that you used for the flooring," and "What inspired you to design and install the world's only jellyfish sphere?" To understand what goes on in the mind of the artist makes the artwork even more beautiful, desirable, valuable, and profitable.

Eventually, of course, your products and services will need to stand on their own as an extension of the personal brand you have created. When Willy Wonka opened the door to the chocolate factory, for example, it was no longer about Willy Wonka. It was about his vision and the way he made his chocolate and other candies. Whenever I open the door to show a potential buyer one of my oceanfront masterpieces, I may lead with the flash of being the Real Estate Rock Czar, but it's the substance of the beauty, luxury, opulence, and never-before-seen touches of the property that the customer is buying. The customer isn't buying me. I'm simply the opening act. When the check clears, I'm on to my next project, and the property needs to stand on its own merits as a reflection of the Frank McKinney brand.

It Takes Years to Build a Personal Brand— and Minutes to Destroy It.

In an experiment at Trinity College, Dublin, designed to demonstrate that pitch (very thick tar or resin) is a liquid rather than a solid, it took *sixty-nine years* for a drip of pitch to separate from a larger blob and drop to the bottom of the beaker below. (You gotta check out the video.)[8] While a bit of an overstatement, that's the kind of patience you need to have when building your personal brand. It's not about making one big splash with a grand opening, or a big push on social media, or one huge win in your business or life. A personal brand is built up day after day, action after action, like an artist layering paint on a canvas, or a sculptor using a chisel to chip away at a block of marble to reveal the beauty inside.

Brand building is cumulative. You must be willing to put in the work consistently to establish and then nurture the brand you want to create in people's minds. This is especially true if the brand you wish to create is one of being the best at what you do. It took years before the Frank McKinney brand was associated with luxurious multimillion-dollar oceanfront masterpieces. And I believe that whether or not I ever build another one (as of this writing I'm retired from creating real estate artistry), the Frank McKinney brand will continue to be one of opulence, showmanship, and pushing the envelope into new, uncharted territories for beauty and risk.

But remember, while building a brand takes years, it can be destroyed in minutes. Just as in your intimate relationship, one mistake on your part can cause irreparable damage to the love and trust you share, one "caught on tape" moment of stupidity on your part posted on social media can wipe out years of prestige and goodwill toward your personal brand. Rachel Hollis is well known as a mega-bestselling author, blogger, and influencer. She built her brand around her life as the mom of four children, and her honesty and transparency about her everyday struggles made her relatable to her millions of fans. Then, in a 2021 livestream, she mentioned the cleaning lady who came twice a week to clean the toilets. When one of her followers called this privilege "unrelatable," she responded with a rant in which she compared herself with women like Harriet Tubman and Malala Yousafzai.[9] The Twitter-storm that followed caused Hollis to walk back her comments and apologize,[10] but, to many, the damage was done to her brand identity as a relatable mom.

Even when you have the best of intentions, you can cause damage to your brand if you get carried away or you don't take care of your customers in the way you should. One of the key tangible aspects of the Frank McKinney brand is that we offer a one-year warranty on *everything* in the home (some warranties have been negotiated out of the deal prior to contract): if anything in the property doesn't function correctly or breaks, we will fix it, no questions asked. That's a great selling point for our uber-wealthy clients, most of whom own multiple residences and want the peace of mind that when they show up at their Frank McKinney house, everything will be in the same working order it was the day they moved in.

Socrates once said, "The way to gain a good reputation is to endeavor to be what you desire to appear." You can come back from a blot on your brand, but it's a lot easier when you've spent many years building up a strong personal brand that's authentic, powerful, positive, and based on you showing up at your best. The whole focus of this section is to show you how to construct the kind of personal brand you'll be proud of and which others will admire and respect. You'll understand the obsession and delight of taking an artist's approach to your life and your work. You'll see how your personal brand is simply bringing out of yourself more of who you truly are at your core. You'll discover the freedom of living your inside on the outside. You'll accept that having the right kind of ego can actually be good for you and for others. And you'll learn why creativity and ingenuity are handsomely rewarded in business today, and why sometimes you need to let your inner little boy or girl out to play no matter how old you are. Throughout section 3, you'll see a lot of references to real estate, as that's where I have built my personal brand. More important, I have helped others to build versions of their unique personal brands that led them to greater success, and you'll read about their examples.

Playwright George Bernard Shaw wrote, "Life isn't about finding yourself. Life is about creating yourself." Many years ago I embarked on creating a brand that would be unique and memorable, yet true to who I am and who I wanted to become. I've structured my personal brand to be an anti-establishment businessman and artist, a combination of Willy Wonka, P. T. Barnum, Evel Knievel, Pablo Picasso, and David Lee Roth. Your personal brand should bring out whatever is unique, memorable, and vital to you, so you can share that uniqueness and specialness with the world.

Take an Artist's Approach to Your Craft

Every child has a god in him;
our attempts to mold the child
will turn the god into a devil.

A. S. NEILL

In 2020, when I was getting ready for the Yugo We-go Tour, I wanted to make my 1988 Yugo look like it was ready to fall apart. To me, my two Yugos *are* works of art, yet I wanted to take that to a whole new level for the hardtop model I would use for the tour. I wanted heads to turn as cars passed me on the highway, and for people to think, "How in the world is that car still running?" So, I went to Valerie Landy, the woman who wrapped the 1941 WWII ambulance I used on the tour for my sixth book, *The Other Thief.* I told her, "I want the Yugo to look rusty, patinaed, and abandoned, like it was left outside in a cornfield or uncovered in a leaky old barn for thirty years." She was so excited as we began this new collaboration. Over the period of a month, she would send me version after version, I'd give her input, and eventually she brought the concept to life. The artistry she created with this wrap is amazing. Every detail, from the faux peeling paint, to the exposed raw and corroded metal, to the rusted gas cap, is exactly what I wanted. (You can see pics at TheAspireBook.com.)

I had a similar experience with Erik Hollander, the graphic artist who designed the cover for this book and three of my other books. I had a very clear vision of the colors I wanted, and I sent him the image of a beautiful watercolor painting. I told him, "When I'm ablaze with aspiration, I close

141

my eyes and I see vivid colors. To me, they represent the creative explosion of the brain and synapses firing as one, authoring their own reality and altering my DNA. I want everyone to see the interplay of that transformative process on the cover of this book." Just look; did he ever get it right?! To many, it's beyond beautiful.

What was exciting about both the book cover and the Yugo wrap was not just the beautiful results but the *passion* and *purpose* with which both these artists approached their craft. I won't work with someone who doesn't have passion for what they do, and they must be willing to collaborate far beyond the four corners of "the box." Erik, who designed the *Aspire!* cover, and Valerie, who did the Yugo wrap, were such a joy to

---

**When I'm ablaze with aspiration,
I close my eyes and I see vivid colors.**

---

work with because they were so passionate about their talent. The same is true about our partners in building self-sustaining villages in Haiti: I want to collaborate with them because their souls have been lit on fire. Their passion for creating a better way of life for generations of Haitians shows in their willingness to overcome monumental challenges in getting materials to the sites and to build our self-sufficient villages from the bare dirt up.

Nowadays the word *passion* is tossed around like a rag doll, but I believe that passion occurs when something lays itself on your heart to such a degree that it drops the blood pressure, raises the heart rate, and aligns you with purpose. That kind of passion is triggered when we're following our aspirations. And art is simply passion with purpose. That's why I believe that in order for your aspirations to be fulfilled, you need to let your inner artist come out and play.

Anyone Can Apply an Artist's Approach

Growing up, I always wanted to be an artist of some kind: either a performing artist, a painting artist, or a sculpting artist. But because I was the son and grandson of bankers on my father's side, and I was raised to follow in their footsteps, I felt like I was a prisoner of the left brain, number-crunching, spreadsheet-analyzing, business-only path I was supposed to walk. I was envious of anybody who was creative, in part because being an artist seemed much more fun. But once I moved to Florida, the analytical side of my brain started to recognize that taking an artist's approach actually could produce significantly more revenue than just being a businessman. I began to see that if you took an artist's approach to your professional endeavors, whatever they might be, you could enjoy a legacy career, one where you build a reputation for excellence first, with an increase in your net worth sure to follow.

So I decided that, while I might not be able to paint or sing, I would spend years reawakening the synapses on the right side of my brain and become a real estate artist. That became one of my life's aspirations, and for the past thirty years, I have created three-dimensional masterpieces on the raw canvasses of multimillion-dollar oceanfront land. Their creation has involved both mind-blowing artistry and five-star craftsmanship, while making a pretty nice living along the way. And I believe that *anyone* can benefit from bringing an artist's approach to their work.

During the Yugo We-go Tour, I visited one of my favorite hotels in the world, The Cliff House at Pikes Peak in Colorado, for a couple of nights. It was my fifteenth city, and I was three weeks and 4,200 miles into my 6,288-mile journey. When I arrived, I was tired and in a hurry to take a shower, get my clothes laundered, eat, and then fall into bed. The next morning I went downstairs to get some breakfast, leaving a mess in my hotel room. But when I came back to the room, it was immaculate; every surface was clean, every detail seen to, every item put away (including my own clothes and toiletries—even the cord to my flat iron was rolled up perfectly). I sought out the housekeeper, gave her a big tip, and congratulated her on the beautiful job she had done. It might be a little over the top to call what she'd done artistry, but she absolutely had taken an artist's approach by doing an exceptional job and taking pride in her work. Anyone can take that approach: It simply requires having a vision for the ultimate result,

being dedicated to excellence in every detail, and feeling passion for what
you produce.

Artists Don't Cut Corners

When I bring up the artist conversation at real estate events that I
keynote, people will say, "Sure, you can be artistic at your level. It's easy
when you can spend tens of thousands of dollars on blue lava countertops
or translucent jellyfish spheres." But I was taking the artist's approach more
than thirty years ago, when I was renovating my first $50,000 crack house.
No one would ever apply the words "artist" or "craft" to rehabbing such a
low-price property, but I wanted to start the way I intended to go on, to
build a personal brand and reputation no matter what the price point. I
wanted to demonstrate what could be created when you take an artist's
approach to your craft.

So I put in touches like granite countertops, under-counter coffee
makers, three coats of paint instead of one, a new roof instead of patching
the old one, and $20/yard carpet instead of $10. I made that house the
nicest one on the block. Yes, I made less money, but people really loved the
finished product, and my business reputation for quality and wow factor
was born. Every time I walked into that first house to show it to a potential
buyer, and even after it was sold, I was proud of what I'd created. It sold on
the third showing. More important to me, however, was that I had *enjoyed*
the process of designing and renovating the property. I was able to let the
artistic, right side of my brain out to play in my new career in real estate.

But the approach and lessons learned from that first house are still
with me today: don't cut corners in art or in life. Even when great masters
like van Gogh, Renoir, Michelangelo, or Monet were first getting started,
do you think they bought the cheapest paint, the cheapest palette, the
cheapest brushes or chisels, or the cheapest canvasses? Not if they could
help it. No artist who is legendary, someone considered a master, would do
such a thing. Instead, I believe they would honor their craft, their art, by
using the best paint, brushes, canvasses, or tools they could afford. And I

believe that taking the artist's approach to your craft means that you, too, should take enough pride in your artistry not to cut corners when it comes to your creations. Remember, work to build your reputation before you build your bottom line.

I'm sure you've run into people in your own profession or line of work who are so bottom-line driven that they think it's good business to buy the cheapest rather than the best. I've seen new and even seasoned real estate investors use one coat of paint instead of two, clean the carpet rather than replacing it, install used appliances instead of new, or patch the roof instead of putting on a new one. But that's not how an artist would approach their craft. And that kind of behavior inevitably leads to a lowering of their personal brand, not to mention what it does to the psyche. I speak from experience: unfortunately, there were a few occasions early in my career when I made a lesser choice on a finish, or went one level down on a fixture when I could have put in something closer to the top of the line. While the business side of me was satisfied, the artist felt his vision had

---

. . . your ROI (return on investment) is significantly enhanced by your ROR (return on reputation).

---

been compromised for no good reason. What was worse, potential buyers noticed the lower-level finishes and it turned them off, and the property took longer to sell. It turned out that the few dollars I saved by cutting corners weren't worth the threat to my reputation.

I sum up this idea in a simple phrase: "DON'T WATER DOWN THE PAINT." You may put a little more money in your pocket, but every dime you supposedly save is a reduction in the quality of your brand. That's not how great artists approach their craft. An artist's reputation is built on the beauty and quality of his artistry, and great artists understand that they must build their reputation *before* they build the bottom line. Great artists pour creative passion into their works to set them apart from the rest. *Every* decision they make about their craft is put through a brand-building filter to ensure the delivery of their artistic vision to their customers.

Never compromise on your artistic vision or the quality of what you produce. You'll find that your ROI (return on investment) is significantly enhanced by your ROR (return on reputation) and is worth every moment and every penny you may spend.

Left Side / Right Side Balance

Let me be clear: I'm not saying an artist should *completely* disregard practicalities. Even though I still love everything about the process of creating an oceanfront masterpiece and I can get so caught up in my passion that I sometimes forget I build houses for a profit, I'm still the executioner. I'm still going to finish the job, sell the property, make money, and move on. And I recognize the need to take market realities into account. You can't put gold-plated faucets and $100/yard carpet in a $250,000 house; you must balance reality with your artistic inclinations. As I emphasized in chapter 4, you must toggle between the left-brain, practical, number-crunching side and the right-brain, creative, artistic side—in nanoseconds. You have to ensure your artistic vision doesn't cause you to over-improve past what is appropriate for your market.

I've been guilty of allowing the artist to get carried away a few times. On my very first property, I made a profit of just $7,000: not bad considering that I'd bought the house for $36,000, but I would have made more money if it weren't for the cost of the higher-quality finishes I used in that house. Then, much more recently, the right side of my brain got so carried away with the Acqua Liana project that the left side, the business side of my brain, went dormant without me checking in on it. That property was an ode to creativity and artistry, but it didn't make a lot of money. I learned a hard lesson, one that all artists need to master if they're not going to end up starving in a metaphorical garret: you must be artistic *and* practical. If you forget the analytical side because of the passion found in the artistic side, you'll end up just as miserable as if you forgot the artistic and focused only on the analytical. I don't care which side of the brain you lead with: just make sure you toggle back and forth between the two. In short, there are too many starving artists out there, and plenty of one-hit wonder success stories. Don't be either.

Ultimately, when it comes to my oceanfront masterpieces, I am a businessman first and an artist a distant second. I'll still get excited and passionate about the beauty and uniqueness of elements like a water floor or an aquarium wet bar, but I view every choice through the lens of ROI and ROR. If it doesn't make business sense, I won't do it. I'm not interested in being a starving artist, and you shouldn't be either. Let both sides of your brain weigh in on your choices.

Three Traits of the Artist's Approach

After three decades of taking an artist's approach to my craft and career, I know three things. First, *when you take an artist's approach, you're more likely to stay passionate about what you do.* Being an artist taps something inside me and gives me enormous passion and energy. I love nothing more than watching people walk through one of my properties for the first time, and seeing the expressions on their faces as they become intoxicated by the sensory delights that surround them. I love hearing them exclaim over the fourteen-foot-tall water wall at the entrance, the fifty-foot-long infinity pool overlooking the Atlantic, the glass-and-black-porcelain stair tower that rises three full stories, and the glass-walled elevator that feels like a space capsule. And I've been delighted when people tell me, "Frank, you're the only one who ever put a jellyfish tank in a residential setting or to use a water floor. You're a true artist!" In those moments, both sides of my brain are happy. I'm just so excited about what I've produced and why I produced it. And I can't think of anything else I want to do than be an artist of such oceanfront masterpieces and cash the checks when they sell.

As I've gotten older, I've realized that I can produce art in many other ways as well. I can take an artist's approach to writing seven books in six different genres, or delivering keynotes and seminars, or filming outrageous videos for my social media feeds. I can take an artist's approach to raising funds for the Caring House Project Foundation. I've even started creating some non-fungible tokens (NFT) and visual art (and pushing what some would consider the boundaries of both art and good taste in the process). No matter what my next project or endeavor is, if I can approach it as an artist, I know it'll keep me excited, passionate, and engaged. After all, Picasso worked up until his death at age ninety-one because he loved what he did. As long as I love what I do, I'll keep doing it, too.

* * *

Okay, pause for a brief public service announcement:
this chapter has me seriously thinking about unretiring.
Now back to our regularly scheduled programming.

* * *

Second, *every artist has a drive to better his or her previous best.* For a while I was building bigger and bigger houses, but then in recent years the market shifted. Wealthy buyers started asking for smaller properties (five thousand to seven thousand square feet instead of over fifteen thousand square feet) with the same high quality of artistic elements and attention to detail. As an artist, it took me a while to change my mindset and to recognize that I could build better by building smaller. But once I understood what my clients wanted, it unleashed a new wave of creativity in me to produce better masterpieces within the constraints of smaller "canvasses." Taking the artist's approach to your aspirations may mean adjusting your materials or changing how you approach your job. But no matter what, every artist I know wants the next canvas, the next hotel room cleaned, the next book cover, the next car wrap, to be better than the one before it. It's that drive to exceed the best of your past endeavors that is the earmark of passion, and the signal that you are bringing an artist's approach to your aspirations.

Third, *artists leave legacies in the minds and hearts of others.* Strange to say, the oceanfront masterpieces I have created probably won't be my longest-lasting legacy. The land underneath them eventually becomes more valuable than the homes I built on that land. Eventually, either a new owner will tear the house down to build something new, or sea levels will rise to the point where the land will no longer be there. But because I have taken an artist's approach to every aspect of my life and career while trying to be a good businessman, husband, father, and Christian, I have faith that my aspirations will be remembered by the people I leave behind.

Taking the artist's approach to your job and your profession will help you build a personal brand that sets you apart from anyone else. Better than that, it will allow you to bring more passion to what you do and to your life as a whole. And that is the kind of reality we all want to create.

Accentuate and Amplify Your Essence

12

Too many people overvalue what they are not and undervalue what they are.

MALCOLM FORBES

About twenty years ago I was having dinner with Don King, the legendary boxing promoter. We were at this fancy Palm Beach restaurant to negotiate the sale of one of my oceanfront homes that he was buying as a gift to Henrietta, his wife of fifty years. As an icebreaker because I was a little nervous, and being ever-so inquisitive, I looked at his hair (which stuck straight up from the top of his head by at least five inches) and asked, "Don, I have to know: after all these years, what's up with the hair?" He looked back at me with my long, flowing blond locks, and bellowed, "Well, ain't that the pot callin' the kettle black!" With a wink he went further to say, "Frank, my hair is a distinguishing physical characteristic."

Don King was a smart man. He knew that he needed to set himself apart so he could be seen as the man who could get the big fights for the top boxers in the world, which he did for more than sixty years. Don's hair, and his flag-waving love of the United States, made him memorable. They reflected the outrageousness and patriotism that are part of his core—his essence, I call it.

What's *your* essence? What sets you apart from everyone else in your field or profession? Bringing out what sets you apart is what will give you a distinct advantage in the business of life and should form the foundation of your personal brand. It should be uniquely yours, unduplicatable. It's not enough to emphasize your expertise, as in, "I'm the oceanfront expert," or "I'm the mortgage king," or to share some forgettable promise about your service, like, "I return phone calls on a timely basis," "I provide great customer service," or, "I put the customer's needs first." Those are lame and should never be uttered again. Go deeper. Find the one or two aspects that represent who you are at your core, then bring them to the surface and amplify them as your trademark.

Years ago I thought I needed to become someone I'm not in order to get a job in real estate. (You'll read that story in chapter 13.) That lasted for less than an afternoon, thank goodness. Instead, I chose to amplify what sets me apart and use it to build a personal brand unlike anyone else. Today my essence might be described as a modern-day Renaissance man: a nonconforming, bombastic artist who is as comfortable with the homeless as he is with presidents, a walking NFT who wears his long hair in different colors and dresses more like a rock band frontman than a real estate businessman, yet who backs it all up with undeniable substance and meteoric results. Because of my willingness to accentuate my essence from the very beginning of my career, even with the lack of education, lack of connections, and lack of money I had back then, I never chose to follow somebody else's path. Instead, living from my essence allowed me to create my own reality.

I don't coach a lot of people, and when I do, it's usually because they have made a significant donation to the Caring House Project Foundation. But most of the time, my coaching focuses on helping someone discover, accentuate, and amplify their essence. One donor wanted to become a high-end real estate salesperson. Well, there are 200,000 realtors in Florida, so we needed to discover how she could set herself apart. I asked her what career she was currently pursuing, and it turned out she was an opera singer, and a well-established one. So we made her the Operatic Realtor.

Whenever she would go to a listing or a showing, she would sing the first few lines of her description of the property. Her voice was her essence, her gift, and accentuating and amplifying it created a memorable personal brand that allowed her to stand out in a crowded profession.

You may be thinking, "But I don't have that kind of talent to amplify!" Relax. You don't have to possess any particular talent. You simply need to explore your personality and background to uncover what can set you apart and then choose to accentuate that. For example, another coaching client came all the way from Canada to spend a few hours with me in my treehouse. He was a mortgage broker with one of the biggest banks in his country, and he wanted to get more clients so he could stand out in that very large organization. I found out that he was a huge Superman fan, so he turned himself into Super Mortgage Man. He started wearing a tee shirt with a big red S on it underneath his dress shirt and tie. When he met a client, he'd reveal the big red S, saying, "Have no fear, Super Mortgage Man is here!"

Sure, you have to have some guts and a good sense of humor to pull something like that off, but identifying this aspect of his essence and letting it shine has caused Super Mortgage Man to reach the top one-half of one percent of all mortgage brokers at the Royal Bank of Canada. As I said in the introduction to this section, your personal brand needs to feel authentic and real to your customers, and when you build a brand based on your essence, they will feel that you are being true to who you really are.

How to Identify Your Essence

Here are a few simple ways to identify your essence. First, ask yourself, "Do I have a trait, physical characteristic, look, tendency, hobby, or interest that I feel is a key part of who I am?" Like the Operatic Realtor or Super Mortgage Man, one of those aspects may be a foundational element of your essence.

Second, if you're having trouble identifying your key traits or characteristics, go to your family members or friends, and ask them, "Tell me straight up: what is it that you think sets me apart?" This also can be a valuable exercise to share with business associates or colleagues in a focus group-type setting—as long as you're willing to listen and be open to perspectives that you may or may not agree with or like.

Third, go back to chapter 1 and look at the list of people you aspire to emulate and see what parts of their personas you'd like to "own." My essence includes pieces of P. T. Barnum and Willy Wonka, mixed with a little Evel Knievel and a touch of Mother Teresa meets Robin Hood, topped off with the frontman style of David Lee Roth. I've never tried to *be* these people, but I've taken the parts of them that I feel will set me apart in my profession. I then absorbed those parts into my DNA so I could become the Frank McKinney I wanted to be.

A word of caution, however: it can sometimes be a painfully long exercise to uncover your essence. Why? It's that *drive to fit in* that you read about in the start of this section. If you live in a world where everybody wears khaki pants and golf shirts, and everybody has the same haircut, it can be hard to find anything unique about yourself. What sets you apart is still inside you, but you've suppressed it for so freaking long that it may take a while to dig it out. Be patient. Trust me, and trust the process. It's in there, so keep exploring, keep digging, keep seeking out the part of you that lights you up and makes you shine.

Remember, this isn't about becoming something you're not. Instead, it's about discovering what's true for you inside, the parts that make you feel, "Yes, this seems a little scary, but this *is* me." And when you bring that essence to light and start accentuating and amplifying it, you'll be able to create a reality that you will love.

Amplify the Positive and Reduce the Negative

Once you've identified the positive qualities you want to embody, you must then accentuate and amplify them. By that I mean, make a conscious and daily effort to be sure your unique qualities are on full display for the world to fall in love with. Don't sit on them or tamp them down: instead, bring them to the surface and then accentuate and amplify their presence in your life and in your brand.

Choosing what to accentuate and amplify should be based upon not just who you are, but also upon what you aspire to be and what kind of

---

What sets you apart is still inside you.

---

personal brand you want to create. Of course, all of us have parts inside that we like, and others that we don't. Your goal should be to build a personal brand based on your best self. You want to amplify the positive qualities found in your essence or to add positive qualities from the people you want to emulate.

Now, you also will discover aspects of those positive qualities that you want to reduce, redirect, or, at the very least, obscure. Even the parts that you want to amplify will have positive and negative aspects. Therefore, you need to identify and then reduce the negative within the qualities that you are accentuating and amplifying. Here's what I mean by that. Throughout my professional life I've chosen to accentuate and amplify the frontman, the showman, to the point now where he's part of my DNA—I know of no other way to be. I've taken a little piece of Evel Knievel, combined it with Willy Wonka, and created a character that the *Wall Street Journal* referred to as "Frank McKinney, Real Estate Rock Czar," with memorable personal style and daredevil stunts as part of the grand unveilings for each oceanfront property. In *Make It BIG!* the Real Estate Rock Czar wrote, "Each day you're on the concert stage of life so you'd better make it rock." Some people have accused him of being too much, of being over-confident, of marketing all the time, but throughout my career that character kept growing and becoming what I've always wanted it to be. So why should I tamp him down?

Well, if that bombastic showman/rock star essence goes too far, I could become the kind of guy who thinks he can throw stuff out of hotel windows into the pool and get away with it. (I left that behind long ago in my early twenties, well before I became the Frank McKinney that my mom is proud of.) Even without going to those extremes, at times the Real Estate Rock Czar is prone to over-excitement. When I tour potential buyers around one of our new works of art, I can get so excited that I'm like a kid in a candy store who has a serious sugar addiction, pointing out this incredible feature and that amazing view, telling stories about where that particular piece of wood, glass, or stone originated and how rare it is, and basically overwhelming people who just want to experience the beauty of the house in their own time. In truth, at those moments I'm not doing either the buyer or the prospect of selling the property any favors by putting the ringmaster aspect of my essence in charge, yet at times it's just so hard to contain my enthusiasm for what I do.

The Real Estate Rock Czar also loves storytelling and can be prone to exaggeration in the heat of the moment. As the Irish proverb says, he never lets facts get in the way of a good story. Like SpongeBob SquarePants—

. . . show the world you're not afraid to be who you really want to be.

---

who my daughter, Laura, and I watched almost every day when she was growing up—he's not above using "sentence enhancers" to expand on the truth and overstate the impact of his tall tales. For example, when I was showing the 3492 South Ocean estate, I'd declare, "Not only did the lava for the countertops come from France, but the volcano erupted after it had been dormant for over ten thousand years and that is the very lava we mined and is what you see before you today!" Sometimes I can't help but to enhance the truth with my take on it, and I've been called out on it by my daughter. She'll say, "Daddy, that's what SpongeBob would do."

Do the Real Estate Rock Czar's exaggerations hurt anyone? No, they don't. And in the moment I'm talking about this or that property as being "absolutely the finest oceanfront home I've ever built" (as I did with 3492 South Ocean), I mean it, just as I meant it when I said the same thing about

La Marceaux, Salacia, Acqua Liana, Ocean Apple, Driftwood Dunes, and many more over the course of my career. But I acknowledge that I have a tendency to go overboard, and I recognize that if I give the Real Estate Rock Czar's over-enthusiasm full rein and represent every single property as being the greatest and best in the history of history, no one will believe me. So, reluctantly but prudently, I've started doing a self-analysis and asking if I should let the showman out for the moment, or let the property speak for itself.

Let's be clear: this chapter is called "Accentuate and Amplify Your Essence" because a lot more people need to amplify their essence than need to tamp it down. Once you find your essence, don't be afraid to bring it out and to let its positive qualities speak for themselves. I believe it's better to pull yourself back if you get too close to the "too amplified" line than to keep your essence under wraps. But if you are amplifying an essence beyond your comfort zone or your ability to deliver, you can bring it out a little bit at a time. If Super Mortgage Man were a little bit shy or a little bit straitlaced, he could start by undoing one button for his first client, and then work his way up to revealing that entire red S on his tee shirt. Eventually, however, you must own your essence: you've got to rip that shirt wide open and show the world you're not afraid to be who you really want to be. It's better to be overrated than underrated!

Back Up Your Amplified Essence with Action *and* Results

While your essence can give you a stronger personal brand that reflects who you are at your core, every brand has to be backed up with action and, more important, results. If Super Mortgage Man didn't deliver on his promises, he wouldn't be super in the eyes of his clients no matter how dramatically he ripped open his shirt. You must be able to walk your talk. Do you think people would put up with the Real Estate Rock Czar brand if every property I created didn't exceed all the hype and pyrotechnics that I used to publicize it? Even when I've had potential buyers be somewhat taken aback by my over-the-top presence when showing a property, afterwards I've overheard them say, "Thank God that guy doesn't come with the house—but this home he built is absolutely stunning." I'm just the opening act for the main performance, which is the experience people will have when they walk through the front door to yes, you guessed it, the most beautiful oceanfront home they've ever seen. Whatever your essence, part of your personal brand has to be, at a minimum, delivering what you promise, and at the optimum, delivering at such a high level that your customers create a line that circles around the block wanting to buy from you or work with you.

Above all, never let fear stop you from letting your essence shine. Too many people are suppressing, obscuring, or even denying their true essence, in order to conform to societal norms or give in to social pressures. That essence burning inside of you is meant to radiate brightly on the outside. Accentuate and amplify it!

Live Your Inside on Your Outside

To be yourself in a world that is constantly trying to make you something else is the greatest accomplishment.

RALPH WALDO EMERSON

I guess over the course of my life I've become known for my choice of clothing, my shoulder-length hair that I dye a different color at the drop of a hat (pun intended), and my unfiltered delivery of my truth. It's a style and approach I've taken since high school, where I wanted to wear white leather pants to class while everyone else was wearing their self-imposed uniform of preppy-ness: pressed jeans and popped collars. But when I was twenty-one years old, I decided that I would someday stop being a tennis pro, which I loved at the time, and get into real estate investing, and I decided to start by getting my real estate license. I took the state real estate license exam and then applied to a couple of brokerages, and one of the Realtors® called me in for an interview. I figured I should change my style to look more businesslike and professional, so I went to the mall and bought a new suit, tie, and shoes, and then to Supercuts® to get what was, for me, a short haircut. The next day I proudly presented myself at the brokerage office. I thought I'd aced the interview and was happy to hear the interviewer say, "Great job, Chuck,"—he called me the wrong name—"on your real estate test. I think you'd be perfect here, but first you have to get a haircut and buy a new suit."

I'll never forget how dirty I felt, like I'd completely sold myself out. I stood up and said in the nicest way I could, "Thank you, sir, but I don't think I'll be working here." I walked out the door, took off my tie and went to 7-Eleven to buy a Slurpee. I gave the clerk my ugly maroon tie then drove to the beach as the sun was setting. I sat on the sand and told myself, "Frank, you will *never* do that again." That was the last time I tried to meet other people's expectations. And it's one of the reasons I'm so passionate about the topic of this chapter: *live your inside on your outside.*

Let's be honest: I've always struggled with conformity. I really don't like khaki pants and golf shirts; instead of belts, I prefer to wear scarves threaded through the belt loops of my jeans. For most of my life I've preferred not to wear a baseball cap or a sweater vest. And not many people in the world today still own a Yugo, much less two. But all of this has evolved to become part of the Frank McKinney brand. It's why I produce the theatrical and legendary grand unveiling events for our properties and for my books. Bottom line, living my inside on the outside makes me feel alive.

The ability to live your inside on the outside is a significant aspect of the art of personal branding. It can be expressed in many ways. It could be what you call yourself or how you identify. It could be in the way you dress, the way you walk, the way you speak, or who you associate with. It *doesn't* mean you have to stand out all the time or be flamboyant: you can be an introvert and yet be an individual. Or you can be incredibly elegant, like my wife, Nilsa, and my daughter, Laura. When Laura went to college a few years ago, the typical uniform of her peers was a hoodie or a midriff shirt and sweatpants. However, Laura's personal style is a cross between Audrey Hepburn and Grace Kelly. It's very sophisticated and tailored, yet it absolutely reflects her inside. I believe Laura's decision to be true to her essence was one of the factors that caused her to be elected vice-president and then president of the 46,000-member student body at Penn State University.

One of the things I'm most grateful for is that God has allowed me to live a life where I could express my individuality so freely. I never had to live in shame or hide who I am. And I'm proud of the example I set for my daughter of living your inside on the outside. (Visit my Instagram account and you'll often see my inside—and occasionally my backside—on *full* display.) Bottom line, it's not about what your inside is like; it's being unafraid to show that authentic self to the world, and to live fully and vibrantly in accordance with the truth of who you are at your core.

The Quashing of Individuality

Unfortunately, it seems like very few people feel they can bring that authentic self out to play. My observation is that quashing one's essence and suppression of individuality is an almost daily occurrence. There are many reasons for it. The implicit or explicit pressure to present a specific kind of image on the job can cause people who go out on Friday night in leather, chains, black nail polish, and heavy eyeliner only to stuff it all in the closet afterward because they won't wear it anywhere else. And while they might share some photos with their friends on a private Instagram account, they would never dream of letting their boss or coworkers see their rock 'n' roll adventures.

The educational system is also a powerful suppressor. Most of us are encouraged to sit down, shut up, and learn stuff to pass exams, so we can graduate from high school, go to college (don't get me started on higher education's societal brainwashing), and then graduate so we can fit ourselves neatly into the little shitbox called a career. Kids like me are told we will never succeed if we don't follow the traditional educational path. Where's the creativity? Where's the freedom of expression of self? Why aren't kids encouraged more often to explore, to create, to think differently, to be themselves, and then to bring that individuality outside and into their lives and professions?

Suppressing individuality shows up in spades when it comes to dating and relationships. I still can't believe how lucky I was to find my princess, Nilsa, who somehow appreciated my unconventionality and didn't care that I was a tennis pro without a lot of money. But many of the women I've met in South Florida tell me how bored they are with the dating scene.

Every guy they meet sports the same office casualwear and baseball cap and tells the same monotone life story while sipping their microbrew beer. The guys tell me that the women they meet want their dates to be successful professionals making tons of money—no artists or creatives need apply. (This doesn't seem to hold with many same-sex couples, which I think is really cool.) When it comes to relationships, both men and women are trying to fit into the mold of what they think is attractive to the other. But as far as I'm concerned, *fitting into* a mold is like to letting mold *spread on your soul* as if it were damp carpet or that yogurt you left in your fridge for three months.

Social media is another place where the need to fit in is on full display. You'd think that an environment where everyone has the chance to shout, "Me, me, me!" would be the ideal venue for people to live their inside on the outside. But all that self-expression surprisingly falls into a relatively narrow range. Too many people use social media to compare themselves

---

. . . it's about breaking out of the shell you've created for yourself and being yourself instead, with all the brilliance and flaws and creativity that's inside you.

---

to others,[1] and unless they already have a healthy sense of self-worth, such comparison can cause them to suppress their individuality in order to fit in and get more likes. Once we post our profile and find our so-called tribe, we tend to do whatever we can to align ourselves with that group, even if it means suppressing our individuality.

Problem is, even the smallest suppressions can have serious effects on the psyche. In 2018 I wrote a Christian romance novel, *The Other Thief*, which faced some pretty significant blowback for its graphic portrayal of sin. In it, I said that stealing a candy bar from 7-Eleven and robbing a bank at gunpoint has the same soul-damning effect. Well, the same is true of compromising our essence. The moment we begin to sell our souls to be like someone else, to fit in, to bow to peer pressure, we are altering our DNA in exactly the *opposite* way than we want. Too many of us think that we're individuals, but what we're really doing is conforming to the societal definition of what an individual is. And who we are and who we really want to be rarely if ever gets a chance to present itself.

Selling your soul for social compliance is too big a price for anyone to pay. If you're not at least willing to let your inside come to the surface, you might as well use the pages of this book as kindling to start a fire, because you'll never create a fulfilling reality. How can you be authentic if you're not bringing forth the essential you? Remember, this isn't about changing who you are: it's about breaking out of the shell you've created for yourself and *being* yourself instead, with all the brilliance and flaws and creativity that's inside you. Yes, of course, if there are self-destructive elements of your inside, you need to redirect those impulses into more positive avenues, as I said in chapter 10. But until you're comfortable with living with your inside on the outside, your chances of a happy and fulfilling life are pretty small. You need to start exploring what your inside is really saying and then give yourself permission to show that self to the world.

Your Inside Is Different from Everyone Else's

Living your inside on your outside means being authentically yourself, not shaping your appearance, behavior, or any other aspect of your persona to fit the expectations of others. I regard it as a key manifestation of altering your DNA and creating your own reality. After all, DNA is the core of your being, right? And while anyone is welcome to attempt to influence your DNA and enlighten your reality, I'm a firm believer that it should always be *your* choice, not shaped by the opinions of other people.

When I was growing up, I didn't want to be like my dad, Frank E. McKinney, Jr. (Yes, I'm the III.) He was the CEO of a bank, and he felt that he had to put on a banker's image in public. He was a different person when we would go out to a restaurant, but then at home he would let his perfectly cut hair down a little. I didn't like that he felt he had to do that, and I swore

I would do it differently. But now I understand that even when you're living your inside on your outside there's a public persona and a private persona: different versions of your inside that you show to the world and to your family. In fact, as you'll see in section 4, showing the deepest, rawest, and most vulnerable aspect of your essence can bond you with a partner in an intimate relationship.

Let me be clear: I don't see a problem with having a public and private persona—as long as the public persona isn't built upon a lie or a denial of who you are inside. My public and private personas are two sides of the same coin: both reflect my creativity and my personal brand. When I am showing one of our oceanfront homes, giving a keynote speech, or meeting with the bankers, I will dress in clothes that are comfortable yet set me apart from the usual real estate developer (a title I don't use for myself). This has been an unconscious decision for decades now. But when I come home and kick back, you're more likely to find me in SpongeBob SquarePants pajamas than ripped jeans and a multicolored jacket. But in both public and private personas, I choose what I wear based on who I am, not what I think other people want me to be.

By the way, living your inside on the outside can include an element of aspiration, too. One of the things that Nilsa taught our daughter, Laura, was always to dress for the job or career you want, not the one you're in at the moment. And long before I became the "Real Estate Rock Czar," I'm sure that my desire to emulate Willy Wonka or Robin Hood led me to want to wear those white leather pants in high school. But remember, the qualities of people you want to emulate are already inside you and part of you. And in truth, acknowledging, accentuating, and amplifying those qualities (as I said in the last chapter) will only let you bring out even more of your authentic self.

What Have You Been Suppressing?

The journey to live your inside on the outside begins with a deep dive within. I hope that in preceding chapters you've learned a lot about who you are at your core: now it's time to discover what you've been suppressing, and how to give freer rein to that true self that is screaming to get out. You begin with an inventory of your life, to evaluate what you have been suppressing, and in which areas you have failed to live your inside on the outside. Here are six questions to get you started.

#1. ARE YOU COMPROMISING YOURSELF BECAUSE OF THE COMPANY YOU KEEP? You are the sum of the people with whom you surround yourself. Are you suppressing who you are or who you want to be because of the friends, family, or colleagues in your peer group?

#2. ARE YOU SUPPRESSING THE WAY YOU LOOK OR DRESS IN YOUR DESIRE FOR A NEW JOB OR A PROMOTION? Are you compromising your artistic or interesting side because you feel as though your colleagues (or worse, your boss) will make a prejudicial judgment about you, or won't take you seriously? (Good news! You can put those strict "anti-discrimination in the workplace" rules to work in your favor.)

#3. ARE YOU SUPPRESSING YOUR PASSION IN EXCHANGE FOR A PAYCHECK? Yes, you may have to put food on the table for your family, but are you trading misery for money that you know you could earn in a different way?

#4. ARE YOU SUPPRESSING YOUR TRUE FEELINGS AROUND INTIMATE RELATIONSHIPS? Are you afraid to be completely open with your partner? If you're not currently in a relationship and you're interested in someone, do you suppress who you are because you're afraid that they won't like your authentic self? (We'll talk a lot more about relationships in the next section.)

#5. WHEN YOU THINK OF BRINGING YOUR INSIDE TO THE OUTSIDE, WHAT FEARS COME UP? What parts of yourself have you been suppressing, maybe for your whole lifetime, because you're afraid of rejection or ridicule? Where have you followed along with the crowd and succumbed to peer pressure, even when you knew you disagreed with others? What would you love to express without the dreaded social media backlash or accusations of nonconformity from friends, family, work, or society?

#6. IF YOU LET GO OF FEAR AND LIVED YOUR INSIDE ON THE OUTSIDE, HOW MUCH MORE FULFILLING WOULD YOUR LIFE BE?

Imagine you were Tom Hanks in the movie *Cast Away*, stranded on an island where it didn't matter that you talked to a volleyball. If you had no fear of society passing judgment on you, what kind of spectacular reality could you create?

For the person who can see easily how they've denied their true nature in order to get a job, a client, or a date, this exercise may be easy. It will be harder for the majority of people who have been culturally hypnotized and bought into the fallacy that what society prescribes for them is what they truly want. I'm talking to all of you out there who believe you were born to wear khakis, golf shirts, and baseball caps (or hoodies, sweatpants, and midriff shirts). If that's truly who you are, great—and I sincerely mean that. But please, be willing to listen to the little voice that shows up in the middle of the night, when you're lying awake and wondering what life would have been like if you'd followed your dream to be a rock musician, or to paint or sculpt, or be a photographer, or to grow that wonderful garden. Go back and read (or update) the list of emulations and aspirations you created in section 1, and ask yourself, "If I were living these aspirations today and emulating these amazing people, how would I show up differently? And would I feel more authentically myself when I do?"

I understand this process isn't easy for you: you've suppressed what sets you apart for so long that you may not know how to dig it out. But no one should have to sell their soul to comply with societal norms or to make other people happy. *There is no price high enough to buy your conformity.* You've got to look in the mirror and inventory exactly what you're holding in and why. And just as we talked in section 2 about building your risk tolerance, you've got to peel away the layers of suppression so you can build up your ability to express who you really are.

Here's Your Membership Card

Today there's a movement gaining momentum around being an individual, expressing yourself, and not being discriminated against for your ideals, preferences, or tendencies. Of course, there's still a ways to go, but it's much better than when my dad had to show up as somebody else's idea of a bank CEO or when my long hair and flashy clothes would immediately alienate some of the stuffier people who came to view our oceanfront properties. In general, we're a lot more tolerant of people who choose to live their inside on the outside. So *why not take advantage of that?*

Congratulations! I am awarding you your own membership card that allows you to live more of your inside on the outside. (You can mail

---

There is no price high enough to buy your conformity.

---

pamela@frank-mckinney.com and ask for an actual *Aspire!* membership card.) It's simple to take advantage of membership benefits: all you have to do is adopt the mindset that you don't care about society's judgment and you don't owe anybody an explanation—because above all, you don't want to owe *yourself* an explanation as to why you didn't live an authentic life. If you find yourself caring in the moment about what people say, simply remind yourself, "I've been suppressing parts of myself for too long, but today I'm choosing my soul. I'm choosing to change the circle of friends that I've been wanting to change for a while." Or, "I'm going to stop being self-conscious about the way I look or dress." Or "I'm finally gonna walk into the office and say, 'Instead of pushing papers around a desk, I want to be a painter, or an organic food gardener, or a forest ranger, archeologist, librarian, or an entrepreneur.'" Living your inside on the outside whether society approves or not will feel more authentic and real and give you greater strength and fulfillment. And really, who cares if society approves or not?

Warning: Society will still try very, very hard to get you back into its mold of what's accepted. You'll encounter people who won't understand you and will say you're ridiculous, like the real estate broker who called me Chuck and told me I needed to get a haircut and a better suit. But I can tell you from experience, the positives of living your inside on the outside definitely will outweigh the negatives. I've created a personal brand that allows me to be authentic *and* stand out in fields that are as crowded as hell (real estate development, real estate sales, being an author, running a charity, running in general, etc.). People may still make fun of my clothes, my style, or my forms of self-expression, but now it comes more from envy. I see it and I think, "That's their sad insecurity. I want *them* to be proud of who they are."

Remember, you can be *completely* different from me or anyone like me. My inside is different from Nilsa's and from Laura's. You can be an introvert or quiet and still bring your inside outside. But the good news is that whenever you live your inside on the outside, it becomes easier for you to give other people permission to do the same. It creates a processional effect that can become part of your legacy. You can inspire friends, family, coworkers, and anyone who knows you to be who they truly are and to experience the freedom of sharing that authentic self with the world.

Here's the truth: Your inside is dying to get out. Are you ready to celebrate who you really are?

Healthy Ego

It's hard to be humble
when you are as great as I am.
MUHAMMAD ALI

When you hear the word *ego*, what's the first thing that comes to mind?

If you're like most people, you probably relate ego to arrogance, self-importance, vanity, grandiosity, megalomania, or something similar. In my experience, ego is considered by many to be a four-letter word that's missing a letter. After all, that's what we were taught, either at home, in school, or in most religious instruction. The only discussion of ego I ever heard was in my psychology class in high school, where it was defined as a negative trait. A healthy ego was never part of the discussion and didn't exist to those who taught on the subject, so it's not surprising that early in my career I was conflicted by my evolving belief in the idea of a good ego. But now I believe that having a healthy ego—which includes an appreciation of yourself, of who you are and what you can accomplish, and the unique qualities that make up your essence—is critical. You need a healthy ego to take an artist's approach to your craft, accentuate and amplify your essence, live your inside on the outside, and bring out your creativity and ingenuity. A healthy ego will allow you to come out of your shell and create a strong and vital personal brand.

To be clear, a healthy ego does *not* mean you have to turn into anything like the confident contrarian I am. I've had this discussion with many of the folks I coach. They often think that my approach to life might be a little too much, and the concept of their own personal brand too egotistical in a negative sense. They would prefer to take a much lower-ley approach to succeeding in life. I get it, and I respect it. But, to me, creating a brand is an art form: it's a right-brained, creative activity, like taking a canvas or clay and designing a brand based upon your unique qualities. To do that, you *need* to have a healthy sense of ego, knowing who you are and how you are different (or better) than other people in your field. Then you must be unafraid to bring that essence out into the world.

Of course, there's a difference between healthy and unhealthy ego. In this chapter I want to explore what I think the difference is, and why developing a healthy ego is so important.

A Healthy Ego Defined

In Latin, the word *ego* simply means "I," the personal pronoun that represents the individual. At the beginning of the twentieth century, Sigmund Freud defined ego as the rational aspect of personality that reins in the demands of the id, or the instinctual drive to gratify our basic desires, wants, and needs.[1] Today the American Psychological Association defines ego as "all the psychological phenomena and processes that are related to the self and that comprise the individual's attitudes, values, and concerns."[2] Do you read anything inherently negative in those two definitions that span 125 years? I don't, but the term *ego* is most commonly used to describe an overdeveloped, inflated, or unrealistic attitude that someone is greater or better than they actually are. The good part of ego—the part that is simply the sense of self that all of us need to function in the world—has somehow been absorbed into the concept of self-esteem. And nowadays people seem to regard ego as bad and self-esteem as good.

I don't agree. The common definition of self-esteem is the value someone places on themselves without reference to the external world, and studies show that good self-esteem is very important for happiness, but it doesn't have the same impact on relationships, health, or success.[3] You need self-esteem to feel good about yourself, and to persist when you are faced with failure. However, high self-esteem can cause problems if it's based upon illusion.[4] Think of the kids who believe they're great soccer players because everyone on their team got trophies for participation. The next year, in a more advanced league, they might think they don't need to practice as hard in order to make the team, only to lose out to players who put in the time because they had a more accurate assessment of their abilities.

I believe that ego—which I define as *a realistic sense of who we are in the world, the unique value we possess within it, and our willingness to let our unique qualities shine*—is foundational to success in life, and is certainly required for a strong personal brand. In my experience, people can have good self-esteem but an underdeveloped ego: they can think well of themselves while lacking an accurate sense of their value to an entrepreneurial venture, team, job, career, or relationship. Most people fall into the category of good self-esteem yet underdeveloped ego. And if your goal in life is to be like most people, then you can skip ahead to the next chapter.

However, I believe that following your aspirations and creating your own reality requires a healthy ego, meaning a clear picture of your unique strengths and abilities, a good-sized dose of ambition and willingness to risk, and, as I tattooed into your mind in earlier chapters, the emotional fortitude to declare your value and worth to the world and go up against its expectations to create your own reality.

A healthy ego is based upon a combination of three elements. First is *exuberance*—a greater-than-normal, bubbling-over, otherworldly passion for your purpose. Second is a *belief* that you are one of the best in the world at what you do. Notice I didn't say "*the* best"—that's unhealthy ego, in my opinion. Frank McKinney isn't the best spec home builder/real estate artist in the world; I know there's somebody who is better than I am at what I do.

But I have heard for more than two decades that I'm *one* of the best, and I'm happy with that. A healthy ego recognizes the value of what you bring to your brand, but is realistic in terms of the value provided by others in the same space.

Third is *a lack of fear* about sharing your belief and passion for your purpose with the world. If I asked you to give me your elevator pitch—your quick, catchy and memorable statement about who you are and what you're really good at—could you do so without the fear of seeming egotistical? Too many people don't have the ability to put humility aside and truly extol their virtues. You can have exuberant passion for what you do and believe you're one of the best in the world at it, but if you're not able to get over the fear of sharing that with others, you haven't met the definition of a healthy ego. And you will *never* build a strong and memorable personal brand.

In chapter 2 I talked about what I do when people ask me for a testimonial or endorsement: I request that they send me what they would like me to say about them first, and then I will fix it and send it back. The results are usually pretty pathetic, because most people are very poor at

---

Too many people don't have the ability to put humility aside and truly extol their virtues.

---

bragging about themselves or their efforts. I do a version of that exercise in my keynotes and seminars, but it originated with my own experience on my very first book, *Make It BIG!*, back in 2001. I wanted to get some big-name endorsements for the cover, so I approached a man who was well-known in real estate circles but not nearly as well-known as he would become: Donald Trump. When I contacted his office, Norma, his long-time assistant, said that Mr. Trump would be happy to give a testimonial because he was familiar with my work in Palm Beach where he had his Mar-a-Lago estate, but he was extremely busy. She asked me to write three versions of what I wanted Mr. Trump to say and then send them to her for his review and approval. So I put myself in Donald Trump's shoes and wrote what I believed he might say (and, more important to me, what I wanted him to say about the book). I must have done a good job, because my favorite endorsement was approved by his office without hesitation and with little modification.

In case you'd like to see it, here's the final quote that appeared on the back cover:

"In the competitive world of ultra-high-end residential real estate, Frank McKinney has managed to do what I've done with projects all over the world. His groundbreaking deals and brand-making attention to detail have enabled him to make it big within his chosen field. Read his book and learn how you too can become a great success."

DONALD J. TRUMP

Getting that testimonial was an example of what I consider the results of a healthy ego contributing to the construction of a personal brand as a bestselling author. I had enormous, exuberant passion for making my first book a success; I believed the book would be exceptional because it would show people how I had become one of the best in the world as the creator of oceanfront masterpieces; and I had no fear about reaching out to people like Donald Trump, Rich DeVos (co-founder of Amway), and Tony Robbins to get testimonial quotes that would help *Make It BIG!* reach more readers.

If you have a negative or neutral view of a healthy ego, I'd like to improve that perspective, because I want you to feel great about being one of the best in the world at what you do and never to be afraid to share it. I would *always* rather be accused of being egotistical than being overly shy or tamping down my essence in business or relationships. If you don't feel ready to share your personal brand because you don't want to be shot down or called egotistical, push through those feelings and speak up. Remember, a healthy ego is about recognizing what is great and unique in you and bringing that out to share with the world. When you believe in yourself and your aspirations, you can use that healthy ego to create an outstanding personal brand.

A Few Healthy Ego Examples

Of all the chapters in this book, this topic is one of the most challenging, because extolling your virtues doesn't come naturally to many of us, including me. But look at the list of people you want to emulate: how many of them do you think fulfill the three criteria for healthy ego? Certainly every single one of the people on my list—Willy Wonka, Rich DeVos, Robin Hood, David Lee Roth, and Evel Knievel—had *very* healthy egos. (Some might argue too healthy, but not me.) Look at some of the famous billionaires on the 2021 list of the world's richest people: Jeff Bezos, Oprah Winfrey, Elon Musk, Meg Whitman, Warren Buffett, Bill Gates, and so on.[5] If you take out those who inherited their wealth, almost all those who made their own billions (including the self-made billionaires above) had healthy egos.

Look at Jamie Kern Lima, whom I talked about in the introduction to this section. She was so passionate about her cosmetic line and believed in her product so much that she kept fearlessly pitching to QVC for three years before they said yes. People in the beauty industry had told her no again and again, but she refused to give up. IT Cosmetics was almost broke when Jamie got that ten-minute slot to sell concealer on live TV. But she sold out every unit, and IT Cosmetics went on to become one of the network's best-selling cosmetic lines. In less than eight years since she started the company, L'Oreal acquired IT Cosmetics for $1.2 billion, and Jamie stayed on as CEO, becoming the first female CEO in L'Oreal history.

If you're not comfortable with the idea of having a healthy ego about yourself and your abilities, maybe like Jamie Kern Lima, or Sara Blakely of Spanx, you can have a healthy ego about your products. Maybe, like Mark Zuckerberg, you can have a healthy ego around your mission to connect the world, or organizing the world's information, like Google cofounders Larry Page and Sergey Brin. Or maybe, like Rich DeVos, Oprah Winfrey, and Tyler Perry, you can have a healthy ego around using your abundance to make a difference.

Let me add another example of someone I believe had a healthy ego: Mother Teresa. Every description of Mother Teresa talks about her passion for her purpose, her belief that she was guided by God to establish the Order of the Missionaries of Charity, and her total lack of fear in spreading the work of the Missionaries of Charity everywhere. To my mind, Mother Teresa created a massively strong and inspiring personal brand. She established foundations in cities around the world and she started associated orders for brothers, fathers, and laypeople to bring them into her work. By the time she died in 1997, there were more than four thousand Missionaries of Charity sisters in 610 foundations in 123 countries of the world.

You may be saying to yourself, "I'm not in the same league as Mother Teresa, or Rich DeVos, or Tyler Perry, or Jamie Kern Lima, or any of those billionaires." Well, as someone who sells oceanfront masterpieces to people like them, I can say with certainty that size doesn't matter—in property, in the size of your business, or in the level of your contribution. Every one of those people started small, with very little, and they used the otherworldly passion, belief, and fearlessness of their healthy egos to build up themselves and their enterprises to impressive levels. (And as you'll see in section 5, they all set the pattern for how they would live and what they would contribute right from the beginning.) No matter where you are right now, if you set your mind to it, you too can develop the kind of healthy ego and personal brand that in time will reach millions.

Healthy Ego Versus Narcissism

Whenever I talk about the need for a healthy ego, inevitably someone says, "Are you sure that's not just a polite term for narcissism?" Even the definition of a personal brand that I used at the beginning of this section ("the art of amplifying your essence to the point where your customers . . .

become subliminally intoxicated—with you first, then your product or service") can be seen as narcissistic because it puts *you* before your product or service. Most people consider narcissism an unhealthy trait, but be honest: if you were to analyze the people you want to emulate, don't you think you'd find at least a little narcissism, or at least some self-promotion, in those individuals?

You may remember reading that I asked my therapist about some of my own narcissistic tendencies. She helped me see how those tendencies could be helpful, as long as I channeled that showman energy in a constructive way. But when I started thinking about healthy ego for this book, I wanted to revisit narcissism to see how the two are different.

Here's the Mayo Clinic definition of a narcissist, whom they classify as someone with a narcissistic personality (a clinical diagnosis of a serious disorder): ". . . a mental condition in which people have an inflated sense of their own importance, a deep need for excessive attention and admiration, troubled relationships, and a lack of empathy for others."[6] Let's break the definition down into its separate elements and see how it compares to a healthy ego.

"AN INFLATED SENSE OF THEIR OWN IMPORTANCE." Does everyone with a healthy ego have an inflated sense of importance—or could it be accurate if it's based on results? After more than twenty-five years, I know that I'm one of the best in the world at building spec homes on the ocean. I also know that we've made a generational impact in the lives of more than thirteen thousand Haitian children through our Caring House Project Foundation; I've sold quite a few copies of my books in more than one genre; and I've finished the toughest footrace in the world seven times, which is more than all but twenty-two other racers. People with healthy egos aren't afraid to pursue important projects and big ideas, and to have a big impact on the world in the process. And that might create a proportional sense of importance about their work. There's a part of me that believes, like Mother Teresa, I was called to do what I do. God gave me this gift, and it would be sinful to not use it. I know that may sound self-important, but these are aspirations that I am proud to have made come true.

"A DEEP NEED FOR EXCESSIVE ATTENTION AND ADMIRATION." I guess the question is, what's the attention and admiration being used *for*? Does someone with a healthy ego seek attention and admiration just for themselves, or to further their aspirations? Many people with healthy egos gain recognition for themselves and their efforts, and some go even further and use that acclaim and admiration to draw attention to their businesses.

For people with healthy egos, attention is a means to an end. Out of eight billion people on the planet, fewer than fifty thousand can afford the oceanfront masterpieces I create, for example, so I need to capture the attention of that relatively small group or else I'm eating out of a dumpster. I'm not going to raise money for Caring House Project Foundation until I draw attention to the fact that we've built twenty-nine villages in the poorest country in the Western Hemisphere. Look at Mother Teresa: over her lifetime she received seven hundred awards and prizes, including the Nobel Peace Prize in 1979, making her "the most awarded person in the twentieth century."[7] But every award was simply an opportunity for her to spread the word about the work of the Missionaries of Charity.

"TROUBLED RELATIONSHIPS." Of course, if you're all about me, me, me, that can definitely cause problems in your relationships. And to a certain extent, I've had challenges that have saddened me with my four sisters and one brother (even though I will never give up working on strengthening those connections). But in my experience, someone with a healthy ego who is in a relationship with someone *else* with a healthy ego can find a balance where both partners fulfill each other's needs for love, acknowledgment, passion—all the good stuff. Suffice it to say that I'm incredibly lucky that whenever my narcissistic tendencies have gotten out of hand, Nilsa's level head and strength of personality have kept me focused on what's truly important, which includes the vitality of our relationship.

"A LACK OF EMPATHY FOR OTHERS." True narcissists care only about themselves; they have no empathy for the challenges other people face. A lack of empathy is the most toxic element of this definition and is the clearest sign of an *un*healthy ego. If you find yourself becoming self-centered, thinking that you're *the* best and disregarding the needs, feelings, and emotions of others, your ego is unhealthy and veering into narcissism.

Thank goodness, as my therapist pointed out, I *bleed* empathy: I care a tremendous amount for other people, especially the marginalized, and

---

. . . when you combine a healthy ego with empathy, then you have a magic formula.

I'm eager to walk a mile in their shoes—literally. During the book tour for *The Tap,* I swapped places with the homeless in sixteen cities. In each city I invited one homeless person who was trying hard to turn his or her life around to stay in a nice hotel with the new clothes we bought for them and the nutritious room service we encouraged them to order. Then I took that person's place for the night, sleeping under bridges, in parks or at shelters. To my mind, empathy is essential for anyone who wants to create a great personal brand, a healthy ego, or a great life in general. As you'll see in section 5, I'm a devout believer in Jesus' statement, "From everyone who has been given much, much will be demanded; and from the one who has been entrusted with much, much more will be asked" (Luke 12:48, NIV). Assuming that your healthy ego will produce a great personal brand and great results, you have a responsibility to be a good steward and help others with your abundance, to take the time, energy, and care to lift them up, to help them if you can, and to inspire them to discover the greatness that lies within. And when you combine a healthy ego with empathy, then you have a magic formula that will counter any potential narcissism and allow you to bring your gifts out to benefit the world.

Are some narcissistic tendencies beneficial, even necessary, in building a personal brand? Yes. You can exhibit a little narcissism and not have narcissistic personality disorder. In my case, some attention-seeking and a belief in myself as one of the best in the world at what I do helped set me apart. But too much of anything can tip you over into dysfunction and take you off the path to creating the reality you want. I know this danger firsthand because it has happened to me. Yet I firmly believe it's okay to sprinkle in a few narcissistic tendencies, if they are balanced with a healthy dose of empathy.

Ultimately your healthy ego—and your brand—should be based on one thing: the belief that you were given a gift from God of your essence, which is unique to you and needs to be expressed if you are to fulfill your purpose in the world. Your purpose, your brand, is yours alone. It won't look like anyone else's. Yet in its own way, your brand is just as important as one that's worth billions of dollars or feeds millions of people. Remember the waiter I met in Albuquerque, who said his aspiration was to "leave a wake of empathy" in his life? He doesn't have a public persona, or a huge following, or a billion dollars, yet, to me, a statement like that shows this young man has a healthy ego. And for the people he encounters, he will be more important and have a greater impact than someone like me, or Mother Teresa, or anyone on that list of the world's richest people.

You're on the earth with eight billion other humans, and you undoubtedly have tens or even hundreds of thousands of competitors. If you're not boiling over with passion for your purpose, if you're not supremely confident in yourself and your abilities, and if you're not willing or capable of sharing that with the world, how will you ever stand out and be found, much less recognized and ultimately remembered? A healthy ego will help you create a strong personal brand so you can fulfill your aspirations. It will allow you to bring your unique gifts and talents out into the world to benefit others and create your own reality.

By the way, just as I was dictating this chapter on the road during the Yugo We-go Tour, I was passed by a big semi-tractor trailer with the logo "Super Ego Holding" on the side. It was the first time I'd ever seen a truck like that in 6,288 miles and twenty-two days of the pre-release tour. Was it just a sign . . . or a *sign?*

Creativity and Ingenuity Are Rewarded

Your shallow men shall dream dreams,
your insightful men shall see visions.

NIKKI SIXX

15

For more than twenty years I've worked from an oceanfront treehouse office perched twenty-two feet in the air and built into a stand of enormous seagrape trees at our Delray Beach home. (Go to TheAspireBook.com to see photos.) I still remember the evening when I became inspired with the idea of building my own treehouse: It was back on New Year's Day in 2001 when Nilsa and I were having dinner in a restaurant along the Intracoastal Waterway in Florida. Because she was much better at drawing than I am, she sketched out on a napkin what would become a 220-square-foot incubator for all things creative in my life. My treehouse has spectacular ocean views out of twelve well-positioned windows that let me peer through seagrape and strangler fig trees. It also has a shower, toilet, sink, air conditioning, hardwood floors, cedar walls, a bamboo desk and cabinets, a loft with a king-size bed, and a forty-foot suspension bridge that connects it to the master bedroom of the main house, keeping my commute to work in the morning and back home at night both quick and fun.

Up until I started working there, I'd been going to a boring old office in some nondescript concrete, glass, and steel office building—but from the moment Nilsa sketched out my concept for the treehouse, I knew it was going to be a fertile home for my mind's potential. Within three months, what we designed on that napkin in two dimensions came to life in three dimensions, and I don't think that it's an accident that it was only a few days later I began writing my first book, *Make It BIG!* The treehouse is an imaginative and magical perch from which I have written all six of my bestselling books (and I'm writing these words from there *right now*). At its built-in bamboo desk, I have designed and sold some of the most beautiful oceanfront mansions in the world. To me, it's the perfect spot, a fantastical place that allows me to tap into the creativity and ingenuity that I believe are essential for success.

Creativity and ingenuity are the two primary qualities exponentially rewarded today in business and in life. They also are foundational to building a dynamic personal brand. *Especially* in today's world of incessant distraction and demands on our attention, if your product or service doesn't apply creativity and ingenuity it won't be noticed, much less rewarded. Seeking ways to access greater creativity and ingenuity will help you amplify your essence and intrigue and intoxicate others when they encounter you. It also will keep people surprised and delighted in your business and personal relationships. (We'll get into personal relationships in the next section, but how many marriages disintegrate simply because both partners become bored with each other after years of the same old same old?) Bringing more ingenuity and creativity into all your relationships will make them stronger and more enjoyable.

In real estate, I believe the qualities that have set me apart are 1) never being afraid to take enormous risks and 2) applying deep creativity and ingenuity to whatever I do. As a result, every oceanfront masterpiece we've built has been a non-duplicatable work of three-dimensional art that sets new standards for luxury, beauty, and opulence. I deliberately set out to find elements that no one has ever thought of using in a private residence before (like a water floor, or an aquarium wet bar where exotic fish swim overhead then find their way beneath your martini glass, or sea glass kitchen countertops, or an all-glass-enclosed three-story elevator, or a jellyfish sphere) and then ingeniously adapting them to create a massive wow factor for our clients. As an author, not only have I used creativity and ingenuity to write seven bestsellers in six different genres, but I also have applied it during our book reveals, launches, and subsequent multicity tours so my books would stand out among the more than 2,700 books that are self-published each *day*.[1] I think most people would say creativity and ingenuity are the hallmarks of the Frank McKinney brand and career.

Getting creative has not only improved my business but sometimes saved it. For years I specialized in building ever-larger, ever-more-elaborate estates here in South Florida, eventually maxing out at $50 million and thirty-two thousand square feet. But in 2016 I noticed a change in the marketplace. While people still loved the spectacular quality of our properties—the heart-stopping aspects of the location and décor, the off-the-charts luxury of the finishes—most of these ultra-wealthy people now had multiple homes all over the world. They would spend only a few

---

> . . . impediments awaken their drive and
> determination and, yes, their
> creativity and ingenuity . . .

---

months at a time in any given location, and usually it would just be one couple living in the home. They wanted the same quality and wow factor but in a smaller space. So I invented a new category of luxury real estate here in South Florida: the micro-mansion. I took the best of what we were putting into our fifteen- to twenty-thousand-square-feet mega-mansions and put those features and finishes into four- to six-thousand-square-foot micro versions. Buyers loved them, and I received amazing publicity for shifting from mega to micro. (If you'd like to see these stunning homes, visit frank-mckinney.com.)

With the pandemic in 2020/2021, many people were also forced to become more ingenious and creative just to keep their businesses running, their kids learning, and themselves sane. I'm excited to say that this fueled a significant increase in entrepreneurship: 4.4 million new businesses

were started in the U.S. in 2020, a *twenty-three percent* increase from
the year before.[2] To me, this is an example of individuals discovering the
greatness that lies dormant within. Whenever people who want to live
their aspirations also face constraints and challenges, rather than causing
them to quit, those impediments awaken their drive and determination
and, yes, their creativity and ingenuity, to push through whatever stands in
their way. And instead of returning to "normal," they build a *more frequent
extraordinary*—a new, better, higher reality instead.

Using Right and Left Brain to Channel Creative Energy

Think of a moment when your creativity and ingenuity were triggered.
Wasn't there a feeling of energy, propulsion, and excitement? Creativity
and ingenuity bring many gifts, and one of the best is the intense energy
they generate. It's as if triggering the right side, the creative side, of the
brain produces an explosion of light and color in the synapses that takes us
to a new level of reality and awareness. (That's what the image on the cover
of this book represents.) But as you read in chapter 4, your creative/big
picture/right side needs to be tempered with the practical considerations
of your analytic/detail-oriented/left side. You need to reengage whatever
side of the brain you've been told is not your strong suit, and then toggle
between both sides in milliseconds. It's almost like taking the raw material
of gold, melting it down, and then pouring it into a form to make a bar:
that's how quickly the brilliance of the right brain should be shaped by the
structure of the left.

I'm referring mostly to decisions about your business and your
personal brand. For example, whenever I evaluate a property or a possible
new project, I always apply both right- and left-brain considerations. But
which comes first? Do I use the business filter to evaluate the marketplace,
assess what's out there and what's not, what's being built, and whether I
can set a new, higher price-per-square-foot benchmark, and then go to
the creative side to make sure the design is never-before-seen unique and

beautiful enough to warrant the premium my creations command? Or do I go to the creative side first and focus on designing something original and spectacularly luxurious, and then put it through the left-brain analysis to make sure the ROI is substantial enough to make it worth my while? Neither. These thousands of evaluations are datapoint interchanges that happen almost simultaneously as I toggle between right and left brain within milliseconds. You, too, should make sure that whenever you feel that explosion of creative energy that at the same time you instinctively let your practical side weigh in.

When it comes to what you hope to build, which is a creative and ingenious brand, I recommend you subject all decisions to three questions that will draw upon both sides of the brain.

Question 1: *"Will this approach build my brand?"* You might be surprised that the first filter is more left-brain-centered. But unless something is going to enhance or advance your personal brand, don't bother with it. And if it stifles, stagnates, or even detracts from your personal brand, you definitely *don't* want to spend a second on it.

Question 2: *"Is this approach creative and ingenious?"* If you want to better your previous best on a regular basis, you must call upon the right brain to come up with new and better approaches to your brand and business.

Question 3: *"Am I willing to put in the time to make this happen?"* Remember the tar pitch drip described at the beginning of section 3? You must be patient throughout the building of your personal brand. It takes time, and time is a finite resource, so any decision must be worth the time you will need to invest in your brand. Note: As you're spending the needed time, if the endeavor later proves *not* to advance your brand, don't be afraid to abandon it.

By the way, you simply can change the word *brand* to *relationship* or *contribution* to apply creativity and ingenuity to other areas of your life. How can you use creativity and ingenuity to become a better spouse or parent or partner or friend? How can you use creativity to make a bigger difference in the lives of others? And how can you harness the power of the right and left sides of your brain to create a better reality for yourself and others?

Let the Little Boy or Girl Out to Play (and It's Okay to Let Them Go Too Far)

When we tap into our creativity and ingenuity, we're accessing the little boys or girls that still live inside us—for some, they're lying dormant in DNA, no matter what the age. We're going back to a time when none of society's handcuffs and restrictions were wrapped around us and recognizing and reigniting the free spirit and boundless energy of childhood. As I wrote in my first book, *Make It BIG!*, "When you can retain that youthful exuberance, that willingness to approach everything as if it were the first time, your creativity can't help but expand. Thinking and acting young allows you to stay in touch with a truly vital part of yourself."

It's very important every so often to let the creativity and the ingenuity of the little boy or girl inside get carried away so you'll learn your limits from experience rather than instruction. In 2001, as Nilsa sketched the first picture of our oceanfront treehouse, I remember feeling the sensation of my own little boy coming to life inside. From ages seven to fifteen, I'd lived on a property with sixteen acres of Indiana woodland, but I'd never had a treehouse. So, when the impulse laid itself on my heart to build one in the strangler fig tree in front of my home, there was no stopping me—and the little boy inside didn't want to wait for permission or to apply for permits from the City of Delray Beach Historical Preservation Board, or HPB. (In my defense, treehouses weren't regulated structures at the time.)

The problem was that, in 1989, before we bought our house—the "Fontaine Fox house," originally built in 1935—the city had designated it a historic structure. As a result of this designation (and buried in the city's land development regulations) there were specific rules and regulations attached to the property. Long story short: as soon as the HPB found out about it, they ruled that I had to get rid of my "illegal" treehouse.

They might have been right according to the regulations, but some things in life are worth fighting for. So, the anti-establishment-juvenile-delinquent-turned-responsible-grown-man who always had followed what he called the Eleventh Commandment ("It's always easier to seek forgiveness rather than permission") wasn't about to take it down just to obey some rules he considered illegal, misapplied, discriminatory, and irrelevant. And the little boy inside me was saying, "Sorry, no way I'm tearing it down. It's my family's treehouse!" By that point the treehouse also had become an important part of my life, as well as my daughter's life (she loved to play in it with her friends) and my business. It was where I felt most creative and in tune with my essence. I'd dreamed there, designed there, written books there, held numerous interviews there; I'd hosted hundreds of donor meetings and lunches in the treehouse to raise millions of dollars for the Caring House Project Foundation and dozens of other charities. Whenever kids would visit with their parents, they'd leave saying, "Dad, you've got to build us a treehouse too!" There was no way I would give up this magical space without a fight.

I protested the ruling to the HPB. They turned me down. I appealed to the Delray Beach City Commission. The commissioners voted 2-2, which the City declared a denial of my appeal. Not understanding how a "tie" could be a loss, I filed a lawsuit against the HPB and the City of Delray Beach. The City then countersued me. For seven long years I fought to keep my treehouse, and eventually the case made it all the way to the Florida Supreme Court. I spent a great deal of time, money, and energy on the issue. Yes, it was affecting my reputation and personal brand with the city (I was even President of the Delray Beach Chamber of Commerce at the time), but I didn't care, because I believed we were in the right. The ACLU even got involved in favor of my case, as they felt I was being subjected to a form of reverse discrimination (but that's another story). So I decided to apply creativity and ingenuity to come up with a solution that would satisfy both parties.

I'll never forget walking into the Delray Beach City Commission chamber in 2009, holding my hands in front of me as if I had on handcuffs. In front of the packed Commission chambers I said, very contritely, "I was wrong. I built this without a permit. I never had a treehouse as a little boy, and I let the little boy get carried away. I have no excuse for what I did other than I did it. I'm at your mercy. But I'm committed to keep the structure on my property. As a compromise I will move it to another tree that won't impede the public's view of the main house, and I'll lower it so it's not taller than the main structure. Ladies and gentlemen, this is just a treehouse. Don't we have more important things to do than have the city waste over a hundred thousand dollars of taxpayer money on attorney's fees fighting my lawsuit? Personally, I'd rather give the money I've been paying my lawyers to the soup kitchen for the homeless that I've been supporting in our town for over ten years. Let's get this resolved."

After my appearance, while public sentiment had always been on our side, that support turned even more fervent, and we started to see rallying cries of "Save the Treehouse!" around Delray Beach. A favorable story even appeared in the *Wall Street Journal*, where the reporter took a private property rights point of view. So, in January 2010, a 120-ton big yellow crane took the treehouse out of the strangler fig and moved it to the seagrape trees it now calls home. Since Haiti had experienced an earthquake a few days before, we turned the move into a fundraiser for the Caring House Project Foundation, and as a tree hugger turned treehouse hugger, I chained myself to the structure as the crane hoisted both of us fifty feet into the air and moved it to its new location. Immediately afterwards we flew to Haiti and spent a week on the ground pulling trapped survivors from the rubble. (You can see a video of the move on my YouTube channel.) The city had their pound of flesh, and I got to keep my treehouse.

I also learned some important lessons. First, I'm a man who is capable of letting his inner little boy get carried away, but the only way to understand those limits is to stretch the boundaries of the playground. Second, never let the right brain/creative side go too far without consulting the left brain/ practical side. And third, with enough creativity and ingenuity you can turn almost any setback into a victory.

How to Trigger Your Creativity and Ingenuity

Since creativity and ingenuity are so highly rewarded, you must find (or make) a place that elicits yours. For me, the treehouse is just such a spot, but most people don't need anything that elaborate. It can be your cubicle, or a desk in the corner of your living room or bedroom, or a special corner of a garden or backyard, as long as you set it up to include views, items, and images that will trigger those creative impulses. But it should be an area you carve out deliberately because you realize the importance of accessing your right brain/creative half. Designing such a space is a key part of creating your own reality.

Here are a few suggestions for setting it up effectively. First, you should have an area that's separate from other spaces and other people. Even if your "office" is the dining room table that you can use for only part of the day, figure out a way to designate "your" end of the table as a creative space just for you.

Second, to tap into the little girl or boy inside, put images from your childhood on the wall, or desk, or computer screen. Go to old scrapbooks for pictures of yourself and your family and your friends when you were young. Find images of your childhood idols (Willy Wonka in my case, Audrey Hepburn for my daughter) or pursuits (tennis, parkour, surfing …) and put those up, too. These images are a representation and reflection of a part of you that's probably been dormant for too long.

Third, include images of nature, especially if you don't have a window that looks out on greenery or water. It's been shown that even looking at pictures of nature can help lower stress levels.[3] I'm fortunate that every day I look out over the ocean from the treehouse or through the North Carolina trees down to the soothing Pidgeon River; both provide ever-changing views that inspire me daily.

Of course, there are other ways you can access the creative side of your brain. Meditation is something you can do pretty much anywhere or anytime; some of my greatest ideas have come to me as I meditate while running. Often I will meditate on some of my happiest, serene, perfect moments from childhood and try to recreate them using all of my senses. Or I'll imagine that I'm back in Colorado, camping all by myself on the top of a mountain in the middle of nowhere, with nothing but sparse vegetation around me and endless skies above.

Solitude is so rare today, yet it can be vital in tapping your creativity. There can be enormous value in being by yourself. It's one of the reasons I get up at four o'clock in the morning, put on my running shoes, and put in six or more miles along Ocean Boulevard outside our front door. It's been shown that walking (or running) increases creativity,[4] and, with over 35,000 miles logged on my legs, I can attest to its power to disengage the prefrontal cortex and unleash your right brain/creative side.

One of the best things you can do for your creativity is to limit or completely block any outside influences. In particular, make it a regular practice to step away from the screen of your computer, phone, TV, or tablet. Twice a year I detox from social media by spending a week cut off

---

. . . the experience of creativity is akin to the sound of opening a soda can . . .

---

from all outside digital input. When you're busy creating your own reality don't immerse yourself in the so-called reality being pushed by TV, news sites, and so on.

Going out into nature of any kind is great for creativity. In the backyard of both our Delray Beach and Canton, North Carolina homes, some of our trees are more than one hundred years old. To me, trees are art, especially the trunks, and the things that cling to them. I can spend hours absorbed in their designs. Venturing out into nature engages a different part of the brain, calming the prefrontal cortex and increasing creative problem-solving ability.[5] Taking a walk in a local park or just going out into your backyard or garden can help your brain to relax and restore its ability to focus, concentrate, and create.

Immersing yourself in the arts can spur the creativity and ingenuity you bring to your life and business. I love visiting museums, art galleries, and, yes, even car junkyards for that reason: visual art triggers something in me that helps me to expand the artistic approach I bring to designing our oceanfront properties. Listening to or playing music does the same thing for many people. For me, listening to the stereophonic sound created by the rush of the Pidgeon River combined with the bubbling of Laurel Branch Creek that surround our Canton, North Carolina, mountain home provides priceless creative energy. Stimulating any of your senses—with a great meal, or a warm fire, or a bracing walk through the snow—can awaken your creativity. Seek out such experiences, and notice what happens when you feed the right side of your brain a sensory-rich diet.

For me, the experience of creativity is akin to the sound of opening a soda can: a veritable explosion of light and sound and color in the synapses. It's something to be embraced and treasured but also channeled through the practical, left side of the brain. Just like every other topic we've discussed in this section—taking an artist's approach to your craft, accentuating and amplifying your essence, living your inside on your outside, and having a healthy ego—creativity and ingenuity are critical filters to apply when making decisions around your personal brand. Best of all, when you bring these qualities to your life as well as your brand, you'll find that the new reality you have designed and built will be rich beyond measure.

Aspire!

SECTION FOUR

Love Life.

Love-Life.

Love Life.
Love-Life.

*The best thing to hold onto
in life is each other.*

AUDREY HEPBURN

The topic of this section isn't one you see covered in many business or personal development books that don't specifically focus on relationships. In fact, if this book were a fancy country club, the other four sections would hang out together while this section would be off in a corner by itself, with the other four sipping their cocktails, pointing at it and gossiping. And to be honest, while I'm qualified to offer insights about aspiration, risk, personal branding, and contribution, I definitely do not consider myself a relationship expert by any means, and it isn't something I cover in depth when I deliver keynotes or seminars.

Yet I wanted to include relationships in a dedicated section for three reasons. First, I'm something of a loner, and I have trouble letting people get close to me. To this day, I have a small inner circle of friends and only a few chosen professional colleagues; I never built the kind of extensive network most real estate developers rely on to help them with their business. Even though I'm not a very good networker, I'm committed to continue to work on that weakness because over the years I have recognized how vital relationships are to business and personal success. Great relationships make it easier for you to reach your aspirations. More important, having friends, family, business associates, and colleagues at your side as you go through life makes the highs higher and the lows more endurable. Bottom line: I have realized that when it comes to creating a life you love, quality relationships are at the top the list.

Second, *problems* in relationships can derail you faster than almost anything else. I've seen thriving companies go under when conflicts between business partners can't be resolved. I've also worked with a lot of individuals and couples and listened as they described how their careers

> **. . . relationships of *all* kinds
> are critical to creating your own reality
> and altering your DNA.**

were ruined by lack of buy-in from a husband, wife, boyfriend, girlfriend, or life partner. It's a terribly sad thing to see people get to the point where they feel they must choose between the work they love and the partner they cherish. It's made me even more grateful for the way Nilsa and I support each other in our business partnership as well as our intimate relationship.

But the most important reason to include a section on relationships in this book is my wife, Nilsa. Whenever I do a keynote or seminar, people inevitably come up to me and ask how Nilsa and I have managed to stay married for thirty-one years, and I always give Nilsa the credit because she provides stability and a calm center in our marriage. I know without a doubt that our relationship has shaped my life more than any aspiration I've ever pursued, role model I've ever emulated, or daredevil grand unveiling stunt I've ever performed. I believe my thirty-one years with Nilsa qualify me to at least render my opinion on why relationships of *all* kinds are critical to creating your own reality and altering your DNA.

I'm also very clear that relationships can be both the most wonderful and the most painful parts of life. My parent's marriage wasn't ideal, and they finally divorced after twenty-five years. On the other hand, Nilsa's parents have been married for sixty-plus years, and they still play footsie with each other under the dinner table. Personally, there have been times for both Nilsa and me that staying in our marriage has been more challenging than selling a $50 million mansion on spec or rappelling down a rope from a helicopter to the roof of one of our oceanfront masterpieces in thirty-mile-per-hour winds. But in my experience, without love in your life—whether that love comes from friends, family, spouses, partners, or even pets—you won't truly love your life at the deep and fulfilling level you deserve.

Even if you feel your path is to be alone (which for some people is a great path), unless you go off the grid and become completely self-sufficient, you're still going to need *some* relationships. Dozens of research studies show how important relationships of all kinds are to our health and longevity,[1] as well as our life satisfaction, professional performance, and creativity.[2] Great relationships can help us embrace new opportunities in good times and to flourish even in times of stress.[3] Of course, there's nothing wrong with being self-sufficient, but why would you want to miss out on the potential richness of connection and experience you can gain from other people? So if you're a veteran of one or more failed relationships (business or personal)—or like me, you don't let many people get close to you—my hope is that you'll find some ideas, insights, and examples in this section that will help you do a better job of creating a reality that includes more joyous, rewarding, and deeply satisfying relationships of all kinds.

Men and Women Need to "Borrow" a Chromosome from Each Other

What I'm going to share now may be somewhat controversial, but I've found it to be true: there are times when both men and women need to "borrow" a chromosome from the opposite sex in order to create better, happier, more successful relationships and lives. Here's what I mean: because my dad was busy with work and not available much of the time, I was raised predominantly by my mom, and I grew up with four sisters. (I have one brother who was born later.) Then, when I came to Florida, I entered a profession (real estate) where women make up a majority (sixty-four percent) of Realtors and brokers.[4] So I've spent a lot of time around women, and I believe they have quite a few advantages over men. They tend to see things in more dimensions than men do, and they have a broader sense that allows them to take into account many more factors in their approach to life. I think it's one reason they're often more effective leaders: in case you're not aware of it, companies with women in C-suite level leadership positions and on their boards of directors tend to have higher share-price performance, better corporate profitability growth, and fewer long-term governance issues.[5]

But there's a flip side to the advantageous qualities that make women excellent leaders and businesspeople. In my opinion, far too many women are not good at extolling their best qualities to others or expressing belief in themselves and their accomplishments. Remember in chapters 4 and 14 where I referred to people writing their own endorsements? In all my years of making that request, I have never seen a woman exceed my expectations when it came to bragging about their success. *Never.* And, while this phenomenon seems to be changing for the better, to my mind, this reluctance to speak up for themselves can hold women back from having a greater impact on the world.

So whenever a woman asks me for an endorsement, I'll tell her to write what she would like me to say but then I'll add, "Before you do, get in touch with the universe's 'Y' chromosome. By that I mean two things. First, remember 'why' you are asking for this endorsement so you realize how important it is for you to write a great one. Second, get in touch with the part of yourself that's more stereotypically male. Most guys are great at bragging about their accomplishments, so get in touch with that 'Y' chromosome if you need to be bolder. Brag about how great you are, because it's the truth."

On the other hand, just as women need to become bolder, I believe men need to add an X chromosome or two—meaning they must get better at empathy and vulnerability. Many men are reluctant to show their vulnerable side because they think it will make them seem weak; and since most men have been trained never to show weakness, we refuse to let ourselves open up emotionally, or to show that we care about what others are feeling. I know this is playing into stereotypes, but I have met only a few men who are comfortable with being vulnerable or demonstrating empathy. But as I said earlier, since authenticity, transparency, and vulnerability are the foundation of every strong relationship, we men need to develop this side of ourselves.

For men to become more empathetic and vulnerable and women to become bolder and more comfortable asserting their strength, it's going to take the kind of healthy ego you read about in chapter 14. It will take an ability to appreciate our unique gifts combined with a willingness to look clear-eyed at the characteristics that we need to strengthen (vulnerability or boldness). Then it will require the courage to ignore the voices inside ourselves as well as the cultural naysayers that tell us it's weak to be vulnerable, or we're too big for our britches if we dare to follow our passion or assert our worth. Even more than that, it's going to take a willingness in *all* of us to see the people who are in relationship with us both for who they are and who they are working to become.

Be Real. Be Honest. Be Open.

In some ways I feel sorry for young people who are trying to form strong relationships in today's world. It seems to me that with social media encouraging us to present only the best parts of ourselves every minute of every day, and with the constant fear of any past or current indiscretion being captured on film or video and posted online (where it remains *forever*), it's harder than ever to reveal to the world who we truly are in all of our unvarnished reality. And when you add to social media the use of dating apps—where people judge you in an instant and then either swipe left or right based on your profile—what chance do most of us stand of getting to know anyone at a deep level?

However, I firmly believe that any relationship—business, personal, familial, friend, lover—has to be based not on how we want to *appear* but on who we truly *are*. So why waste time creating a false identity when the truth is going to come out eventually anyway? For a relationship to last, it requires each person to be authentically, vulnerably, and transparently him- or herself. You must start by applying the R.I.S.K. acronym, Risk = Requires Intense Self-Knowledge. You must know yourself and your negative tendencies so you can seek out people who will accept you for who you are. But here's what's more challenging: you must do the same for the other person.

I'm a smart enough man never to give dating advice to my daughter, Laura, and I'm not one of those fathers who thinks it's funny to stand on the porch with a gun anytime she brings home her boyfriend for the first time. But the only recommendation I would ever make to her (or to anyone getting into a relationship) is to *give the other person a chance*. Far too many people use any negative trait as an excuse to reject a relationship out of hand. They've read books that recommend getting a legal pad, drawing a line down the center of the page, and on one side writing down all of the person's positive qualities, and on the other side writing all their negative qualities. Well, you know what happens: the negative side fills up first, and they end up either dumping the other person right then and there or continuing to focus on the negative aspects to the point where both people are so miserable that they end the relationship by mutual agreement. But if you simply give someone a chance to show you the best of themselves as well as the worst, it can open things up to create a beautiful reality together.

So yes, you should go into any relationship with your eyes open and be aware of any negative traits in your partner, just as they should be aware of yours. Let your potential partners see who you truly are so that you're both starting the relationship from a position of honesty. Don't waste time trying to conceal your negative qualities: they're gonna come out anyway, and odds are your partner is already aware of them. Besides, if you start a relationship based on a lie, how long do you think it will last without both of you being miserable? However, make sure you also are looking past the surface or any perceived negative qualities to see the real, beautiful person they are inside. One of the many things I'm proud of in my wife and daughter is their willingness to see past the surface of people and look for what's inside. Sometimes they'll say to me, "I see you beneath all the endorsements, the accolades, the clothes, the hair, the earrings, the fancy shoes, all the accoutrements—I see the real person underneath." How many people take the time to do that? Well, Nilsa and Laura have, and they always will.

As you'll see in many of the stories in this section, Nilsa was all too aware of my negative tendencies. From the time we first started dating, I was never afraid to show her my soft "underbelly," and I didn't hide any of my tendency to be addicted to excitement from her. On our second date, I took Nilsa out on my Suzuki GSX-R 1100, the fastest production motorbike ever made at the time. I decided to show off, so I dropped her by the side of the road and did wheelies at nearly 70 MPH up and down a main highway, U.S. 1. (The feat didn't impress her. She was even less impressed when a cop pulled me over and started to arrest me and put me in handcuffs until he was called away unexpectedly for something more pressing.) Then, after dating for about six months, when I *was* arrested as a habitual traffic offender for a long list of speeding tickets, fleeing and attempting to elude, and other traffic violations. I was deeply impressed when this incredibly beautiful, refined woman came to visit me in the county jail. (You'll read the full story of that visit later in this section.)

Nilsa could have easily decided I wasn't worth the trouble, but she didn't. She believed in me. She was always so elegant, and she certainly wasn't impressed by my big hair, rock and roll attitude, and fancy car with the back seat full of speakers that shook your bone marrow. What made the difference? She felt my heart. From our very first date she noticed how I paid attention and cared for every person I met, from the busboy to the waiter to the dishwasher back in the restaurant's kitchen. She could feel that I had a deep care and concern for the downtrodden, the forgotten, the invisible, the persecuted. She'd never met a man like that before, and that was why she said yes when I proposed (again, more on that later).

I know that for Nilsa, being married to me has been like being married to a circus inside a high-speed blender on a rocket ship traveling at the speed of light. But for me, being married to Nilsa has been a gift rarer than the Pink Star Diamond. Of course, it hasn't been a bed of roses for either of us. Every long-term relationship is going to be tested, and we've had times when we didn't think we were going to make it. But still, I believe God gifted me with the only woman on earth who could love me like Nilsa has. Without Nilsa, there would be no Frank McKinney or Laura McKinney. There would be no real estate artistry, no forty-four oceanfront masterpieces. There would be no Caring House Project Foundation, and more than thirteen thousand kids in Haiti would be living in mud huts by the side of the road instead of in self-sustaining villages with renewable food, clean water, churches, clinics, and schools. Without Nilsa there would be no Badwater Ultramarathon finishes or bestselling books—nothing. (Well, maybe I'd still have the 1988 Yugo, but that isn't saying much.) In truth, I probably wouldn't even be alive if it weren't for the blessing of being married to Nilsa. So I hope you understand why I believe so deeply in the power of your relationships to shape—and even save—your life.

While this section focuses primarily on intimate relationships, I believe there are things to be learned from them that can apply to every relationship you might have—with friends, family, children, colleagues, employees, clients, customers, and so on. In the next chapter we cover "significant others," those key partnerships that shape your reality for good or ill more than anything else. In chapter 17, you'll see how your relationships with people whom I call "guardian angels" can help you redirect your energies and tendencies toward new, more positive directions. After that, you'll discover insights and suggestions for using the pressures that every relationship faces to transform it into something precious, rare, and lasting. Then we'll explore the topic of "magnetic-ism," or how to amp up your ability to attract the people/relationships/clients you want into your life and business. Finally, we'll take the doors off the bedroom (metaphorically speaking) to talk about the importance of satisfying your partner's sexual desires to keep the spark alive in your long-term intimate relationship.

One final word before we start. The date 9/11 has a special significance to most people in the world, but for the McKinney family it holds a different, special meaning. My father died in a mid-air plane crash on September 11, 1992—not *the* 9/11, but *our* 9/11. So every September 11, I wear a Christian Dior suit jacket my dad bought me when I first got into real estate because he wanted me to look more like a businessman than a rock star. I wear it for many reasons. To honor my dad's memory. To thank him for the love and advice he gave me (even though as a teenager I didn't want any of it). But most of all, I wear it as a reminder that tomorrow someone I love could board a plane and never return.

Make sure that every day you love deeply and live with no regrets. And remember to love life, love yourself, and love others. Nothing you will read in this book is more important than that.

The Significance of a Significant Other

I love her and that's the beginning and end of everything.

F. SCOTT FITZGERALD

In 1987 I was a young tennis pro just starting out in real estate. I had an office in one of those executive suite buildings in Boca Raton, Florida, where all the tenants had tiny offices (mine was eight feet by nine feet) and a shared reception area, conference room, and copy room. One day I walked into the building, still in my tennis clothes, and saw this beautiful, elegant, well-dressed woman with long blond hair sitting with her back erect and legs crossed, reading the *Wall Street Journal* in the conference area/copy room. I remember thinking, *Wow! She's gorgeous but waaaaay out of my league!* But I figured, what the hell, nothing ventured, nothing gained, so I went into my office, grabbed a piece of paper, ran back to the copy machine, put the document on the glass, and selected one hundred copies as an excuse to be in her presence for a while. (The truth is that I'd inadvertently put a blank piece of paper in the copy machine.)

Do you remember a scene from the 1994 movie, *Dumb and Dumber*, where Jeff Daniels (Harry) is talking to a girl in the foreground, and in the background Jim Carrey (Lloyd) is leaning on a bar and sticking out his butt so the girl will see and admire his "assets"? Well, that day I did my own version of the Jim Carrey move. Because I'd spent hours on the tennis court, my legs were tanned and muscular, so as I leaned against the copier, I figured I was showing this beautiful woman my best side, so to speak. I introduced myself to Nilsa and, after some small (very small) talk, asked her out.

She promptly said, "No, and by the way you just printed one hundred blank copies."

If I could have, I would have crawled into the tiny cabinet beneath the copy machine and shut the doors.

At the time, Nilsa was a successful interior designer for houses as well as yachts and planes, and her firm had multiple offices (including the corner office) in the building. She was mature for her young age, and she probably thought I was ridiculous. She was probably right, too—but I was persistent. The next day, and the day after that, I found another reason to talk with her and ask her out again. Her response: still no. So I thought, *She's an interior designer: I'll ask her to be the designer on one of my projects. She doesn't need to know that I'm renovating crack houses in a bad part of town.* I went to Nilsa's office and told her I wanted to hire her.

"Fine. The retainer is $500 up front," she said. I agreed and wrote the check. (What I *didn't* tell her was that $500 was nearly my entire budget to renovate the interior of the house.) She agreed to make an appointment—once the check cleared.

A few days later we met in the office lobby at 2 P.M., and I drove her to the property in a questionable neighborhood. As we pulled up in front of the house, I saw Nilsa reach over and lock her car door.

Being somewhat egotistical (the unhealthy kind), I said, "Hey, babe, what do you think?"

Unamused, she looked at me and answered, "You don't need an interior designer. You need a bulldozer."

I started laughing, but she was serious: she wasn't going to get out of the car. So I said, "Okay then, let's go get some drinks."

Her reply? "I'm not going to get a drink with you because I don't date my clients. I'll come back later on my own to look at the house."

This was *not* going the way I planned. I said, "You don't date clients? Well, then, you're fired."

"Fine," she said. "I'm keeping your $500. But I will go out with you—to lunch."

On August 5, 1987, Nilsa and I went to lunch. (I remember the date because I still have the credit card receipt, on which I drew a heart around the name of the restaurant.) After a courtship of a few eventful years, we were married on August 3, 1990. I tell people that I may have lost that $500 retainer, but I gained the best wife a man could have—not a bad ROI in my book.

Who you choose for your closest relationships will shape your reality, but *the most significant influencing factor in life is your relationship with your significant other*—wife or husband or spouse or partner, whatever term you use. If Nilsa hadn't married me, I would not be the man I am today. My relationship with her has altered the trajectory of my life. In fact, I firmly believe that had God not sent Nilsa to me, I'd likely be dead or living in a beat-up old trailer somewhere in the backwoods of West Virginia, chewing tobacco, smelling like motor oil, and married to the bearded lady from the circus. And I guarantee that if she'd chosen someone else, her life would have been radically different too.

The guidance and advice I've given you in each chapter of this book will be influenced dramatically by your significant other. If he or she is willing to encourage you, cheer you on, and help you pursue your aspirations, you'll get there faster. If they doubt your intentions, disparage your abilities, diminish your dreams, or sabotage your efforts, then it will be nearly impossible for you to succeed. More than the family you're born into, the profession you choose, the mentors you encounter, or the level of success you experience, your significant other is a determining factor when it comes to influencing your DNA and creating your reality.

Now, I get that you may or may not have—or want—a significant other right now. If you look at statistics, as of 2019 only 48.2 percent of U.S. households contained a married couple, 8.3 percent of men and 11.1 percent of women in the U.S. were divorced, and 36 million people were living in single-person households.[1] But even if you're reading this and saying, "I'm not interested in a relationship; I'm perfectly happy being alone," *no one can exist all by themselves*. Relationships are a necessary part of being human. Think back over your life: wasn't there at least one relationship you would consider significant—with a parent, sibling, child or grandchild, best friend, teacher, business partner, or colleague? Even a momentary connection with the barista who hands you coffee or the homeless person you give money to has the potential to transform your life as well as theirs. The goal of this chapter (and this section) is to help you get better at building strong relationships with everyone, especially your significant other, because he or she can be either the greatest help or harm to the reality you want to create and the aspirations you want to pursue.

How a Significant Other Can Shape Your Reality

Here are just a few of the ways in which your significant other shapes your life and reality.

#1. THEY CAN MAKE YOU HEALTHIER—OR NOT. Researchers have long seen a connection between the quality of your relationship and health. Married people tend to live longer than unmarried people,[2] and couples who are in stable, happy relationships have lower risk of heart disease, lower blood pressure, less stress, less depression, and better outcomes for cancer and surgery.[3] Happy relationships can improve endocrine and immune functions by lowering cortisol and increasing oxytocin[4] (the "love hormone" or bonding chemical in the brain). On the other hand, poor health habits in significant others can have a negative impact on the other party's health. For example, partners tend to have similar levels of physical activity and fast-food consumption. In fact, if your significant other is obese, the likelihood that you're obese as well increases by thirty-seven percent.[5] What's worse, problems in a relationship can create or worsen health concerns like sleep issues, metabolic issues, and diabetes.[6] And God forbid you actually split up: the brain processes the pain of a relationship breakup in the same way as it does physical pain and withdrawal symptoms.[7]

#2. THEY CAN MAKE YOU HAPPIER—OR NOT. Multiple studies show that, in general, people in relationships are happier and their life satisfaction and general well-being are higher.[8] Being in love can elevate dopamine, which is the "reward" chemical in your brain, and oxytocin, the "love" chemical that creates attachment and bonding.[9] And as long as your relationship is in good shape, these chemicals can continue to be elevated for years, long after the honeymoon stage is over.[10] Of course, factors such as trust, understanding, and open communication between partners will have an effect on how happy your relationship is. Poor relationship quality produces lower happiness, satisfaction, and even self-esteem in partners.[11] It's even been shown that marital discord can increase the risk of depressive symptoms by a factor of ten.[12] And if people decide to separate or divorce, in many cases the negative effects of the previous unhappy relationship may last for a lifetime.[13]

#3. THEY CAN MAKE YOU MORE SUCCESSFUL—OR NOT. They say behind every successful man there is a strong woman. In my case it is not nor has it *ever* been behind, because Nilsa has always stood *beside* me and supported me every step of the way. As I described in *Make It Big!*, back in 1992 she supported the decision for us to sell everything we owned (including our house, cars, and most of our clothes) and move into an efficiency apartment so we could put every penny into our first oceanfront property. That efficiency was so small that I could flip the pancakes that were on the stove while I was *in* the shower! We have been partners in all forty-four of my oceanfront transactions, and she's created the stunning interiors for each property. And while I might be the primary decision maker in our business, I'm smart enough to listen to Nilsa's advice. In 2010, following the global recession and subsequent plunge in high-end real estate prices and demand here in Florida, we were struggling financially, to the point where we were on the verge of losing everything and would have had to sell our house. Nilsa had the idea to keep the house and lot surrounding it, subdivide the remaining property and sell three newly-created lots that were undeveloped and very desirable. That sale gave us the funds to get through a financially stressful time *and* keep the oceanfront home we've lived in for twenty-five years.

As you read in the introduction to this section, I've seen dozens of men and women who have had more natural talent, better connections, and access to financing, but whose careers never reached their full potential because their significant others weren't on board. To achieve your aspirations and create a new reality, you and your significant other should be like the two rails of a railroad track: separate and equidistant from each other, but always heading in the same direction. That way, your ride on the train of life will be less problematic and more enjoyable.

#4. THEY CAN HELP YOU REDIRECT YOUR NEGATIVE OR SELF-DESTRUCTIVE ENERGY AND TENDENCIES—OR NOT. Chapter 9 advised redirecting the energy from your negative tendencies into more positive outlets. Well, the best person to help with that is your significant other. Sharing with your significant other from an early stage your desire

---

. . . you and your significant other should be like the two rails of a railroad track . . .

---

to bring out what's inside (even if painful) and then rewire and redirect that energy can give you the best ally possible, one who can encourage you and support you in finding the constructive outlets you need for that destructive tendency.

Conversely, *not* involving your significant other in the redirection process from the very beginning can cause them to accidentally or inadvertently sabotage your progress. Say your doctor says that you have become pre-diabetic and need to lose weight and eliminate sugar and alcohol immediately. You don't tell your significant other because you're ashamed that you've let yourself go to this extent, and decide you'll simply say no to desserts and drinks whenever they're offered. But your spouse (who loves to cook and entertain) can't understand why you're turning down invitations to parties and won't eat the baked goodies they create. He or she starts making comments, like, "You don't like my food anymore?" or "Are you on a diet? You don't need to lose weight," or "What's wrong with a few drinks now and then?" And when you finally tell them why you're trying to redirect your health habits, they're upset because you hid the diagnosis! In such a scenario, how much more likely are you to go back to the unhealthy old way of doing things?

New circumstances are uncomfortable enough without having a significant other not understanding what's going on and resisting your efforts along the way. When it comes to following your aspirations and creating a new reality, your significant other doesn't have to pursue them with you. But you'll find it easier to follow through if you have their understanding, support, and buy-in.

What to Look for in a Significant Other

It was about a year after we met that I knew for sure that Nilsa was the woman I would ask to marry me. (I'll tell you that story in chapter 17.) And looking back from a vantage point of thirty-plus years married, here are a few things to think about when selecting a partner. By the way, these same criteria can be applied when looking at your relationships with business associates, friends, or colleagues.

First, *recognize your relationship role models, good and bad.* Growing up, we all observe the relationships of people we are close to, especially our parents or other caretakers, and that becomes what we believe a relationship should be. And if you've had a previous relationship that ended (in particular if it ended badly), that will affect your expectations and ideas. You may say to yourself, *I promise I'm never going to fall in love with someone like my ex again!* But remember, there was *something* about your ex-partner that you found attractive, even if their traits drove you crazy. So if you're not aware of your tendencies and attractions, you may end up with a different "bad" boy or girl, for example, or another successful, driven partner who puts career before you.

I'm not saying that you should reject someone you're interested in because they remind you of your parents' relationship or the ex who you dumped (or who dumped you). What I am saying is to be aware of the role models you're bringing into the relationship, so you can make a more conscious choice of partners. And if you're smart, ask that prospective significant other to tell you about their family and their past relationships as well.

Second, *decide what you want in a significant other, but be flexible.* In the start of this section I said that people who are dating today have a more difficult time of things than I did back in the "Stone Age" (i.e., before the Internet). It's far too easy to reject potential partners before you even meet them, much less get to know them. You may be turning down someone who is a possible nine out of ten because you don't like their haircut or their choice of clothing, where they went to school, or their job. Sure, you need to have some basic criteria to decide whether you want to go out with someone, but limit those requirements to a few and be willing to flex on the ones that aren't super-important.

Third, *find someone who balances you out.* You've heard that opposites attract, right? Well, I believe the reason is that unconsciously most of us are seeking to find a significant other who will have strengths and attributes we don't possess. For example, as a self-admitted adrenaline junkie, I don't expect, nor would I ever ask Nilsa to rescue me or to save me from myself, but I do rely on her to be the voice of reason when it comes to some of my riskier endeavors. (Yes, there are some pursuits that are too much even for me.) She always has been the calming presence in our relationship, and I think she appreciates the energy and excitement that I contribute to her life. If you've done the work to get to know yourself, your strengths, and your weaknesses, you should have a better sense of the qualities that will help you pursue your aspirations and become the person you want to be. Then as you're looking for that significant other, ask yourself if he or she can bring some of those qualities to your relationship—and conversely, if you have great qualities that they will find valuable as well.

Fourth, *look for someone with whom you can be honest, and who will see clearly who you really are, good and bad.* After I had to work so hard to get that first date with Nilsa, you'd think I would have been smart enough to treat her like the classy lady she is from the very beginning. But being young, naïve, and somewhat self-absorbed, I was over thirty minutes late to meet her at the restaurant for that first lunch date. I finally zoomed up in my fancy convertible Mercedes 450 SL with the top down and my big 1980s hair blowing in the wind, stereo blaring and tires screeching—and I saw her standing at the valet station, ready to get her car and drive back to work. It took a lot of fast talking to persuade her to come back into the Bridge restaurant with me, and, luckily, we had a very enjoyable lunch. But I guarantee she never would have gone on a second date if she'd just seen the selfish side of me, which was on full display. Thank goodness she also saw my softer, empathetic side, in the way I spoke to the waiter and the busboy, asking their names and treating them kindly. I think she was amused at how consumed I was with feeding each one of the fish that were swimming just beneath our table with our leftover french fries. She also noticed that before we left the restaurant I went back into the kitchen to give the dishwasher five dollars. From the earliest days of our courtship, Nilsa saw many facets of me, and I always could sense her deep care for others, her strength, her commitment, her elegance, and her heart. I believe that our willingness to be honest and open with each other from the very start laid the foundation for our marriage.

No truly great relationship is ever based on a lie, so don't waste time trying to put on an act when you're looking for a significant other. You will never be fulfilled in any relationship if you can't be yourself, with all your flaws and faults as well as your awesomeness—and neither will your significant other. While it's natural to want to put your best foot forward on that first or second date, any relationship worth pursuing should be able to withstand you both being true to who you are.

A Few Thoughts for Creating a Great Relationship

I believe any great relationship is just as much of a work of art as any of the oceanfront masterpieces I've created. Indeed, building a great relationship takes the same kind of dedication, artistry, passion, and plain hard work as it does to build the most beautiful property in the world. Now, I'm not Oprah or Dr. Phil or any other kind of love guru, and I don't have a list of guaranteed secrets to help you make your relationship legendary. What I can do is share some hard-won wisdom (HWW) and my perspective from the artistry that Nilsa and I have put into our marriage.

HWW #1: HAVE THE OTHER PERSON'S BACK. There have been things that I've done and stunts that I've pursued during our marriage that I know were waaaaaay outside Nilsa's comfort zone. (Setting myself and my motorcycle on fire for the *Aspire!* book launch trailer comes to mind.) But never once has she talked me out of something or told me it was scary. If she felt I was passionate about and monomaniacally focused on pursuing a project or idea or stunt, she was behind it one hundred percent. She trusts me enough to go along with these pursuits even if she's watching me from the sidelines with a rosary in one hand and a scotch in the other. Conversely, there are a lot of things that our daughter Laura chooses to share with her mom and not with me, and I know that Nilsa will give her exactly the advice she needs, and tell me if there's anything I need to know. Studies of intimate relationships show that strong, secure partners demonstrate qualities like trust, connection, reliability, and belief that the other person will support them.[14] Make sure your partner always knows that you are in their corner.

HWW #2: SHARE AND LISTEN. This may be Relationship 101, but after a few years in a relationship, how many of us start to take someone for granted and stop listening to what they are saying—and more important, we stop paying attention to what they're *not* saying? Partners who stop sharing about their lives are usually in deep trouble. Healthy relationships require open communication so that each partner feels heard and understood.[15]

Now, this can be interesting when you work together, like Nilsa and I have done from the earliest crack house and throughout all our oceanfront homes. There can be a temptation to bring business into the bedroom, so to speak, which can create problems, especially when issues crop up on the job. I have to acknowledge Nilsa for her handling of this. Through the years I've made a few bad decisions on properties, locations, finishes, margins that weren't high enough, and so on, but she's never brought them into our relationship. In the evenings when I come down from the tree house, she leaves her office in our guest house, and we go into the main house

---

Partners who stop sharing about their lives are usually in deep trouble.

---

together. We may *talk* a little business but we don't *argue* about business. And for most of the time, we leave business for business hours and focus on the other things we share.

HWW #3: THINK ABOUT THEIR NEEDS. This is an area where I definitely need to do a better job. I've performed what many people perceive to be extremely risky stunts as part of our grand unveilings for our oceanfront properties, and for each one I have spent countless hours on planning everything down to the last detail. But I *didn't* spend enough time putting myself in Nilsa's shoes and thinking about how she would feel as she watched me risk life and limb. Being in a relationship requires you to develop empathy for your partner and to put their needs ahead of yours at times. For example, I continue to work on being more cognizant of "Nilsa time," which to me is placing all of my attention on her. It's okay not to set the world on fire every moment. It's okay to stop and watch the sunrise every now and then. Sure, I'm not ever going to be that way 24/7, and Nilsa wouldn't want me to be that laid-back anyway. There's a part of her that says, "I'm glad I'm married to my Renaissance Man, this daredevil of a husband, and not Mr. Boring Khaki-pants." But we both work to find that balance, to understand the other person's happy place, and to seek to make space for their needs to come to the forefront.

By the way, meeting your partner's needs may very well require being okay with being apart—for a few hours or days, for that matter. I get that sometimes Frank's world is not a place that Nilsa wants to be in because it's exhausting. And all those mornings when I get up at 3 A.M. to go running, I truly enjoy being by myself in the dark and silence, putting in the miles on the road. But when I come back to the house every morning, I always go in the kitchen and make Nilsa a cup of coffee or squeeze her fresh lemon juice so it'll be ready for her when she gets up.

Bottom line: one plus one equals more than two. If (when) you find your significant other, I encourage you to create your own reality; then every day, pursue the impossible within that reality as an unbreakable team.

Marry Your
Guardian Angel

All God's angels come to us disguised.
JAMES RUSSELL LOWELL

I knew Nilsa was the woman I would marry when she came to visit me in jail, and I saw her sitting on the other side of bulletproof glass. We'd been dating for around six months when the dozens of speeding tickets I'd accumulated during my early years in Florida finally caught up with me. I owned the fastest production motorcycle in the world, so, of course, the owner's manual said I had to break the speed limit, right? I'd even been cited for "fleeing and attempting to elude," meaning I had managed to evade the police who were chasing me. And the times I went to court for a ticket, I was able to charm the judge out of suspending my license or, worse, giving me any jail time.

Eventually, however, I was confronted by a particularly smart prosecutor. When I went into court and presented my plea as to why I should be let go with nothing more than a slap on the wrist (a small fine), the prosecutor held up a document (one of those old continuous computer printouts) above his head, and it unfolded and unfolded and unfolded until it hit the ground—more than seven feet of citations. He looked at the judge and said, "Your Honor, he's snowing you." So I was sentenced to three days in the Palm Beach County jail for being a habitual traffic offender. Yes, it was time for me to suffer the consequences and pay the price for my destructive past.

Now, since Nilsa and I had been dating for such a short time, while I'd been up front with her about going to jail, I really didn't expect her to visit me. But she did. In the visitor's log where it asked which inmate she wanted to see, she wrote, "Frank McKinney." Then she went into the visitor's room, sat in front of the bulletproof glass, and waited for me to arrive.

Imagine her shock when the door from the jail side opened, and in walked a three-hundred-pound Black man. She started crying, turned to the guard and said, "What happened to my Frank?" Turns out there were two Frank McKinneys in jail at the same time!

So the other Frank went back inside (no doubt dejected at the loss of his new love), and the guards came and got me. I walked through the door and saw Nilsa's tearstained face on the other side of the glass, and I knew, in that very moment, one day I would ask her to marry me. If ever there was a time for a woman to say, "What am I doing here, sitting in some dirty old jail where I had to be frisked before I came in, waiting to talk to a tennis pro playboy/wannabe real estate investor loser who's been incarcerated for his self-destructive, irresponsible behavior? I don't need this in my life! Forget this guy. I'm going to move on," this was it. But she didn't. Instead, there she was, and at that moment I knew that she was my guardian angel, sent by God to love me like no other woman ever would or could.

According to the catechism of the Catholic church, every person has a guardian angel: "Beside each believer stands an angel as protector and shepherd leading him to life."[1] (CCC 336) I've even known people in my inner circle who swear they've seen two angels hovering around me. (I'm not surprised that I need more than the usual quota.) But I believe that I'm married to my *real* guardian angel, Nilsa. She has made my life, saved my life, and gotten me to realize what life is all about. I know there is a heaven because God has allowed me to experience what it will be like due to Nilsa's presence in my life.

I think she'd say the same, yet she'd put it in a very different way. For Nilsa, being married to me is like putting on a beautiful flame-retardant

Dior dress each morning and, with that rosary in one hand and that scotch in the other, strapping yourself into a rocket-fueled rollercoaster, all the while knowing that when the ride hits 100 MPH the cosmos will switch off gravity and the coaster will career off into space, leaving you wondering (again) if you'll land on a beautiful new planet or disappear into a black hole. It'd be exciting for a while, but every night you'd have to decide whether you want to ride the coaster all over again tomorrow or say, "That's enough. I'm done." There were times that I'm sure Nilsa wanted to trade me in for a slower, more stable ride that had fewer rocket boosters and less defects. I'm so glad she didn't, and every night I thank God that she has been willing to hop on the ride with me for another day.

This entire section on relationships will probably make Nilsa very uncomfortable. While I'm an open book (bordering on exhibitionist), Nilsa is the polar opposite: she cringes when praised or given attention. But this beautiful woman (who is all of five feet and one inch tall when she teases her hair, and who can still fit into her wedding dress after more than three decades) has not only been an angel in my life but in the lives of many other people as well. She's an incredible mother to our daughter, Laura, and a devoted daughter to her own parents. She drives for more than seven hours round trip every two weeks to visit them and make sure they get to their doctors' visits. She's been crew chief for thirteen Badwater 135 ultramarathons, more than any person in history. She devotes many hours of volunteer work in our local community and has been recognized as a Woman of Grace by Bethesda Hospital and the Woman Volunteer of the Year by the Junior League of Boca Raton. And she co-founded the Caring House Project Foundation with me. It's with her effort and support that CHPF built twenty-nine self-sufficient villages in twenty-four Haitian cities over the past two decades, caring for over thirteen thousand children and their families.

When I was so sick at the beginning of 2020 that I couldn't get out of bed for over a month, every time I opened my eyes I saw Nilsa sitting in a chair across from our bed, making sure my chest was still rising and falling. Whenever I've done risky, daredevil stunts through the years, Nilsa has always stood on the sidelines, praying for my safety. I know how hard it has been for her, yet she never has told me I'm crazy or tried to talk me out of doing anything that was important to me. Before I left Florida to embark on the Yugo We-go Tour, she wrote me a note in which she said things like, "I believe in you. You're able to do this. This is a sign that God is giving you your health back. I can't wait to see you when you return." (After a life-threatening illness, it was a big step to spend twenty-two days all by myself, driving 6,288 miles in a thirty-three-year-old car that could hit sixty miles per hour, maybe, if was lucky and heading downhill with a tailwind.) I kept that note with my rosary and Bible and read it every night I was on the road. There's no way I could have pursued the Yugo We-go tour without Nilsa believing in it, buying into it, praying over it, and hoping that the car didn't break down. It never did.

Those are just a few examples of how my guardian angel Nilsa loves, protects, and supports me more than anyone else in the world. Even though you probably don't need a guardian angel as much as I do, my greatest hope is that you are lucky enough to find a wife, husband, or partner who fills the role.

Four Signs of a Guardian Angel

I get that not everyone can relate to the idea of a guardian angel. (In fact, Nilsa isn't fond of it when I describe her that way, because she feels that I'm my own keeper and she's not responsible for me.) And I'm sure that if you're lucky enough to have a guardian angel as your partner, they'll have their own unique qualities. But here are a few characteristics that I consider important when it comes to my relationship with Nilsa. I hope these signs will help to identify some of the unknown and unseen angels in your own life.

First, *guardian angels see the good inside you, even when you're at your worst.* I was never reluctant to reveal my "bad boy" nonconformist side from the very first date with any woman, and if she didn't like it, I'd simply move on to the next candidate. You read in chapter 16 how I was late (and somewhat obnoxious) for our first date, and in the introduction to this section you learned that she spent part of our second date standing on the side of the road as I did wheelies on my motorbike while inebriated. After the cop who almost arrested me had to leave to answer another radio call, Nilsa—who'd been very quiet and stoic the entire time—hopped on the back of the bike and asked me to take her home. She never freaked out, even when I spent the entire ride back to her house sneezing and covering the inside of my helmet with snot. But even with that, and even with having to visit me in jail (something I'm sure she never thought she would have to do for a boyfriend), somehow she focused on the good that she knew was inside me, even when it was obscured by my behavior. She chose to believe that the deep, caring concern for the invisible, the downtrodden, the people who are ignored by most of the world that she sensed on that very first date would always win the day. Her willingness to see and remind me of the good inside has helped me to become a more caring, compassionate man.

Second, *guardian angels accept all of you.* Nilsa was very aware that my compassion and empathy were mixed in with some self-destructive tendencies—the addiction to excitement, for example—which had created a tortured existence from time to time and a lot of ongoing issues. Yes, it's exciting to jump onto moving freight trains, for example, or jump *over* a replica of my first house on a motorcycle, or buy a second multimillion-dollar property when all our available cash was tied up in building the first, or to rappel forty feet down a line hanging from a helicopter above our latest oceanfront masterpiece, or to run 135 miles non-stop in the burning heat of Death Valley as the bottoms of your feet are peeling off and you're hallucinating from dehydration and heat exhaustion. A lot of other women would see such behavior and leave, saying, "He may have a great heart, but I just can't cope with the rest." But Nilsa accepts *all* of me: the insecurities, sensitivities, the risk taking, and the big heart. It's her acceptance of both the good and bad sides of Frank McKinney that creates the space for the good side to show up more often.

Third, *guardian angels don't try to change you. But they can help save you from yourself.* According to the Catholic faith, no one, not even God, can mess with your free will to act or not act as you decide. It's your choice to do what you're going to do. But there have been instances where I felt that Nilsa's presence caused me to alter my free will—not because she wanted me to be different, but because she made me *want* to choose another path for myself.

I have a tendency to act very quickly on impulses, and that often has served me well—but at times it's also gotten me into a lot of trouble. My "oppositional defiant" approach to life makes me want to prove to everyone that I can shape reality the way I want it no matter how high the odds. While Nilsa has never tried to change my mind if she feels that I'm truly passionate about something, upon occasion she has offered her opinion in between the onset of the impulse and its implementation. She might not have changed my mind, but she has redirected my impulses to healthier avenues.

It is enormously powerful when a guardian angel's love is so deep that it causes the other person to alter his or her free will. Without preaching or nagging, and simply by being her elegant, strong, loving self, Nilsa showed me that I could make the choice to redirect my energies to become a better version of myself. Then it was my responsibility to rewire that energy and redirect it into more constructive avenues.

Fourth, *guardian angels are there for life.* Some of Nilsa's girlfriends admire her for many reasons and look up to her for being so patient, but others have asked her, "He's charming and different, but why in the world do you stay with him? Isn't it time to leave him and focus on you?" And to be honest, if the tables had been turned, I don't know if I could have

---

It is enormously powerful when a guardian angel's love is so deep . . .

---

stuck with Nilsa during the difficult times I've created for us over the past thirty years. I'm sure there are periods on the roller coaster ride of our marriage—when the universe switched off its gravity and it felt like she was shooting off the tracks (again), not knowing if she would land in a black hole or end up in a new, unpopulated, Garden of Eden—that she probably asked herself why she was still with me. But a guardian angel is there for life, and marrying your guardian angel means he or she will be with you no matter the circumstance.

A word of warning, though: if you're not careful, you may find yourself taking your guardian angel for granted. And then it's all too easy for them to choose to leave and go be with somebody else more deserving than you, or simply choose to be alone and love themselves. If you push your angel to the breaking point, he or she may choose to waft over to love someone else who has less baggage and creates less trouble. While every relationship will have its challenges, never push any relationship to the breaking point. I've come close to that, but luckily through introspection, therapy, and self-examination I realized it before it was too late. And as you'll see in the next chapter, with some skill, commitment, and a lot of understanding and love, a relationship with anyone—including a guardian angel—can come back from the breaking point even stronger than it was before.

When My Guardian Angel Said Yes

Strange but true, even after I realized that I wanted to marry Nilsa, we never discussed marriage for the two-plus years we were dating. But on her birthday in 1989 I told her to put on her prettiest outfit because we were going to a fancy place for dinner, The Gazebo in Boca Raton. It was a wonderful evening, and I was on fire with excitement—and nerves.

After dinner I gave her presents, and saved the best for last: a large wrapped box, with a smaller box inside, and a smaller box inside that, and a tiny box inside that one. Before she could open the fourth box I handed her a blindfold and said, "Put this on, but keep that last box handy—we're going somewhere else." I led her to the car, and we drove around for forty-five minutes to disorient her. When we finally stopped we were only about a block from the restaurant, but she had no idea where we were. We had circuitously arrived at the base of the Boca Raton municipal water tower.

Unbeknownst to Nilsa, earlier that evening I had criminally trespassed on the city's water tower property. I had put on a full Army camouflage outfit, complete with face paint and climbing ropes, and proceeded to scale the tall barbed-wire fence protecting the tower. Then it took nearly an hour to climb the water tower carefully all the way to the top, where I hung a large, thirty-foot banner that said, Nilsa will you marry me? I also had asked a neighbor who lived close to the tower if I could use their yard for one of those *huge* Hollywood-style searchlights to illuminate the banner.

I parked the car at the foot of the tower, opened the door and helped Nilsa out. She was still blindfolded and had no idea what was going on. The spotlight was as bright as the noonday sun, shining on the banner. I turned her to face the side of the tower with the banner and, down on one knee, said, "Okay, take off your blindfold, open the box, and look up."

For what seemed like an eternity she didn't say anything. All she was doing was staring up at the tower, then back at the box in her hand. Terrified, I thought she was actually saying no to my marriage proposal. What I didn't know was that she couldn't see the banner because she was literally blinded by the intensity of the sixty-thousand-watt spotlight!

But I wasn't going to take no for an answer. "If you don't say yes, I'm climbing back up there until you do!" I told her. Once her eyes adjusted and she saw the lofty love note and the engagement ring, my guardian angel said yes to all the years of mayhem and joy that would follow.

I wouldn't have lived this long and probably would have squandered a tremendous amount of talent had it not been for the woman whom God sent for me to marry. And if something ever happened to Nilsa I'd be lost. She's said a few times that if she passed away there are dozens of women who would line up to take care of me, but I don't want to be taken care of. I can take care of myself. No one could ever take the place of Nilsa's love. And every night as I close my eyes and thank God for the blessings he has given me that day, my guardian angel Nilsa is at the top of the list.

P.S. If you go to TheAspireBook.com you'll see newspaper images of the water tower with the marriage proposal. It stayed up there for over a month, eventually blowing down in the wind. I retrieved it and still have it to this day!

Relationship Pressure Creates Diamonds

You don't develop courage by being
happy in your relationships every day.
You develop it by surviving difficult times
and challenging adversity.

EPICURUS

As I wrote in a recent social media post—one that included an image of one of my first paintings where I applied an unusual choice of paint materials (more to follow)—it seems to me that over a lifetime many people cycle through different stages in their romantic relationships.

STAGE 1: YOU FALL IN LOVE. A frozen and steeled heart begins to thaw and unlock as you battle the hurts and scars from past loves. Whether your first love or your tenth, the rational and fearful mind tries mightily yet fails to shut it all down, finally succumbing to the power of the irrational heart.

STAGE 2: YOU'RE ALL IN—BUT ARE THEY? The fall is complete. You're In Love. The heart has shifted, grown a new chamber, yet the words are suppressed behind frightful trepidation, until they can no longer be contained and come bursting forth.

STAGE 3: YOU SAY THE WORDS FOR THE FIRST TIME. With raging vulnerability and a racing heart, *I love you* is shared for the first time. As the words roll off your tongue, the feeling is orgasmic—but only if you hear, "I love you, too." Your world has been turned upside down in the most beautiful way.

STAGE 4: THE HONEYMOON BEGINS. You're blissfully in love with the most perfect person on the planet. Sure, you notice a few things you'd like the other person to change, but you can ignore those little defects— right?

STAGE 5:"I LOVE YOU, BUT I WISH YOU'D . . ." The honeymoon appears to be over. Now those defects are starting to bug you, and you're amazed that your partner doesn't think you're perfect either! You both find yourselves disagreeing, or maybe even arguing about the areas of your relationship that aren't up to snuff in your opinion.

STAGE 6: IT EITHER GETS BETTER—OR WORSE. After stage 5 most relationships hit a crossroads where you and your partner either learn how to handle conflict or your disagreements and arguments start to pile up. And if you don't learn to handle them with an open, communicative mind, eventually the pile gets so high that it turns into a wall between you. The fights get bigger, and you stop feeling that you should even bother trying to see the other person's point of view. By that point "I love you" has become "You don't love me," or worse—"I don't love you." And whether you walk out the door or stay in what's now a "cohabitant zombie" relationship where both of you are miserable and in pain, you're left with half of a broken heart—your partner took one half and you're left with fragments of the other. (I used my own blood as "paint" to depict the deep pain felt in this stage.)

I think most of us are realistic enough to find it hard to hold onto the belief of "happily ever after." Any long-lasting relationship will go through times where you wonder if it would be better to just call it quits. The problem is that even if you do leave, you may find that the cycle begins all over again, only with a new partner, who is often a new version of the old. (Because we tend to be attracted to similar people, it's not surprising that while forty-one percent of first marriages end in divorce, that number goes up to sixty percent of second marriages and seventy-three percent of third marriages.)[1] So what's the solution? You need to learn how to drop your expectations and ride a relationship's highs and lows with the grace of an eagle soaring on the thermal updrafts and downdrafts of nature, knowing that no one, and I mean no one, is responsible for your happiness but *you*. It starts by both of you becoming expert fighters. Sounds counterintuitive, right? But let's be realistic: no relationship lasts, much less thrives, without conflict. So if you want longevity in your relationship,

---

**. . . learn how to drop your expectations and
ride a relationship's highs and lows
with the grace of an eagle . . .**

---

you and your partner must learn to deal with conflict in such a way that will make your connection as strong, durable, and brilliant as the world's hardest substance: a diamond.

Diamonds are formed 90 miles below the earth's surface, in upwards of 725,000 pounds of pressure per square inch and temperatures of at least two thousand degrees Fahrenheit.[2] Most minerals crumble or liquefy under such extreme circumstances. In the same way, most relationships can't withstand even small amounts of emotional stress, pressure, and heat. However, you want your relationship to be able to pass any test and come through stronger and better each time. And whether the conflict in your relationship produces divorce or diamonds all depends on your approach. After all, nine divorces take place in the two minutes it takes for you to say your wedding vows,[3] yet over four hundred new diamonds are discovered in those same two minutes![4]

The Value of Conflict

I will never forget seeing Nilsa on her dad's arm as she walked down the aisle of the church on our wedding day. I also remember the beautiful custom lace and beaded headdress she was wearing underneath her veil— it reminded me of a slimmer, fancier, more elegant version of motorcycle headgear. (In fact, my first words whispered to her at the altar were, "Nice helmet.") I often tell Nilsa that her choice of headpiece was probably her unconscious recognition that our marriage was going to be one heck of a ride—and that she'd need a crash helmet to make it through the bumps, bruises, and collisions we'd experience, not only in the world but also in our marriage.

I've talked with other couples in long-lasting relationships, and almost every single one of them tells me that they've all gone through very rough patches during their time together. I'm sure this fact doesn't surprise you, but Nilsa and I are no different: we've had times when we were thinking of not being a couple anymore. And I'm not proud to say that there have been times where most of my energy was dedicated to fixing things that I have broken in our relationship with my addictive, self-destructive tendencies. I grew up with four sisters and my mom, and I've always been very comfortable having women as close friends. But I've also encountered women who, with my complicit ignorance, mistakenly thought they could take me away from Nilsa because I appear to live an extreme life as an exciting "bad boy" who has a little bit of money. Knowing that I'm regularly confronted with that kind of temptation has been painful for Nilsa and caused tension between us over the years. And when you pair that with the stress of our working together (more on that later), you can see why our marriage has had its share of ups and downs.

Look, I'm very aware of my failings as a man and husband. It's still a journey every day to try to be a better husband and father, to understand and have more empathy for Nilsa's needs, and that will never change. But I do believe the stress and pressure we both have gone through has produced a dynamic, vital, loving, legendary relationship. One of the secrets to our long marriage is understanding that relationship pressure either will crush our union or create a diamond. We choose to believe that conflict equals growth. We welcome conflict, because we believe it will produce a jewelry box full of glittering diamonds.

Even if it's just about how to squeeze the toothpaste tube, or who is going to take out the trash, or whether the toilet paper roll should face up or down, no couple is going to agree about everything. Conflict in relationships is both natural and healthy. In fact, in 2018, a study of more than 3,400 couples in Germany showed that when partners thought their relationship had serious problems, their level of conflict went *down* rather than up![5] Researchers believed this was because the couples were no longer

---

. . . conflict equals growth.

---

invested enough in their relationships to feel that it was worth spending their emotional resources to work through issues. No wonder that in a different survey "lack of commitment to the relationship" showed up as the top reason to seek a divorce, ranked higher than "too much arguing and conflict"![6]

The greatest danger to a relationship, in my opinion, isn't conflict but complacency. Once you start to take your partner for granted, you head down the road of being satisfied with a relationship that's "good enough." And when you're satisfied with "good enough," you stop putting in the effort to make your partner feel loved, appreciated, and special, and you won't feel loved or appreciated either. I'm not saying you have to look for disagreements, but if you let yourself become complacent and stop dealing with issues you really should bring up, then the relationship is sure to die a death by a thousand cuts—maybe not quickly, but over time. However, if you accept conflict as healthy and view it as an opportunity for growth, you will appreciate it as a sign that your relationship is alive and vital.

Learn to Fight Effectively

Now, ignoring things or stuffing down feelings isn't really my approach to any personal or professional relationship. I am pretty much an open book, and when something bothers me, I'm not shy about letting others know. But for a lot of people, conflict registers as a threat to their safety and triggers the "fight, flight, or freeze" impulse in the brain and body.[7] If their tendency is to fight, they start that argument with their partner. If their habit is to flee or freeze, they'll ignore the upset, push their feelings down, or walk away. But avoiding conflict actually can increase stress levels and make things worse, especially in intimate relationships.[8]

Over the years Nilsa and I have learned the importance of immediately bringing up the little things that are bothering us so we can take care of them before they become big things. As the artist for our oceanfront masterpieces, I make the business decision to buy the land and then create the grand vision for the design and marketing of the property. As the interior designer, Nilsa does all the space planning and makes hundreds of choices on finishes, furnishings, and accessories. And as we are both strong-willed people with clear ideas of what's best, inevitably there are conflicts along the way. But if we bring our conflicts out into the open, even if the exchanges get heated and prove painful in the short term, we can deal with issues and then move on.

No one thinks that conflict is fun, but it's going to happen any time two human beings are together for an extended time. You're going to fight with your partner, period. So the question is, how can you do it effectively? Speaking not as an expert but as someone who has dealt with conflict many times in my relationships, here are a few ideas to help you disagree, even argue, and then come back together stronger than before. If you have a significant other, I strongly encourage you to read the following aloud with them. Heck, read this whole section together!

First, *approach any conflict with a sense of mutual respect—for yourself, your partner, and your relationship.* Respect yourself and your feelings enough to bring the issue out into the open. Respect your partner enough to believe that he or she is willing to deal with this issue to help make the relationship stronger. And respect the relationship enough to feel that it can endure the pressure and become better once the conflict is addressed.

Second, *recognize that conflict may cause your rational, thinking brain to take a back seat to your raw emotions.* When the fight, flight, or freeze impulse is triggered, biochemicals produced by the amygdala (which regulates our emotional responses) block responses from the prefrontal cortex, which is responsible for reasoning and problem-solving.[9] In other words, when we're upset we're not thinking clearly, and then it's all too easy to turn an argument about one specific action ("You didn't call me when you were running an hour late," for example) into a fight about a habitual pattern ("You *never* call") or worse, about personal defects ("Why are you so inconsiderate and disrespectful"). Therefore, when you find yourself in conflict with your partner, take a moment to let your emotions settle and let the rational part of your brain provide a better perspective.

Third, rather than blaming your partner, *take immediate responsibility for your own feelings and actions.* Most of us tend to start a fight by saying, "*You* did this," which immediately puts the other person on the defensive. Instead, be honest enough to start with what you're feeling: "I'm upset about X," or "X is causing me to think or feel Y." In the example above, rather than starting off with "You didn't call me when you were running an hour late," say something like, "I was really worried when you didn't call me. I thought you might have been in an accident or there was real trouble at work." It's a better way to express your emotions so your partner can hear them.

Fourth, *listen to what your partner has to say, and be willing to concede when they make valid points.* "I was wrong and I'm sorry" are six of the toughest words to string together in the English language, and they can be especially hard to say when you feel you're in the right (which most of us do during conflict) or you're on the defensive because what your partner is saying hits home. But the more you both can feel respected and heard, the more likely you are to end up feeling better after the argument. So try to keep yourself centered and open, and listen in a way that your partner believes you hear them. In fact, I suggest you both practice actively listening to each other in situations that aren't as emotionally charged, so you can use the skill when conflicts arise.

And be willing to put your pride aside and give way whenever appropriate: conceding even a small point can help defuse things when the energy gets too high. If you can find something to agree on ("You're right, I should have called you when I was held up at work"), it can help create the psychological and emotional space to move the bigger discussion forward. For example, "Sometimes it's not practical for me to break off a meeting to call you, and I don't like feeling that I *need* to check in with you. Can we come up with a better way of approaching this in the future that'll work for us both?"

Fifth, *if things get too hot, take a short break and cool off, but agree to come back and finish the discussion.* In an experiment at the Gottman Institute (founded by top relationship experts Drs. John and Julie Gottman), researchers studying couples who were fighting interrupted the arguments after about fifteen minutes, using the premise the equipment filming the interaction needed to be adjusted and asking the couples to read magazines for thirty minutes. After the enforced break, the heart rates of the couples were significantly lower and their subsequent discussions far more productive.[10] If you feel the argument with your partner is going nowhere (or worse, escalating to the point that you are both going to start saying things you don't mean), stop and ask to take a break so you both can cool off. Then do something that gets you into a better, more centered place: listen to music, bang on your drum set (or the wall), take a walk or a bath—anything that relaxes you. Don't use the time to tell yourself how unreasonable your partner is being or to plan your next line of attack. The goal is to calm yourself down so your brain and body can rebalance themselves and you can go back into the discussion from a more centered place.

Sixth, *approach conflict not as a threat to the relationship but as a problem to be solved.* I don't think anyone goes into a relationship with the idea that it's going to break up, so try viewing arguments not as irredeemable flaws in the relationship but as evidence there is a problem to be solved—and *you can solve it together.* Approaching conflicts from a problem-solving framework can help to lower psychological stress,[11] engage your rational prefrontal cortex, and perhaps even tap into the creative part of the brain to come up with new ideas and approaches to the challenges you are facing. Simply turning a "me versus you" argument into a "we can solve this together" discussion may be all that's needed for your conflict to subside.

Face it: there is never a point in any healthy relationship where there won't be differences and disagreements. But if your relationship isn't growing and evolving, it's dying, and conflict is a vital part of growth. And when conflict is approached correctly and dealt with effectively, the end result will be that beautiful diamond.

The Perils of Working Together

Many couples work together in the same business, but this adds another potential source of conflict to their intimate relationships and opens new avenues for disagreement. If you share an office and have a bad day, for example, chances are your spouse did too—and you're probably not going to get away from that bad day when you go home. It's also very likely that much of your time at home will be devoted to talking about business, and you'll lose sight of what I call the "underside of the pillow": the sensitivities and commonalities that are vital to keeping the connection with your partner strong. It's all too common for couples who work together over time to devolve into a business relationship instead of a romance. If that's what you want, fine—but you're sure missing a lot of the juice and joy that comes from having an intimate partner in your life.

Through the years, Nilsa and I have made a conscious effort to keep our marriage vibrant while also working together on forty-four oceanfront creattions and other endeavors. Here are a few of the things we've found to help keep the spark alive. (Again, read this aloud with your partner.)

First, *create ways to separate your business and personal lives.* As I said in chapter 16, in the mornings we both leave the house and go to our respective offices (mine in the treehouse, Nilsa's in the guest house). If we need to discuss work, we meet in our offices, or by the pool, or go to lunch, or go to the general contactor's office and meet there. We rarely have work meetings in our home because that's our personal space.

Second, *we almost never discuss work outside of work hours.* It's not a hard and fast rule, but if one of us starts to bring up a work question in the evenings, the other will say, "Hey, it's after six, so let's talk about the size and location of the jellyfish tank tomorrow."

Third, *work always stays out of the bedroom.* We choose not to have a TV in our bedroom, and cell phones are off limits there too. While those two things aren't allowed, almost everything else is—more on that in chapter 20!

Fourth, *we make a conscious effort to share other interests outside of work.* We both work to create rich lives outside of business. Some of those interests, like the Caring House Project Foundation and Badwater, we both are involved in pursuing. Other interests are different: Nilsa does a lot of volunteer work in our local community, while I have my second career as an author and speaker. We enjoy supporting each other's efforts and relish the excitement and diversity these outside interests bring to our relationship.

Finally, *we do little things for each other frequently to show that we care.* I make Nilsa coffee or lemon juice every day. She hides little sticky notes with cute sayings on them for me to find when she leaves town to take care of her parents. None of these are big or expensive gestures, but they remind us that we are in each other's minds and hearts. It's never the gifts of jewelry, fancy clothes, or exotic trips that cause a marriage to thrive. Instead, it's the smallest reflections of love and the random reminders of affection that keep the diamond of your relationship polished and shining brightly.

Relationships Are Not Meant to Be in Balance

There's one more pressure that comes up in relationships, and that occurs when life gets out of balance—which it *always* is. Pregnancy, for example, or a new baby, or a family business crisis can create enormous pressure. Even the passion and joy created when one or both of you is monomaniacally pursuing your aspirations can upset the stability of your relationship. But you can't let that pressure drive you apart. Remember, whenever we undertake a new project, a big risk, or anything significant, we will be focused exclusively on that particular purpose, and that's completely normal and healthy. Homeostasis—the supposed "golden mean" where everything is in balance—doesn't exist except in fleeting moments, whether it's in nature or in relationships, and that's perfectly okay. Like the mid-point of a pendulum swing, we will pass through that point of balance briefly and then head off to one side or another.

Trying to preserve the status quo is unnatural. It stops growth and leads to boredom, in life and in your relationship. So don't beat yourself up when things are out of balance and both you and your partner are feeling pressure. Instead, recognize that this can be a time of enormous growth and excitement, as long as you focus on adapting to new circumstances and finding your equilibrium, however fleeting it is supposed to be.

It's never the gifts of jewelry, fancy clothes, or exotic trips that cause a marriage to thrive.

Nilsa and I accept that our life is going to be out of balance simply because we are very different people in some ways. I thrive on the extremes; Nilsa likes a calmer existence. There are times when I need my adrenaline fix, and there are times she needs to escape the very intense world of Frank. But we accept that about each other and feel it's okay to take breaks from the pressure of being in our relationship. That was one of the best things about the Yugo We-go Tour. After an intense year—one when we sold our final oceanfront masterpiece, I started writing *Aspire!* and I was bedridden for more than a month—it was very healing for me to spend twenty-two days on the road, fifteen of them by myself. And even though we would talk nearly every night, Nilsa too got a valuable break by staying in Florida for that time. When she flew to Colorado to join me for the last seven days of the tour, we were really looking forward to seeing each other again. I arranged for us to stay in The Cliff House, the nicest hotel in Manitou Springs, and there I welcomed her with flowers, and we went out for a special dinner together. Oftentimes being apart can remind you of how much you love and care for that special person in your life.

I started this book by saying we're not meant to stay motivated or inspired every moment. Well, we're not meant to stay balanced either. We're meant to pursue our aspirations, alter our DNA, and create the reality we desire, and that takes the ability to withstand enormous amounts of pressure in our lives as well as our relationships. Well-known twentieth-century minister and writer Dr. Norman Vincent Peale once said that problems are a sign of life. Well, pressure and conflict are signs that you and your relationship are healthy, vital, and growing. You owe it to yourself and your intimate partner to learn to welcome pressure, because it will turn your life and relationship into the most magnificent diamond the world has ever seen, and that's a reality that we all want.

Magnetic-ism

The meeting of two personalities is like the contact of two chemical substances: If there is any reaction, both are transformed.

CARL JUNG

In January 2021, I found myself in front of a live audience for the first time in many months. Because of the pandemic it was a small group, fewer than two hundred people, all socially distanced and seated throughout a large hotel ballroom. I was speaking about how to address the fear that's associated with taking a risk or facing a big change or challenge, and because I was in the middle of writing this book, I really went deep into the topic. It was one of those events where you know you're on fire, delivering tremendous content and value. A sense of invincibility had returned after a nine-month hiatus, an excitement that was contagious. It's a feeling that I activate and use on a regular basis, a feeling that attracts confidence and repels insecurity. It's what I call *magnetic-ism*.

Now, that's not a word you'll find in any dictionary other than mine, but it represents a practice that I believe is critical to anyone who wants to build incredible relationships and a life they love. It's rooted in the word *magnetic*, which *National Geographic* defines as "able to produce a force field that can attract or repel."[1] You might have done an experiment in grade school where you placed a magnet on a flat surface and put a piece of white paper on top of it. Then you shook some iron filings on the paper and watched as the filings created lines corresponding to the invisible force fields created by the magnet beneath.[2]

It's my experience that humans have a similar energetic field that can either attract or repel others. Some people describe this force field as charisma or presence, but it's more than that. Magnetic-ism is a radiance that comes from essence, an aura that others subconsciously sense and are attracted to whether they want to be or not. In the same way that iron filings have no control over their attraction to the magnet, we can't resist the pull toward someone who is magnetic in this way.

There's a line in the Van Halen song *When It's Love* that is about looking at the faces in a crowd and seeing some of them shine while others keep you guessing. As I looked out on my audience that January night, I noticed five or six people with their own magnetic energy, and throughout the keynote I found myself focusing on them. There was a beautiful energy exchange going on between us, a mutual amplification of essence that elevated the

> ... magnetic-ism is based upon essence,
> the deepest, truest part of who you are ...

state of the entire crowd. That night benefited everyone who was there because of the energy that was created. It's why people love going to concerts or other performances: that magical exchange and amplification of magnetic-ism energy uplifts everyone present.

The word *magnetic-ism* ends with a suffix, -ism, which represents a distinctive practice, system, or philosophy, typically an artistic movement or ideology.[3] In other words, it's something that you do again and again and make a part of who you are. With practice, therefore, anyone can develop magnetic-ism within themselves and use it to amplify their relationships.

What Magnetic-ism Is and Isn't

Some people use the word *charisma* to describe the quality of magnetic-ism. But while they may be related, at their cores, charisma and magnetic-ism are different things.

- Charisma is based on attractiveness and charm.[4] Magnetic-ism is much stronger; it's an almost unwilling attraction that the other person cannot resist.

- Charisma can be appreciated from afar. It can impress you, but it doesn't necessarily influence you. Magnetic-ism turns appreciation into influence. It's as if there's an internal compass that turns you toward this person and causes you to pay attention.

- Charisma can be either awe-inspiring or aww-inspiring: you can look at someone with charisma and think, *What a cool guy!* (awe-inspiring) or *What an ass!* (aww-inspiring). Have you ever met someone for the first time and noticed some aspect of their personality that you like, but after you got to know them you found that is not who they really are, and you're no longer attracted—in fact, you're repelled? There are idiots who have charisma, but as soon as they reveal their true colors, you're no longer attracted to their energy. Charisma goes no deeper than the surface, but magnetic-ism is based upon essence, the deepest, truest part of who you are, so anyone who is attracted to you is likely to stay that way.

- Charisma is like fireworks: you are enthralled by the show, but once it's over, you stop staring at the sky and go home. Magnetic-ism is like looking at the northern lights: they go on and on, deeper and deeper, swirling as they become more brilliant and enthralling. You want to be around that person because there's always more to see and discover.

To me, magnetic-ism happens when you have become so good at amplifying your essence that you know that when you walk into a room, part of the air leaves, and the vibrational frequency is altered in an "or-cosmic" way (another word from my dictionary, orgasmic + cosmic). As you walk into any situation where you want to have an impact, your magnetic-ism starts to ooze out of your pores. There's a sense of invincibility, because the pull of your magnetic-ism is irresistible. It's an unfair advantage, yes, but one that's available to anyone, from Miss Universe to the hunchback of Notre Dame. It's simply a matter of taking your natural gifts and then amplifying that essence consistently to create a new reality.

Magnetic-ism affects anyone who comes into your orbit, from babies to grandparents. In fact, kids are some of the most accurate gauges of magnetic-ism. One of the things I'm proudest of is the way kids were attracted to a ritual I shared with my daughter, Laura, when she was growing up. From the time she was in pre-kindergarten all the way through to the end of eighth grade, I walked Laura to school every single day (1,652 consecutive times). After a few years, other kids at her school started showing up at our house wanting to go with us. Eventually over one hundred kids and some of their parents were joining us for the "Mr. McKinney Walks," held on the first Friday of every month. We would play fun games I made up that let kids be kids, like setting off fireworks at 7:30 A.M. and choosing two or three "lucky" kids to attach their school clip-on ties to bottle rockets—and a melted tie was considered a badge of honor. In the "ritual of roadkill," all the kids would lay in the middle of the road and strike their best "roadkill" pose, and in the good luck circle dance, the kids would dance, one by one, in a special circle Laura and I drew in wet cement in 2004. And finally, the flying lunch boxes game was the biggest hit: kids would toss their lunch boxes off a bridge that crossed the Intracoastal Waterway on the way to school. The closer your lunch box landed next to a particular rock (the "T" rock) and not in the water, the more points you got, and the points were redeemable for a trip to 7-Eleven, where you could take home as much candy, soda, or chips as you could grab in twenty seconds. (Of course, the kids had as much fun scurrying down the embankment to retrieve their lunch boxes by the famous "T" rock as they did tossing them!)

Even though it's been more than ten years since the last "Mr. McKinney Walk," many of those kids and their parents still talk about the experience. To me, those Friday walks were magnetic-ism at its best, and a reflection of essence in its purest form. By the way, the adventures found in those 1,652 walks over a ten-year span are the story behind my bestselling young reader fantasy novel, *Dead Fred, Flying Lunchboxes, and the Good Luck Circle.*

How to Develop Your Magnetic-ism

To get to the point where your magnetic-ism is irresistible, you must be aware of what is magnetic in you already, so you can accentuate it in the sincerest way, without feeling inauthentic or contrived. If you're typically shy and reserved, for example, yet you believe you have to act like Mick Jagger or Beyoncé to be magnetic, you'll come across as fake or trying too hard. (If you've ever been on a really bad first date and felt like the other person was trying to be someone they aren't, you know what I mean.) Instead, you need to accentuate and amplify your own unique qualities, whatever they may be, for others to feel that magnetic, irresistible pull to you.

Take Nilsa, for example. If she ever tried to be like me—flashy, bombastic, showman-like—she would look and feel uncomfortable. Ask her to do her "Frank" impression sometime: it's ridiculously hilarious! But Nilsa is the most magnetic woman I know. She is reserved, doesn't say a lot, and is more comfortable sitting in the back of the room than onstage, but her ability to listen is amazing. That's her magnetic gift, and people of all ages are attracted to her constantly for that reason. Almost everywhere you look, you'll find quiet people whose magnetic-ism may not show up instantaneously, but it becomes apparent over time. They don't necessarily broadcast their essence, but boy, is it there, and it runs very deep.

My daughter Laura has her own brand of magnetic-ism. She always has a quiet elegance about her, like a young *Breakfast at Tiffany's* Audrey Hepburn or Grace Kelly, with a sense of style and authority that sets her apart. She isn't trying to be like me, or Nilsa, or any of her contemporaries, yet her authentic essence makes people want to be around her and helped her get elected president of Penn State's forty-six thousand student body. Her magnetic-ism comes from owning and amplifying her unique essence.

Once you've identified the essence you want to amplify, becoming more magnetic is simply a matter of "turning up the volume" on your energy. We all do this unconsciously: it's akin to speaking louder in a big room so someone on the far end can hear you, only in the case of magnetic-ism, you turn up the volume of every aspect of yourself. When you're meeting someone for the very first time, for example, you turn on your magnetic-ism so the other person will be attracted and want to develop a relationship. Imagine you're getting ready for a date with someone that really excites you. You'll dress so that you look your best, not like you're going out at 10 P.M. to walk the dog in your sweats. You'll slowly walk into the restaurant where you're meeting your date with your best posture. You'll be aware of your body language, and the inflection and resonance of your voice. And you'll watch and listen more acutely to how your date is responding. Essentially, you'll dial up your presence as well as your awareness of its effect on your date.

Magnetic-ism is so much more than what you say or don't say: it's in your posture, body language, tonality, inflection, the physical energy you exude—your aura, for want of a better word. But ultimately, magnetic-ism is nothing more than your essence magnified and expanded to touch others. You just need to get used to turning up the dial so your volume is loud enough to reach the people who need to hear and feel who you truly are.

Magnetic-ism in Context: When and Where to Turn It Up or Down

There are multiple stories of movie stars who look and seem like nothing special when they're walking down the street, yet once they step in front of the camera you can't take your eyes off of them. They know how to turn their magnetic-ism on and off. You too need to develop the ability to dial up your magnetic-ism at certain times and dial it down at others. In getting ready for that date, for example—by choosing the right clothes and shoes that bring out your essence, doing your hair, ladies doing their makeup and spraying on perfume, men shaving or getting our facial hair on point, and tying that tie just right (if you wear a tie)—we subconsciously dial up our magnetic-ism to irresistibly attract the person we'll be seeing later, and hopefully even later than that. But sometimes we need to dial down our magnetic-ism for self-preservation. Say you go out on that first date and you feel something is off with the other person: they come across as dangerous, weird, or even crazy. You need to be able to turn off your magnetic-ism quickly so you can extricate yourself from the date or situation with ease while you still can.

Dialing magnetic-ism up and down is an essential skill in business. You may find this hard to believe, but I'm fundamentally a loner and can be somewhat of an introvert. Yet when I step onstage or in front of a microphone and camera, I will dial up my magnetic-ism to have a greater impact. On the other hand, I don't want to blow people away with too much energy, so I have to adjust to fit the situation. When I walked onstage for the first time in nine months, for instance, my energy level was at seven or eight out of ten because there were only about two hundred people in the room and being at level ten would have been too much.

You always should start an interaction by assessing the level of magnetic-ism you need to bring to the table. Whenever I'm presenting one our oceanfront masterpieces to buyers, for the first few seconds I'm listening and observing to understand exactly how much I need to dial up (or down) my energy. Then, depending on the couple (and typically my buyers are married couples), I will adjust my posture and body language so that the customers know they are the big shots in the room. When we get to the negotiation phase, I'll usually dial back my energy again. In high stakes negotiating I'd rather you think *you* won than us both winning—it's one place where I don't subscribe to *win-win*. The only place I will let my magnetic-ism shine is when I am describing the property in vivid detail. If the customers compliment the countertops, or the jelly sphere, or the water floor, or the property's beauty and craftsmanship, I'll ramp up my magnetic-ism as a storyteller, extolling the property's magnificent virtues exactly as any world-renowned artist would do. I'll make the product irresistible, not myself.

Arrogance versus Magnetic-ism

There's a danger that your magnetic-ism can come across as arrogance to some people, especially those who may be struggling with their own self-assurance or self-confidence. And yes, there is a fine line between self-confidence and being arrogant. To my mind, self-confidence is endearing; arrogance is alienating. And people know the difference.

If you believe you're being perceived as arrogant, there are a few simple fixes. First, adjust your body language. A woman I know always held her head tilted slightly back, causing her to look down her nose at others— literally. Turns out she was sensitive about her double chin and tilted her head back to make her neck appear longer, but this posture caused others to think she was stuck up. There's a guy I was working with who walked (strutted actually) with one hand always in his pants pocket. I suggested he try taking it out and walking normally, not like a Ralph Lauren model on the runway. It worked. There are postures that convey confidence and others that convey arrogance, and you can see the difference almost as soon as people walk in the door, even before they open their mouths. If you find yourself being accused of arrogance (I know: how dare they?!),

---

. . . self-confidence is endearing; arrogance is alienating.

---

you might want to take a good look in the mirror to see what's conveying that message, or ask a confident friend to give you some honest suggestions on changing the way you stand and move that will make you appear more friendly and approachable.

You also can check how you express yourself verbally. Nine times out of ten people feel someone is arrogant because of the words, tonality, and inflections he or she uses. Try saying "we" rather than "I" when you talk. Ask a lot more questions. Listen more. Make sure the volume of your voice is suited to the space you're in. Try mirroring back the way someone is speaking to you, matching how loud they are and the speed at which they talk. These are simple ways to create connection with the people you are speaking to and prevent you from seeming as if you want to dominate them with your energy and presence.

Next, be self-effacing rather than self-absorbed. If you feel you always must talk about how great you are, you're not magnetic, you're a boastful ass. This is different from the criteria of a healthy ego you read about in chapter 14: there you are talking about the greatness of your *purpose*, not yourself. On the other hand, there's nothing more fascinating than a magnetic individual who takes the focus off of themselves and puts it on the other person, asking to hear everything about them. Whenever you do talk about yourself, make sure to incorporate a healthy dose of humility and a little self-deprecating humor. Never be afraid to say, "I'm not all that I'm cracked up to be, and I continue to struggle just like you," or to tell a humorous story at your own expense. For example, as part of my keynotes, and even when I meet someone new who has prejudged me, I share that I'm a lot less exciting than I look. I go to bed at 9 P.M., don't drink, smoke, do drugs, gamble, overeat, oversleep, etc., and my wife calls me a nerd in sheep's clothing! It takes a very self-assured person to be vulnerable with others. Have faith that your true essence, with all its flaws as well as its strengths, is beautiful and worth being shared.

Finally, you can make sure that your actions convey respect rather than arrogance. A couple of years ago I was promoting what I called a "Dueling Announcement—My Final and My First," a big reveal party for my final oceanfront property combined with the launch of my first Christian romance novel, *The Other Thief*. I asked the people who follow me on social media what transportation I should use to deliver the invitations: a McLaren (one of the most exclusive and fastest sports cars in the world, more expensive than a Ferrari) or my 1988 Yugo. Unfortunately, the McLaren won, but by a smaller margin that you would expect. So for an entire day I drove this beautiful, sleek, powerful McLaren sports car to all of the real estate offices in the Palm Beach area. I would get out, walk in the front door, and then look around for the least "important" person in the building, usually a receptionist or member of the cleaning staff, and that was the person I spoke with first.

Now, if I'd marched in and asked for the head of the office without first paying attention to the people who are typically considered the least important in the room, I would have been perceived as being an arrogant ass. But as I hope you know by now, the "unimportant" folks are the ones I *want* to approach. I want to connect with the receptionist, the cleaning staff, the waiter, busboy, and dishwasher at the restaurant, and get their perspective. It's not an act; it's a reflection of my essence. And I've found it not only helps insulate me from accusations of being arrogant, but it also produces stronger, deeper, richer connections across the board.

Ultimately, your ability to attract people comes down to the way you treat others and the way you utilize the gifts God has given you. The gauge of your magnetic-ism is not how you feel but how other people feel about you. Be prepared, though: when you have developed your magnetic-ism, every time you walk into a room people may choose to make ignorant judgments about you simply because they feel your energy and attractiveness. They may think, *Wow, he or she is really full of themselves to be so confident. What makes them so great?* Do not let occurrences like this reverse the polarity, or otherwise affect, your magnetic-ism. Take the first opportunity possible to show your true, irresistible essence, which needs to include doing the little things that mean so much to others. Saying people's names while looking them in the eye as you greet them. Complimenting them sincerely on their appearance or accomplishments. Mentioning something you remember about them the next time you meet them. Petting someone's dog or cat. None of these take much of your time or energy, but they tell the people you meet, "You are important. You matter. I see and feel your essence as you feel mine."

When you display a magnetic-ism that includes treating others well, at the end of an interaction you're likely to hear, "Wow, you're much humbler and more approachable than I thought." That's one of the best barometers for the right kind of magnetic-ism, the kind that will create richer and more vital relationships—in business, in love, and in life.

Oh, and Give Mind-Blowing Sex

Sex is a part of nature.
I go along with nature.
MARILYN MONROE

L et me start by saying that I considered removing this chapter after I wrote it because I'm not particularly comfortable writing or talking about sex. But I decided otherwise because sex is just so damn important. And just as I'm no expert on relationships, I'm certainly not an expert on your physical intimacy. After all, everyone's sexual drive, preferences, and positions are personal and unique, and they are of no concern to anyone other than you and your partner. But I wanted to include this chapter primarily for two reasons. First, I've seen that it's a topic that most everyone gets excited about (pun intended). In a recent celebration of Nilsa's and my wedding anniversary, I put up a lengthy social media post that included the advice, "Give mind-blowing sex at least once a day, often twice." While that statement was certainly quite aspirational, boy, did it get a reaction! Since Nilsa and I appear to be complete opposites in terms of our physicality—Nilsa's style is very elegant, timeless, and classy, whereas I (while very much a sapiosexual) can come across as having as much culture as a cup of low-fat yogurt. People have always wondered, and some have been bold enough to ask about our sex life, so I'm sure the post caused a lot of comments behind closed doors in our small Florida community. But sex is an important part of the vitality of our relationship, and I believe in being open about that truth.

Second, according to hundreds of psychologists and social science researchers, a good sex life is essential to the health of intimate relationships—after all, you can't have one without the other. Multiple studies show that sexual satisfaction contributes to greater relationship quality, satisfaction, and well-being;[1] in interviews many couples describe sex as a barometer of the health of their marriage.[2] Good sex also makes us happier: when approximately one thousand women were surveyed about the activities that gave them the greatest amount of happiness, "intimate relations" topped the list.[3] (I know, guys, you'd love to meet the respondents to that survey.) Another survey of sixteen thousand Americans showed a strong link between sex and happiness for both men and women.[4] It turns out that the more sex you have, the happier you are: indeed, having sex four times a week adds as much happiness as getting married in the first place![5]

Unfortunately, lack of sex decreases relationship quality—and on average, most couples have sex only two or three times a *month* (for women over forty, it's only once a month).[6] After the first six months of a relationship, only fifty percent of couples report being happy about their sex lives, while the rest are either neutral or dissatisfied.[7] That's really sad. What's worse, conflicts around sex can become common in many long-term relationships,[8] yet far too many couples fail to address this vital area due to embarrassment or lack of knowledge. It's no wonder that some of the top reasons for divorce include infidelity, low libido, sexual dysfunction, and lack of physical and emotional intimacy.[9]

To maintain the health of our intimate relationship for the long term, it's imperative that we talk about how to keep its physical side fresh and vibrant. I hope that some of the non-clinical insights Nilsa and I have discovered about pleasing a partner after thirty-one years married (thirty-four years together) can be helpful for anyone who wants to keep the spark alight in their intimate relations.*

---

* Please note: while everything I talk about is put in the context of a heterosexual relationship, because that's what I know, I believe that it would apply to a same-sex relationship as well.

Let's start with the most important point that's summarized in the title of this chapter: **You should always seek to *give* mind-blowing sex, not *have* mind-blowing sex.** "Have" can be selfish; "give" means that you put your partner's pleasure and satisfaction at the forefront of your mind, often ahead of your own desires. Yes, of course you should enjoy yourself, too, but here's the good news: in giving your partner mind-blowing sex, you're way more likely to receive the same in return. So, with *giving* great sex as the framework for this chapter, let's talk about desire, sensuality, foreplay,

---

"Have" can be selfish; "give" means that
you put your partner's pleasure and
satisfaction at the forefront . . .

---

orgasms, experimentation, avoiding "not tonight, dear" moments, and above all, how to keep the passion between you hot enough to turn your relationship into a steamy romance novel.

What Is Mind-Blowing Sex?

Of course, what I regard as mind-blowing sex may be very different from whatever rocks your world, so to speak. But to me, mind-blowing sex is where both partners make each other feel appreciated, desired, sensual, sexy, alive, connected, hot, replete, and incredibly happy. Mind-blowing sex means seeking to satisfy your partner's needs first, which will serve to enhance your own experience in the heat of the heat. Mind-blowing sex is authentic; each partner should feel free to ask for what they want and to give the other person what they desire. It includes communicating what is pleasing to you in the moment, through words, movements, sounds, looks, touches—whatever lets your partner know how you're responding. Mind-blowing sex is a sensual dance between love and lust: love sweetens and deepens the connection between you, and lust fans the flames of passion and takes both partners over the edge to completion. (Does mind-blowing sex usually include orgasm? Probably—and we'll talk more about that later.) Ironically, the best mind-blowing sex shuts the mind off completely, because partners are fully focused on each other's physical and emotional responses, to the point where mind and body gladly surrender control.

Of course, not every sexual encounter will reach the level of mind-blowing: if you've had a bad day at work, or your partner's not feeling well, or the kids have been acting up, sex in general might be the furthest thing from your mind. But don't you think your partner will appreciate your goal of giving them mind-blowing sex? And when it occurs, isn't the sex likely to be more sensual, passionate, and exciting? Even if you only succeed in giving mind-blowing sex twenty-five percent of the time, you're still doing better than ninety-five percent of couples. And if you make it to fifty percent, you deservedly will be a legendary lover.

In truth, even when you've been with the same partner for years, every sexual encounter is still unique. So let's dive into a few ideas on how to make those encounters not just fulfilling but otherworldly.

Get in the Mood with Fore-Foreplay

To set the stage for mind-blowing sex, it's important to engage in what I call "fore-foreplay." These are the things you do to make your partner feel desired and desirable at any point during the day. It lets your partner know you're attracted to them and you're thinking of them as a sensual being as well as a wife/husband/parent/partner/significant other. And I believe the three most important aspects of fore-foreplay are *thoughtfulness, appreciation,* and *sensuality.*

First is thoughtfulness, making your partner's needs a priority. Small, thoughtful gestures throughout the day are points of connection that remind your partner how much you care. For instance, I often wake up at 4 A.M. to go running or to the gym, and I'm out of bed long before Nilsa. When I get back I make her coffee or lemon juice so it's ready for her when she gets up. Since our thirtieth anniversary I put her coffee or lemon juice in the cup I bought her at Waffle House. (Yes, we celebrated our thirtieth anniversary at Waffle House in Canton, North Carolina.) The fact that I take the time and effort to make her coffee and put it in that particular cup reminds us both how much we care for each other.

Nilsa and I rarely indulge in big, romantic gestures, but we are good at the little things. I'll write a love note on a paper napkin and put it with her coffee in the morning. I'll light the candles in her prayer area. I'll empty the dishwasher and take the laundry out of the dryer. Nilsa will pick up my favorite potato chips and sugar-free chocolate covered raisins at Fresh Market, and make a special breakfast served on our riverfront porch during a drizzling rain in North Carolina. Even though she's an empowered woman and she has her own strength and independence, she is very proud of the fact that she's a doting wife. While none of these gestures are particularly sexy, they are a demonstration that we are always thinking about each other's needs.

The second aspect of fore-foreplay is appreciation: acknowledging that you find them attractive. When you're with someone day after day, it's very easy to stop paying attention to them or to take them for granted, but I believe that partners need to feel seen and appreciated to keep the spark alive. The other day Nilsa came home from the beauty salon with her hair three inches shorter. I didn't notice it right away, however, and it hurt her feelings. She had to ask me, "Do I look pretty?" And a few years ago when we were going through a rocky point in our relationship, I was hearing from other people how exciting and handsome I was, but I wasn't hearing it from her, and it didn't feel good.

Bottom line, fore-foreplay should include noticing and appreciating your partner physically. If they're wearing something new, comment on it favorably. (Even if it's not that new, you'll still get points for noticing and complimenting their attire.) If they get a haircut or even just a trim, notice it and compliment them on it. Make an effort to say that you find them attractive and sexy. Everyone wants to feel that they are not just desirable, but they are actively *desired* by their partner in the moment.

The third critical aspect of fore-foreplay is sensuality. It makes me feel like a man when Nilsa feels sensual, and I want her to *want* to feel sensual when she's with me. So I look for ways to draw out her sensuality throughout the day. A hand on her back. A lingering kiss. Smelling the perfume she puts on her neck and wrists. Whispering in her ear something loving or hot or even downright dirty. And even though Nilsa is far more restrained than I am, on occasion she will give me a look or smile that says without words, "You are the sexiest man on earth," and it makes me feel like I'm just that. When you regularly pay attention to your partner and find moments to awaken the sensuality in you both, fore-foreplay will last for hours and make the mind-blowing sex even hotter.

Kindling and Fulfilling Desire

Not long ago I was journaling in front of a warm fire on a cold morning in North Carolina, and the mesmerizing flames reminded me how intimate, romantic, and deep love relationships are like a cozy fire in a fireplace. Something special—maybe the fore-foreplay you've been engaging in?— sparks the dormant fuel in your bodies. The flame starts slowly, almost imperceptibly, often flickering and struggling, needing a gentle nudge to keep it from extinguishing prematurely. Once the chemistry takes, though, the flame swirls and builds until it reaches a crescendo, an inferno so intense, so hot, it's the most enveloping and beautiful sensation in the world.

There's nothing more magical than feeling desire arise in yourself and then feeling it answered in your partner. Mutual desire is one of the cornerstones of a successful intimate relationship;[10] yet just like a fire, a couple's desire will burn hot, then smolder, whether it's in a single encounter or over the course of a long-term relationship. Navigating and directing the ebb and flow of desire is a central skill that you must master to give mind-blowing sex. The techniques you use to arouse your partner will be unique to your relationship, but here are some general principles that I believe will help you make sex even more fulfilling.

First, *focus on your partner and his/her needs.* Sex is a team sport, one in which your goal should be to help the other person "win"—meaning, you focus on increasing and fulfilling your partner's desires rather than just your own. For example, in general, a woman needs quite a bit of foreplay and titillation to reach arousal and then orgasm, so a lover who wants to give mind-blowing sex needs to take her desires and extended timeline into account.

One of the advantages of a long-term relationship is that you get to know what your partner responds to sexually. One of the disadvantages, however, is the temptation to believe that once you have the formula for mind-blowing sex, you can do the same thing over and over again. Sorry, there *is* no formula that works every time; eventually both you and your partner will become bored with the "same old romance novel." That's why you need to be present with your partner, focusing on how they are responding today, in the moment, and (as we'll talk about later) be willing to bring an element of spontaneity into your sex life.

The second principle is to *communicate—both what you want and what you are enjoying.* Mind-blowing sex rarely involves a guessing game (unless you're into that kind of thing), so it helps if you have an idea from your partner as to what they like, both in advance and during lovemaking, and to be able to communicate your needs during the process in return. Unfortunately, many people are terrible at talking about sex with their partners. They're embarrassed and concerned that expressing their feelings might threaten their self-worth, or their partner's self-worth, and even harm the relationship itself.[11] But assuming you are focused on fulfilling your partner's needs, wouldn't you want to know what those needs are? And wouldn't you appreciate feedback in the moment to know that what you are doing is driving your partner crazy or turning them off? And don't you think that your partner would like to know the same about you? Studies show that more open discussion about sex between partners, and more communication during sex itself, leads to greater intimacy as well as greater satisfaction.[12]

As a man, the thing that is most important to me during sex is pleasing Nilsa. My raw, male, sexual energy wants those cues that let me know, "Yes, this is good for me." Whether it be through looks, words, sounds, sighs, or physical responses, communication between partners can fan the flames of desire. So when it comes to the kinds of physical intimacy that you and your partner prefer, you both have to communicate what you want, respect each other's desires, and get over any embarrassment you might have. Believe me, the increased pleasure will make the momentary discomfort worthwhile!

The third principle is to *take your time and enjoy the dance of love and lust.* Many years ago I did some research on how long it takes for a woman to reach orgasm versus a man. For men, it can be five minutes or less.[13] For women, the average time is fourteen minutes[14]—and in many cases it exceeds twenty minutes. Problem is that according to sex therapists, the average length of a sexual encounter is *only* 5.4 minutes[15]—great for men, not so great for women. So in other words, guys, *slow down and take your damn time.* Even when you're able to reach orgasm, don't be selfish and leave your partner unsatisfied. You may be fine with a quickie (and you both may like that, depending on the moment), but do what you can to help your partner reach their own point of mind-blowing-ness.

Mind-blowing sex is a dance between love and lust, one where both partners agree to explore, enjoy, and give delight to the other. There will be times when you'll want to be romantic. Other times you may want to say screw it (pun again) and forget foreplay—let's just go for hot, quick, sex. And still other times you'll start off one way and things will change in the moment, based on your mood. But in my experience, the most important part of mind-blowing sex is *generosity:* putting the focus on giving to your partner fully, being present with their needs, and, in the process, having your needs fulfilled too. That's what kindles and fulfills desire, and leads you both to the point where you lie, exhausted and replete, in each other's arms.

What to Say Yes and No to in the Bedroom

It might surprise you to learn that sex between couples can continue to grow both in intimacy and eroticism over the years. According to professor of sociology and intimacy Jacqui Gabb, "What makes sex successful—in relationship terms—is that it works for each individual and the couple, something that builds upon intimate knowledge accumulated over the partnership duration."[16] In other words, after a few years together, what you learn about your partner's likes and dislikes can make your mutual sex life better. On the other hand (as I can attest), you have to be willing to keep learning as your sexual relationship will continue to evolve over time.

Here are some suggestions of what to let in—and keep out of—the bedroom in order to keep the sexual flames alive and blazing.

- **Say YES to novelty and experimentation.**

Well-known relationship and sex therapist Esther Perel says, "If intimacy grows through repetition and familiarity, eroticism is numbed by repetition."[17] That's why it's important to be open to trying new things, both in the bedroom and in life. Various surveys show that adding new positions, new locations, new techniques, or anything new to the mix of your sex life can lead to greater sexual satisfaction, as long as both partners are open to the experience.[18] And remember, suggesting something new is not an implication that the old ways of pleasing each other no longer work, nor is it a judgment about your skills as a lover. Think of it more like going to the ice cream shop together. You both may love chocolate and order it every time, but then one day your partner says, "Hey, let's try the rocky road!" and you discover you enjoy that flavor too. You both still love chocolate ice cream and probably continue to order it often, but occasionally you like changing things up by sharing a little rocky road. (Truth be told, our bedroom is more like the thirty-one flavor Baskin-Robbins menu than a Dairy Queen.)

While I may be more of a routine guy, Nilsa is great at helping me see how I need to break out of my routines. That said, there were a few things my therapist suggested that we try to liven things up in the bedroom, and Nilsa wasn't interested. However, other things we've experimented with (some at my suggestion, some at hers) allow us to keep our sex life exciting and fresh. I would add that making experimentation playful is important, too. Some of the things you try may be exciting for you but not for your partner and vice versa (like fish-flavored ice cream being very popular in Japan, but here, not so much), or the fantasy that gets you both going one day falls flat the next time you try it. But if you approach sex with a sense of adventure and fun, even if you try a technique or toy or fantasy that falls flat, you both can laugh about it and then do something else to re-light the flames.

- **Say YES to being authentic and generous.**

One of the reasons sex is called "intimate relations" is that it's supposed to be the place where you reveal your most intimate, authentic self. So I believe that when it comes to their sexuality, both inside and outside of the bedroom, partners need to feel they can express who they are authentically. Nilsa has always given me the freedom to express that gift outside of the bedroom. She is much more restrained and conservative in her appearance (yet oh so sexy), but she has always encouraged me to project my inherent sexual energy because she has faith that I won't cross the line with that energy. I love her because she gives me the freedom to express myself, and I do the same for her. Even though I consider her an incredibly sexy woman, I don't push her to wear clothes she's not comfortable in or to flaunt her sexuality in public. We allow each other to be authentic to who we are.

In addition to being authentic, I believe you should be generous in the bedroom. One form this takes for us is when one partner is in the mood and the other one isn't. Nilsa and I have one simple rule: the person who is interested in sex is always the one who prevails, and the other person acquiesces out of love. Naturally, there's a caveat to this rule: the partner who's interested in sex needs to have some consideration if the other person isn't feeling well or has some other physical problem. If Nilsa has a migraine, for instance, I'm not going to come knockin'—unless I feel her "ache" is not in her head, but elsewhere. But our baseline is that the most important gift we can give each other is the gift of ourselves, so that takes priority.

- **Say YES to changes in your needs and desires.**

Every relationship will go through stages and cycles, and so will a couple's sex life. It's tougher to find the time (or energy) to be intimate when the kids are young, for instance, and if one or the other partner is going through a tough time with their health or business, their libido may be affected. On the other hand, when the last child leaves home, or when one or the other partner leaves a job or retires, it can be a time of sexual re-awakening for a couple. Remember, the only thing that stays the same in life is change. Changes in desire are inevitable, so see them as opportunities to learn about this *new* version of your partner, and to explore new ways to have even better sex than you did before.

- **Say NO to sacrificing intimacy in your relationship.**

Every couple should have a great relationship that includes mind-blowing sex, but too many people settle for what they can get rather than what they want. They feel they have to sacrifice an exciting physical relationship because of the kids, or because they're focused on business, or they're reluctant to talk with their partner about what's not working for them in bed. Frustrated, they will complain to close friends about their lousy sex life, and then say, "But he/she is a good man/woman, so I guess that's just how it is." Please, do yourself a favor and leave that kind of attitude outside the bedroom door—heck, leave it outside the front door of your home. You and your partner *deserve* to have a great physical relationship, and you can create it (or recreate it) at any point with some honest communication and a little willingness to experiment together.

- **Say NO to treating your partner like your child.**

I've seen this happen with people who become empty-nesters: once the kids are gone they transfer their parenting instinct over to their partner. Now they're advising their significant other on what to eat, what to wear, and what to do. I love being taken care of, but I also need to feel like the man in my relationship, not a little boy. Nilsa loves being taken care of, too, but she also needs to feel that she doesn't have to be my parent or my child, but instead can be the strong, sexy, passionate woman she is.

As sex therapist Esther Perel writes, "Caretaking is mightily loving, [but] it's a powerful anti-aphrodisiac."[19] It can be a beautiful, natural instinct to want to provide for your partner's needs, but beware if it turns into treating your partner like a child.

- **Say NO to using sex as a battleground for other relationship issues.**

Sex is when we should be able to feel the most vulnerable and open with our partners. Unfortunately far too many couples use sex as a channel to express their upset about other problems in the relationship. Even something relatively small, like, "You forgot to take out the trash again," or "You brought home fish ice cream and I specifically asked for chocolate," can affect your sexual response to your partner if you let it. Of course the relationship with your partner includes everything from finances, kids, and work to trash and ice cream, and if you're really upset about something, it's really difficult *not* to let it affect your sex life. But you know that old advice for a happy relationship, "Never go to bed angry"? Well, if you want great sex, you should expand that to, "Avoid bringing your upsets into bed with you." If you and your partner are facing a problem that's diminishing your desire and attraction for each other, be honest with each other about it, and then hash it out together before you have sex. Or just have sex and all the other stuff might just work itself out (not).

Remember in chapter 18 you read about how pressure can turn your relationship into a beautiful diamond? Well, the desire and passion of mind-blowing sex can bring the equivalent of the two-thousand-degree Fahrenheit heat that it takes for that diamond to solidify. But for that relationship heat to continue to blaze, you need to feed it frequently with great sex. Without consistent fuel, the fire of desire in both you and your partner can begin to fade, and your passionate, mind-blowing relationship will become only companionship. Certainly, companionship is a nice, temperate bed of warm coals that will keep your home toasty. But most of us want to feel the flames of passion continue to blaze no matter how long we've been together.

Good news! Even if the flame of desire seems to be extinguished in your relationship, the heat lasts long after the flame dies. The coals, the burning embers of love and lust for each other are there, so just keep feeding the fire with the right "fuel"—your attention, your love for your partner, your sensual appreciation, your honest communication, your playfulness, and sense of adventure—and that passion will blaze brightly whenever you wish. Then your sex life will be of the altered reality type—mind-blowing and legendary. And don't we all want that!

... for that relationship heat to continue to blaze, you need to feed it frequently with great sex.

WARNING!

Sections One to Four all lead to this.

If you truly want to alter your DNA, create a new reality, and fulfill your aspirations, what follows are the most important chapters of the book.

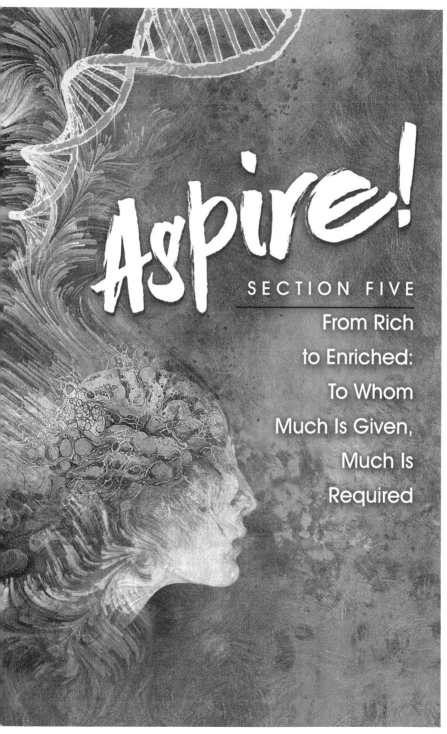

Aspire!

From Rich
to Enriched:
To Whom
Much Is Given,
Much Is
Required

From Rich to Enriched: To Whom Much Is Given, Much Is Required

The price of greatness is responsibility.
WINSTON CHURCHILL

f you'd seen the eighteen-year-old Mickey McKinney—corn-fed country boy from Indiana, born and raised in the little town of Carmel, the oldest of six, his father a banker and mother a retired schoolteacher; a guy who attended four different high schools in four years and finally graduated with a 1.8 GPA, not even enough to get into community college, with an adrenaline-addicted personality that had resulted in seven stints in juvenile detention—arriving in Palm Beach, Florida, with just $50 in his pocket and all his belongings in a duffle bag, you'd have been sure that the best job he could ever aspire to was digging ditches. And you'd not be far off, as the first job he got was digging sand traps at a posh golf course for $180 a week. He was the only white guy on a crew of Haitians, and he was proud when they dubbed him "The White Haitian" because he worked as hard as they did. (That was my first connection to Haiti. You'll read more about Haiti in this section.) But within a year, that guy had started his own business as a tennis pro, teaching wealthy people at affluent Palm Beach oceanfront residential communities how to improve their forehands, backhands, and serves. He was making $50 an hour, or $400 a day, $2,000 a week, and $100,000 a year. By the time he was twenty-one, he had enough to buy his dream car, a Ferrari.

After hanging around with all his rich tennis clients and grilling them to discover how they'd succeeded at such a high level, he decided to go into real estate. He started going by his legal name, Frank, and, using all his savings, he bought his first piece of property at a HUD auction on the courthouse steps. It was a $36,000 crack house in a bad neighborhood that he fixed up and sold for a $7,000 profit. Within five years after he sold that fixer-upper, he acquired his very first piece of oceanfront property for $750,000 and built a spec house that sold for $2.2 million. Thirty years later, he retired from real estate, having designed, built, and sold more than forty spectacular multimillion-dollar oceanfront masterpieces, including the most expensive spec house ever sold in Palm Beach County at the time ($50 million). What's more, he did this without backers (other than the bank) or outside partners (except the IRS and his wife).

How did all of that happen? How did a guy who barely graduated from high school, with little formal education and no formal training in architecture, design, construction, marketing, etc., and no network or resources, manage to fulfill all of his aspirations, alter his DNA, and create his own reality? I believe the only way that someone like me could achieve the success I have is due primarily to three things: 1) an unrelenting and monomaniacal entrepreneurial spirit, 2) a lot of hard work, and 3) the grace of God. In the preceding four sections and twenty chapters I've tried to give you some insights into the secrets of my success. But no advice contained in those chapters is worthwhile without the spiritual foundation that I will describe in this section. Without spirit, any success you have will be transitory. Worse: it will feel inadequate, unfulfilling, and hollow.

I speak from experience. Ten years into my real estate journey, I was featured on the front cover of the *Miami Herald* as having designed and built what was then the most expensive spec home ever sold in Palm Beach County. You'd think I would have been ecstatic, but instead I was depressed and unhappy. As you'll read in chapter 21, it took what I believe was a "tap" on the shoulder by God that day to open my eyes to the need all around me and point me in a new and different direction, one devoted to helping those to whom no one pays attention or who are invisible in our society.

It started small, with volunteering to serve meals one hour a week at a local soup kitchen. And over the years it became a mission that transformed the materialistic twenty-one-year-old kid with the Ferrari into a man in his fifties whose Caring House Project Foundation will have built twenty-nine self-sustaining villages in Haiti as of the beginning of 2022 (and be starting on our thirtieth), providing more than thirteen thousand children and their families with sturdy concrete housing, clean water, renewable food, schools, clinics, community centers, churches, and the means to support themselves through some form of free enterprise.

That tap has brought me more happiness and fulfillment than any multimillion-dollar sale, mega-bestselling book, or sold-out keynote could ever do. It also has driven me to achieve more in my life and business, so I could use the proceeds of all those endeavors (and my public profile) to serve a cause much bigger than one man's personal success. Most important, it taught me the lesson that lies at the core of section 5, the precept that will create more success and fulfillment in your life than any other aspiration or accomplishment: **feeling a connection to something bigger than yourself and a responsibility, a stewardship, to promote the welfare of others, and then putting those feelings into immediate action, is the difference between mere achievement and deep fulfillment, between being rich and feeling** *enriched.*

As I wrote twenty years ago in my first book, *Make It BIG!,* "Each of us is fortunate to be blessed with the ability to succeed at some level, not for our sole benefit, but so we may apply the results of our success to assist others." Money, wealth, riches, success, are all just means to an end. If you want your riches to truly *enrich* your life and produce greater happiness, then your vision for yourself, your profession, and your beneficial impact on the world needs to include sharing your blessings with others.

Everyone Prays for More . . .

I don't care if you're a Christian, Muslim, Jew, Hindu, Buddhist, atheist, agnostic, druid, wiccan, or none of the above, and it doesn't matter to me if you read the Bible or the Koran or the Talmud or the Upanishads or the Buddhist Tripitaka or Christopher Hitchens or *Mao's Little Red Book* or *People* magazine. But I do believe that regardless of faith (or lack of it), most of us at some point close our eyes and send up a prayer to whatever we call God, to ask either for blessings for ourselves and those we love, or relief from a problem. If we inventory our prayers, however, they all come down to simply asking for *more*. More health. More wealth. More love. More happiness. More peace. More healing. More joy. Or fewer problems, which would mean more happiness, wealth, love, and so on. In essence, like Jabez in the Old Testament, we are asking God to bless us and "enlarge our territory" (1 Chronicles 4:10, NIV)—in other words, to give us more.

And there is *nothing* wrong with that. Hundreds of verses in the Old and New Testaments, in the Koran, in the Upanishads, and many other holy books describe the abundance of God's blessings that are available to us all. So here's the question: how can we show that we are worthy of and ready to take on the "more" we are asking for? That's where the quote that inspired the title of this section comes in, Luke 12:48: "From everyone to whom much is entrusted, much will be required." Before God will enlarge our current "territory," we need to demonstrate that we are responsible stewards of what we already possess.

You may recall from section 1 my advice that you identify the people you want to emulate and the qualities they possess that you can add to your personality and thus achieve your aspirations. Well, one of the people I emulate is Rich DeVos, philanthropist, co-founder of Amway, and my mentor and good friend for many years. In his endorsement for my book, *The Tap*, Rich wrote: "The gaining of material wealth means little without responsible stewardship for those blessings." It's clear to me that the secret of moving from rich to enriched is simple: *become a responsible steward for the blessings you receive, no matter how small or large.* I believe that starts by taking the focus off of yourself and your needs and using your resources to help others with no expectation of personal benefit or reward.

Now, you might be thinking, "But Frank, the reason I'm praying for more is that I don't have enough!" Sorry, I must challenge you on that, because I believe we all have a responsibility to share at least a portion of *whatever* we have in the form of time, talent, and treasure, no matter how little that may be. This is for two reasons. First, it's a signal to our minds and hearts that we are grateful for what we already have, and gratitude is a sign

> ... the secret of moving from rich to enriched is simple: *become a responsible steward for the blessings you receive, no matter how small or large.*

of responsible stewardship. Second, and most important, when you make giving a regular practice, it will alter your DNA and create a profound new reality in a way that links you directly to both your Creator and the rest of humanity.

I saw this clearly on the Yugo We-go Tour in Manitou Springs, Colorado, when I met an earthly angel named Stevie. You'll read the full story in chapter 24, but Stevie is a homeless twenty-eight-year-old transsexual autistic savant who is the den mother/father for numerous other transient souls in a park near the hotel where I was staying. This beautiful young person had nothing by most people's standards, yet whatever was given to them was immediately given away to others residing in this little park by a stream. Stevie is a shining example that responsible stewardship has nothing to do with how much we have and everything to do with our willingness to look outside ourselves and our own needs and prioritize the needs of others. When you take the focus off your own problems and focus on somebody else, your problems dissipate. They may not go away forever, but they go away in the moment—and sometimes that moment is exactly the "more" we need.

I'm not so arrogant or stupid to declare that God requires *anything* from you for him to bless you with what you ask. He already knows what you want and is keenly aware of what you need. After all, I've been the recipient of far too many undeserved blessings in my life, so I know God doesn't keep score! But when I look at people like Warren Buffett, Bill Gates, Oprah Winfrey, and others who have been hugely successful in business and then ultimately in philanthropy, I can't help but believe that those successes are linked at some cosmic level. Bottom line: something transformative happens to the responsible steward who shares what he or she has been given. If you want to create a new reality for yourself and your family that includes greater success, prosperity, *and* happiness, the secret is simple: start looking for opportunities to do more for others.

By the way, if you ever think that you don't have enough to share, come to Haiti with me sometime: you'll return home feeling that you're the richest person in the world. While extremely beautiful, Haiti is the poorest country in the Western Hemisphere, where most people live on $2 a day, the average life expectancy is forty-seven years, and in some rural areas there's a twenty-two percent chance that a child born there won't live to see his or her fifth birthday. Some of the children we have cared for live in mud huts with palm frond roofs, and they eat dirt pies flavored with bouillon and lemon juice just to fill their stomachs. I am grateful for God's gift of awareness that has allowed me to help more than thirteen thousand of those children to grow up in new communities with clean drinking water and renewable food. And when I think about it, in the end, the multimillion-dollar mansions I've created will be rendered meaningless when compared to our efforts in Haiti and elsewhere. The Caring House Project Foundation mission has enriched my life by giving meaning to the blessings God has bestowed upon me.

Five Ways to Move from Rich to Enriched

I believe being a responsible steward for your blessings happens when you live in accordance with the lessons of each chapter in this section.

Here's a preview:

#1: YOU MUST MAXIMIZE BOTH YOUR PROFESSIONAL CALLING AND YOUR SPIRITUAL CALLING. God gave me the ability to create beautiful oceanfront mansions for the ultra-wealthy, and to waste the gift of that professional calling would have been a sin. But I have used the proceeds of my professional calling to fund my *spiritual* calling, which is to uplift the poorest of the poor in Haiti and elsewhere with housing, food, water, and education. How can you marry the gift of your talent and the source of your treasure with a mission that will improve the lives of others and perhaps the world as well?

#2: YOU MUST NOT ONLY FEEL COMPASSION: YOU MUST ACT UPON THOSE FEELINGS TO MAKE A DIFFERENCE. In the New Testament, James 2:17 (NIV), it says, ". . . faith by itself, if it is not accompanied by action, is dead." The same is true of the feeling of compassion: unacted upon, it is worth nothing. When I felt called to help people who were homeless, that feeling meant nothing until I put it into concrete action by volunteering at the local soup kitchen.

You learned in section 2 about the need to take on more and more risk in order to expand your sense of who you are and what's possible in your life. Well, you must exercise that compassion muscle regularly by taking action to help others. Compassion plus action will lead you directly to an expanded territory and a more enriched life.

#3: CONSUMERISM AND MATERIALISM LEAD ONLY TO GREATER DISSATISFACTION AND UNHAPPINESS. INSTEAD, YOU MUST FIND WAYS TO USE YOUR GIFTS TO HELP OTHERS HELP THEMSELVES. That's philanthro-capitalism: taking the best of philanthropy and combining it with the best of capitalism. Repeated charity only serves to exacerbate poverty, while philanthro-capitalism solves the problem—for good. Human beings aren't wired to handle excess, so why not engage your head, heart, and wallet to seek out ways to help others lift themselves up? It'll provide you with more lasting fulfillment than any purchase or experience,

while giving people the tools they need to create their own sustainable abundance.

#4: YOU MUST RECOGNIZE THAT ANGELS WALK AMONG US, AND THEIR SMALL ACTS OF KINDNESS TRANSFORM LIVES. Over the past few years I have become fascinated with the New Testament verse Hebrews 13:2: "Do not forget to show hospitality to strangers, for by so doing some people have shown hospitality to angels without knowing it." These angels are people we randomly encounter who radiate a divine yet everyday presence. They were sent by God to enrich our lives by making us better stewards of the gifts we've been given. Throughout the Yugo We-go Tour, I would ask people to tell me stories of any earthly angels they had encountered in their lives. I also came across dozens of men and women like Stevie, angels whose presence enriched and uplifted others. My hope is the stories of earthly angels in chapter 24, written by *you*, the reader, will help you to notice and be grateful for the small miracles you may encounter, and to seek out opportunities to be an angel to others.

#5: YOU MUST UNDERSTAND THAT YOUR ASPIRATIONS CAN CHANGE THE WORLD. I began this book by saying that motivation is like soap washing off in the shower, and inspiration lasts about as long as a bad sunburn, but aspiration will alter your DNA and help you create a new reality. Well, that new reality isn't for you alone: your aspirations have the power to change the world. And it's far simpler to change the world than you might think, because every time you impact a life, you have changed the world for that person as he or she perceives it. When you feed a little girl in an orphanage and show her you care, you have changed her world. When you make time to mentor someone, you have changed their world. When you give of your time, talent, or treasure to a cause you believe in, you have changed the world for each person that cause touches, creating a new reality for them and a lasting legacy for yourself.

Throughout this book I hope that I've touched your aspiration "nerve" and caused you to aspire to leave a lasting legacy that you and your kids and their kids will be proud of. That legacy is far more likely to be inspired by your spiritual rather than your professional calling. For example, I know that the multimillion-dollar oceanfront mansions I created will be rubble in twenty or so years. No one will remember the theatrical grand unveiling events we did, and the only thing that will remain of the seven Badwater 135 Ultramarathon races I completed will be my name on a list of finishers and a few belt buckles that I'll leave to my daughter in my will. My real legacy, what I will be remembered for, is the work we've been doing in Haiti for the past twenty years. And that spiritual calling will continue to inspire and drive me for years to come.

Throughout my life I have used "To whom much is entrusted, much is required" as a life mantra, but did you know that verse continues with, "From those to whom *more* is given, *even more* is required"? When I read that, I think, "I've been given so much, I've got to continue to build more villages in Haiti and save more children and their families." So I don't intend to stop working on my spiritual highest calling until my ashes are sprinkled across the Badwater racecourse, because it enriches my heart and soul every time I look in the eyes of one of the Haitian children and see hope and love instead of despair. My wish for you is that you find a spiritual calling that enriches your life equally, so that God may bless you, continue to enlarge your territory, and bring you greater joy and success.

Your Highest Calling

A job is how you make money. A career is how you make your mark. A calling is how you acknowledge a higher vision, whatever it may be.

DEEPAK CHOPRA

I'm sure, at some point in your life, you've been featured in the newspaper for something you have accomplished, and I'm sure you remember how special that made you feel. Well, in 1999, when the *Miami Herald* asked to do a front-page article on me and the oceanfront home we had just sold (the most expensive spec house in Palm Beach County at the time, $14 million), I was honored. After all, there's nothing like third-party validation for your work! So, as usual, I accentuated and amplified my essence during the interview and photo shoot, making sure the reporter and photographer represented every detail exactly as I wanted them to, and then eagerly awaited the article's publication a few days later.

At 5 a.m. that day, I drove to the nearest newspaper vending machine (you might remember those from the days when we actually read printed newspapers). I put my quarter in the slot, opened up the machine, and grabbed ten copies to share with my friends—I was in a hurry and had only one quarter with me, so it was okay, right? Then I raced back home and sat down in my favorite chair, ready to enjoy reading about another moment of triumph.

On the front page was a photo and headline teasing the longer article inside. I can still hear the sound as I snapped open the newspaper and turned to page three. There it was, the culmination of all my work and aspiration, revealed to a worldwide audience! The full-page article looked goooooooood. There was a big picture of me, big hair, suede pants with a lace-up front, huge grin on my face, hands raised above my head in victory, with the magnificent oceanfront mansion I had built in the background. I rechecked the photos carefully. How's my outfit? Sharp! Hair blond and flowing? Yep! How's the house look? Magnificent—worth every penny of that $14 million. I scanned the text of the article: yep, they'd quoted me perfectly. If I had written the article myself, I couldn't have done it better. It was like a freaking advertisement for me and my brand on the front page of a renowned publication! I sat back in my chair with satisfaction. This is excellent!

Then I happened to glance at the left-hand page of the newspaper… and there was a photo of a guy about my age, skinny like me, straggly long blond hair (resembling my hairstyle when I don't use a blow dryer, flat iron, and tons of hair product), wearing a dirty sweatshirt and ripped jeans that looked like he'd been wearing them for weeks. He was standing in an area directly underneath the I-95 overpass in Delray Beach, only two miles from where all my glory had taken place. He was being handed a meal by someone from the back of an old, beat-up Econoline van that said "Caring Kitchen" on the side. It was clear the guy was homeless and had been sleeping under the girders of the freeway.

Have you ever had a friend point at someone and say, "That guy looks like you!" and nine times out of ten you think, *No, he doesn't—he's too fat or thin or his nose is too big*? But on a rare occasion you realize, yes, there's a strong resemblance. Looking at the photo of this homeless man, I realized he could have been my doppelgänger, and I had the strangest feeling of, "There but for the grace of God go I." A few wrong turns back in Indiana, a different choice when I left juvenile detention for the seventh time, another adrenaline-fueled motorcycle chase, and I easily could have ended up on the left side of the newspaper that day instead of the right, living underneath that overpass just like that guy. I could have been *that* guy.

Wait a minute, I don't want to read about that, I thought. *Today's about me, man, and how great I am. Who cares about that homeless guy?* I quickly snapped the newspaper into a fold so I could no longer see my twin's picture and started to re-read the glowing article on me. But as I looked at my photo on the right-hand side of the page, something came over me. My triumphant grin looked so fake, and I could see the deep depression and unhappiness behind my eyes. This was the biggest achievement of my real estate career, the culmination of over ten years of hard work. Yet I felt a complete void inside, as if I had lost all the heart in my soul, or soul in my heart.

"This isn't how I'm supposed to feel sitting on top of the world," I said aloud. I slowly unfolded the paper and looked at the homeless man again. Why hadn't I ended up on the left-hand side of the page? I'd taken a right turn and ended up on the right-hand page; he'd taken a different turn and ended up on the left, being fed a meal donated by strangers from a soup kitchen. He had nothing—yet why did I perceive real joy in his eyes and despair in mine? I spiraled into a deep funk. I had no purpose other than being the best at my profession and making sure the world knew it, by accumulating more than other people to prove I was successful. I'd focused completely on putting more cars in my garage and clothes in my closet and food in my pantry. The adulation and the ascent to the heights of my profession were all rendered meaningless in an instant. I needed to find something to give me back a sense of who I was, what I could become, and why I was doing what I was doing.

I believe that article was the most epiphanous "tap moment" in my life, a message from God telling me I was meant to do more than just line the Palm Beach coast with beautiful mansions. As a real estate artist, my buyers are the ultra-wealthy who probably don't need another house, and I'm an expert at moving them from need to desire, to the point where I can charge over $3,000 per square foot for one of my oceanfront masterpieces. That is my professional highest calling, and I'm extraordinarily good at it. But by showing me that photo of the homeless man who looked like me—who could have *been* me all too easily—God was asking, "What are you doing with your blessings, Frank? Why are you so focused on the 'I' and the 'me' instead of the 'you' and the 'we'? Are you truly being a responsible steward for the gifts I have given you? Are you ready to discover your spiritual purpose and experience true success?"

As you'll see in chapter 22, I believe that the way to give purpose to any "tap" is to take action on it as quickly as possible, so that same day I picked up the phone and called the soup kitchen whose name was stenciled on the side of that old Econoline van. I asked what I could do to help, and they signed me up as a volunteer to serve food to the homeless once a week. Every Monday (before *Monday Night Football*) for almost a year I handed out meals to people who lived on the streets of Palm Beach County, men and women just like the guy whose life-changing picture I'd seen in the paper. Few of us really look at these forgotten people; if we slip them a dollar, we usually do it without acknowledging them then hurriedly walk away, either embarrassed or afraid, perhaps thinking, as I did, "There but for the grace of God . . ." But for whatever reason, I've always been aware of people whom others don't see or notice. And when I looked into the eyes of the homeless men and women as I served their meals from the back of that rusted-out van, it set my soul on fire. I knew I could help those whom society had forgotten or chosen to ignore, to provide them the resources to live with dignity and respect. In a beautiful life-altering moment, I knew this would be my spiritual highest calling.

Inspired by the name of the Caring Kitchen, in that same year my wife and I created the Caring House Project Foundation (CHPF), with the mission of supporting the desperately poor and homeless by providing them with food, housing, and opportunities to become more self-sufficient. Caring House's first project was to buy a small, one-bedroom house in Delray Beach, fix it up, and then rent it to Buster, an eighty-three-year-old homeless man, for $1 a month. (Charging rent gave the formerly homeless tenant some dignity and the opportunity to take responsibility for his housing, and it allowed me to circumvent having the home be designated a homeless shelter.) Through the years, CHPF has continued to provide assistance to hundreds of homeless families throughout the United States, and it has expanded its mission to deliver food and aid following natural disasters, including the 2010 earthquake in Haiti. And in probably its most meaningful work, in 2002 CHPF built its very first self-sustaining village. In 2022, twenty years later, we will have constructed our thirtieth of these in Haiti, sheltering thousands of children and their families.

None of this ever would have happened had I kept that newspaper folded in an attempt to conceal the "tap" God was sending me.

Through the years I've been privileged to experience a lot of success in my career, but at the same time, one of the lowest points of my life came when I didn't have a purpose other than my professional highest calling. To succeed in the business of life requires purpose, and I have learned that you can't have purpose without spirituality. My spiritual highest calling has given my life more fulfillment and meaning than any house I ever built, more excitement than any adrenaline-fueled grand unveiling stunt I have executed, more creative satisfaction than any bestselling book I have written, and more impact than any keynote speech delivered to an enthusiastic sold-out audience of thousands. It's also stretched me more than running 135 miles nonstop in the 125-degree heat of Death Valley. Most important, my spiritual highest calling has allowed me to put the abundant gifts I have received from God to use in service of a much greater cause. In this chapter I want to show you how to discover and follow a spiritual highest calling that will give your life greater meaning and help you create a new reality—not just for yourself and your family, but for the people and causes who need you.

Your Professional and Spiritual Highest Callings

As I acknowledged in section 3, most of us have a professional highest calling, defined as something that we do a little better than most, and that's usually the skill/ability/talent that puts food on our table. But too many of us spend our lives pursuing this professional highest calling only to discover that the success we achieve feels hollow. So we keep upping the ante—more success, bigger challenges, more money—and we become addicted to the search for "more." Unfortunately, as the heartbreaking examples of people like Anthony Bourdain and Kate Spade demonstrate, no professional "more" is ever going to be enough to fill the void inside our hearts.

I see the effects of this need for "more" in some of the people who make a significant donation to our Caring House Project Foundation in exchange for a coaching session with me in my oceanfront tree house office. They climb up, gaze wide-eyed at the stunning view, and tell me they're excited to learn my secrets to creating success in real estate. But at some point during our conversation they'll fall silent and then admit that something's missing in their lives, and what they really want is to find out what and why. "Treasure this moment," I say to them. "Because that feeling might just lead you to your spiritual highest calling, which is the real reason you were put on this earth. Fewer than twenty percent of people ever identify then pursue their spiritual highest calling, but if you do, it will give more fulfillment to your life than any material success."

Even though identifying your spiritual highest calling will be a deeply personal journey, here are a few "signposts" that might point you in the right direction.

First, *whenever you feel a strong desire to contribute to something greater than yourself, that's a sign of your spiritual highest calling.* Like me, you might see a photo in the newspaper or online of a homeless person camped on the street, or an animal in pain, or a kid raising money to relieve child hunger. Or perhaps someone mentions they're sponsoring a run for Alzheimer's or Parkinson's. Or you might see a post on social media about an event happening to benefit college scholarships for the underprivileged, or a link to a GoFundMe project sponsoring disaster relief. Whatever it is, it creates a feeling inside of, "I need to do something!" You always should pay attention to such promptings because they are designed to awaken you to your spiritual highest calling. (In the next chapter we'll address how important it is to act on such feelings.)

Second, *a spiritual highest calling invariably involves service to others.* Malala Yousafzai was only eleven years old when the Taliban took control of her village in Pakistan in 2008 and banned all girls there from going to school anymore. Malala courageously decided to speak out on behalf of girls' education, even after the Taliban threatened her with death. In 2012, a gunman shot her in the head while she was riding on a bus. Miraculously, Malala survived, and she was flown to the U.K. for treatment. After two years of rehabilitation, she continued with her mission to guarantee girls everywhere access to free, safe, quality education. Because of her courageous efforts, in 2014 she became the youngest person ever to be awarded the Nobel Peace Prize.[1]

While Malala's mission might have started out advocating for a cause that benefited her personally, it quickly evolved into a spiritual highest calling that served others. There's no such thing as a selfish spiritual highest calling. Instead, it connects us with a purpose that's in service of others, as well as the greater good.

Third, *there's no spiritual calling without love.* As part of our CHFP fundraising to build villages in Haiti, for eleven consecutive years we used to host what are called "Survival to Thrival" events. They began with an elegant outdoor reception at my oceanfront home in Delray Beach, including a visit to my tree house, for upwards of sixty guests. Very early the next morning everyone boarded a plane to Haiti, where we spent two days interacting with the people in the villages that the donors' contributions

. . . a spiritual highest calling speaks directly to the heart . . .

built. We would play games with the kids, teach in their school, and feed children in the village orphanage. Some people would stay overnight in the village to experience life as some Haitians do. After each trip our attendees invariably came back with their hearts opened. They were shocked by the poverty that exists throughout Haiti, but they also were deeply moved by the families they met. "All these kids want is to be loved and to feel that someone cares enough to help them create a better future," one donor told me.

Everybody has a heart for something that is beyond what they do for a living, and a spiritual highest calling speaks directly to the heart, not the head. It touches you emotionally, which engages a completely different kind of energy and drive than your mind. Princess Diana, Malala Yousafzai, and Nelson Mandela were all powerful advocates for their causes, but more important, these leaders passionately cared about the people they served. When you encounter something that you believe might be your spiritual highest calling, be completely open to *allowing* your heart to be moved by the needs of others.

Dovetailing Your Professional and Spiritual Highest Callings

I'm not saying you should leave behind your profession and pursue only your spiritual highest calling. To me, if you don't take advantage of your professional calling, you have wasted one of the greatest talents that God gave you. But I believe that when you bring both spiritual and professional highest callings together, it's like two hands coming together in prayer. When I felt called to help the homeless, as I was serving meals for the Caring Kitchen, I would say to myself, "Frank, you provide houses to the world's most wealthy people. There's no judgment on your profession, it's just a fact. You love what you do and are really good at it. But what about the people who *don't* have any housing and are living on the streets, in parks, under bridges, or in homeless shelters? What can you do to provide shelter for them?" The origins of the mission of Caring House Project Foundation lay in dovetailing my professional and spiritual callings.

In the New Testament it says, "As each has received a gift, use it to serve one another, as good stewards of God's varied grace" (1 Peter 4:10, NIV). Yes, there is a way you can use your professional skills, abilities, talents, and connections in the service of others. For example, I've used my skills as a real estate artist to design sustainable villages for CHPF's Haitian projects, I've publicized our efforts via my books and keynotes, and I've raised millions of dollars with my connections. What talents do you use in your profession that could also serve your spiritual highest calling? Are you a good organizer, fundraiser, writer, speaker, designer, executive, or chef? Are you good with budgets, drawing, childcare, physical fitness, or design? Do you have skills or abilities that are part of your hobbies that you could use? Perhaps you love to sing, dance, or play a musical instrument. Could you teach those skills to kids in shelters who can't afford lessons? Could you go to a retirement home and perform for the residents?

In chapter 4 you read that the reason we are here is to create greater happiness for ourselves and those we love. But much like motivation, happiness is fleeting, washing off like soap in the shower at night. What if you could skip over happiness and spend more time in its more desirable and longer-lasting cousin, *joy?* That's what linking your professional and spiritual highest callings will give you.

Uniting head and heart, profession and spirit, is the best way I know to be a responsible steward for the gifts you have been given. And as I said in the introduction to this section, I believe God rewards responsible stewards with more. At times that "more" is greater professional success. At other times it is more demand on your resources. But regardless, the "more" that I guarantee you'll receive when you follow your spiritual highest calling is more fulfillment and meaning, and yes, more joy. And that's the kind of new reality we all want.

Compassion Without Action Is a Waste of Emotion

22

Compassion is an action word with no boundaries.

PRINCE

O n Tuesday, January 12, 2010, at 4:53 P.M., a 7.0-magnitude earthquake[1] struck Haiti just outside of the capital city, Port-au-Prince. It knocked down almost every building in the city and surrounding areas, killing hundreds of thousands of people and burying thousands more in the rubble. All three local hospitals as well as Port-au-Prince's airport and seaport sustained significant damage. Aftershocks throughout the night brought down more debris and made rescue efforts dangerous, if not nearly impossible.

That evening I was giving a keynote at the Junior League in Boca Raton when someone came up on stage and whispered in my ear the horrible details. I wrapped up my talk and sped home. I raced across the suspension bridge into my tree house, where I watched Anderson Cooper on CNN, and I was sickened by what I was seeing. *I've got to do something right now!,* I thought and stepped unhesitatingly into "executioner" mode. Even though I've never put together a search-and-rescue team, I reached out to numerous first responder organizations around the country, seeking to secure qualified and trained volunteers to immediately go to Haiti with me. I went online and worked the phones, asking anyone in my network with search and rescue experience to contact me ASAP. I raised money like a fiend to finance the trip, and of course put up a bunch of funds myself because time was so short.

Early in the afternoon of Thursday, January 14, I dashed out of a pre-planned media event (to mark the court-ordered move of my tree house from one spot to another at my Delray Beach home) and boarded one of two large private jets I had charted to carry eleven top-notch search and rescue experts from Florida and Colorado, along with supplies and all the gear necessary to excavate people from underneath collapsed buildings. Less than forty hours after the initial earthquake struck, this group of superheroes set out for Haiti. We had no idea what we'd find, but we knew that we'd been called there to save lives.

As I've said before, to create your own reality and alter your DNA you must take action consistently. But nowhere is taking action more important than whenever you feel compassion. According to Merriam-Webster, compassion is "a sympathetic consciousness of others' distress together with a desire to alleviate it."[2] But feeling others' pain and having a desire to help is *never* good enough. Compassion is a signal from God that we must *do* something. **Compassion without action is a waste of emotion.** Sure, it may make you feel good in the moment, and it's better than simply ignoring all the suffering in the world—but without taking action on that compassion you're feeling, you're missing a God-given opportunity to do good in the world and, in effect, turning your back on your Creator.

In the New Testament it says, "As the body without the spirit is dead, so faith without deeds is dead" (James 2:26, NIV). When you feel compassion, you must act: maybe not in that very moment, but very soon. If you don't act right away, you may never do so, and you'll begin to develop a habit of not acting. My hope and prayer is that this chapter is your wake-up call and a reminder always to see compassion as a tap on your shoulder from God, indicating that it's your turn to step up and take action to help those who need it.

Compassion in Action Saves Five Lives

It should be very clear by now that I strive to act every time I feel the "tap" to help someone less fortunate. We've provided disaster relief after hurricanes in Louisiana, New Jersey, and Florida, and helped hundreds of homeless families and the elderly throughout the U.S. to get off the streets and into safe housing. But as I say in every keynote or speech, I've had a special place in my heart for Haiti for decades. When the earthquake hit Haiti in 2010, CHPF had already built fourteen self-sustaining villages there, and I knew and loved the Haitian people's spirit and heart.

However, nothing could have prepared me for what we found after our plane touched down on the runway at the Port-au-Prince airport. (Literally touched down: the pilot practically pushed us out of the door, then turned around and took off again. It was that bad on the ground, with the taxiway still shifting from aftershocks.) Had I known what we were up against as far as the logistics, or how prepared we should have been but weren't, I don't know if I would have been brave enough to attempt the rescue mission. In this case, I believe that ignorance wasn't bliss: it was God's way of saying, "Go, and I will provide."

As soon as our eleven-member team got out of the planes, the first thing that hit us was the smell. Haiti's sewage infrastructure is nonexistent at the best of times, but laid on top of the usual stench was the pungent whiff of bodies beginning to decay in the tropical heat. We walked to the tent where search and rescue teams were required to register. Since we were not officially sanctioned, we weren't on their list, so we just made up a name for our team (Colorado Two, because there was a good chance there already was a Colorado One on the list) and acted like we were supposed to be there. It's a sign of how chaotic things were that the lieutenant colonel in charge shrugged his shoulders and assigned us a specific quadrant of the city to search. That night we slept in our little camping tents right next to the airport runway, so there was no chance of a building falling on us in an aftershock. (Yes, we felt many during four sleepless nights.)

The next morning we set out for our search quadrant. We were accompanied by an Ecuadorian security detail with machine guns to make sure we weren't attacked by people who not only might have been desperate to steal whatever supplies we had but also would have done anything to save their loved ones trapped under collapsed buildings. A Peruvian squad was also assigned to us that had dogs trained to sniff out the living from underneath rubble. It broke my heart to turn away dozens of men and women pleading with us to help them reach the bodies of husbands, wives, children, grandparents . . . but we were there only to rescue the living. People wailing and crying, the smell of decay coming from every building we passed, seeing dead bodies being scooped up by front-end loaders: it was a sensory assault that I will never forget.

Even though I was officially the team's leader, I have no expertise in search and rescue nor any medical background, yet I was always a pretty skilled driver, so I was to take us on our odyssey. (The adrenaline-fueled motorcycle and car-racing exploits of my misspent youth could finally be put to good use.) Somehow I managed to commandeer two large SUVs, the type that could navigate the shattered roads and roll over concrete chunks from crumbled buildings that covered the ground, and we got to work. We knew we were in a race against time because it was now fifty-two hours since the quake struck. According to search and rescue statistics, after ninety-six hours we'd be unlikely to find anyone alive under the rubble.

The Peruvian team and their eager dogs led the way. It took twelve hours of painstaking work, chipping and scraping away at piles of concrete chunks and twisted iron rebar, before we found Isabel, an older woman who was still trapped under a three-story house. With the skill of our expert first responders, we pulled her and her daughter free, and, after taking them to a local medical tent, we moved on to search other buildings. Our team spent four heart-breaking days in Haiti: hours in the hot sun, choking on the dust, faces covered with bandanas to mask against the horrendous smell, hoping every minute to hear one of the dogs barking to indicate someone was alive under the debris, all of us exhausted from the physical and emotional toll.

On our final day in Haiti we found Pierre in the ruins of a hospital run by Doctors Without Borders. He'd been taken there before the earthquake to be treated for a stabbing, and when we uncovered him we discovered that the knife was still in his back. I remember Pierre taking the bottle of water we handed him and saying, "l'eau de vie" (water of life), as he drank—it was the first drink he'd had in over three days. We put him in our makeshift ambulance, knowing that Pierre was beginning to lose his battle to stay alive as he still had blood dripping from the IV tubes protruding from his arms. I drove like a man possessed, through the streets, into and out of the woods, against traffic, on the sidewalk, over boulders, until we reached a military hospital tent. One of the ex-military guys on our team had told us that once a patient made it inside the tent the doctors would have to treat them, so we pulled up, shoved Pierre inside the tent, and then fled.

All told, of the forty-three people who were documented as being rescued alive from the rubble left by the earthquake, we saved five, a remarkable record for a rag-tag team of eleven men and women, assembled in less than forty hours, led by someone with no search and rescue experience but with a burning need to help. In all my life I don't think I had ever been more resourceful than I was during those one hundred hours. Everyone involved in the Haitian earthquake "miracle"—first responder teams from around the globe, all the governments and NGOs that stepped up to provide supplies and flights, and people everywhere who donated to the "Hope for Haiti Now" global telethon held only twelve days after the earthquake—are tributes to what can happen when compassion triggers action. (If you'd like to see a short compilation video of our Haiti rescue mission, there is one at TheAspireBook.com.)

The Upward Spiral from Awareness to Action

I get that this idea of letting compassion move you to immediate action may be new to you. Not everyone starts off being aware of the needs of others. And I consider myself fortunate that God gave me the desire to notice and then want to help people whom most of us ignore. But I believe that anyone can learn to let compassion become the catalyst for action that will make a difference in the lives of others. In fact, I wrote an entire chapter about this seven-stage process in my book, *The Tap*. Here's a short recap. (For a full explanation, go to my website and buy *The Tap*.)

STAGE ONE: Almost a complete lack of awareness or care for others. At this stage you have no connection with anything outside yourself and your own needs. You don't even see the homeless woman crouched on the sidewalk.

STAGE TWO: You begin to notice others' suffering but it only makes you uncomfortable, and you're certainly not willing to take any action. "I get it, but it's their fault, and I'm not interested," you say, averting your eyes as you walk past the homeless guy.

STAGE THREE: Finally, there's enough guilt, shame, or social pressure to cause you to take action because you feel you have to, but you only do the minimum amount. You hand the woman in tattered clothes a dollar and keep moving.

STAGE FOUR: You are willing to share your blessings more abundantly, but only if you think others in your position are doing the same, and you want public attention for your gift of time/money/talent: your name on the building, or your donation listed in a charity's annual report, for example. Instead of handing a homeless person a small amount of cash, you'll write a modest check for the homeless shelter and then make sure you're recognized for it.

STAGE FIVE: This is where your response comes more from the heart than the head, and you begin to feel the first stirrings of real compassion, where you want to alleviate the suffering of others. But there's also a sense of "There but for the grace of God go I, so I'd better do something to help, or I might find myself in those circumstances." This was the stage I was in when I saw the newspaper photo of the homeless man that looked like me.

STAGE SIX: Compassion produces a sense of purpose: you feel that sharing your gifts and helping others is what you were put on earth to do. You seek out ways to help because it offers more fulfillment than any other activity or reward. Some of the donors to our Caring House Project Foundation are in stage six. They love feeling they are making a difference by helping to build our villages in Haiti.

STAGE SEVEN: Acting on compassion is so engrained that it is no longer what you do but who you are. Helping others is a spiritual calling that inspires others to act and perhaps to find their own spiritual calling as well. Think of Bill Gates and Warren Buffett and their Giving Pledge,[3] where they committed to give away ninety-nine percent of their respective fortunes during their lifetimes and challenged other billionaires to do the same. Their action inspired many other ultra-wealthy people to join them in using their success to fund important causes around the world.

Please don't think that these seven stages are either exclusive or linear. Even if you sometimes find yourself at stage seven, where acting on compassion is just who you are, there may be other times when you feel disconnected and separate, or stretched to the point where you think, *I'm too exhausted; I just can't give anything right now.* And far be it from me to discourage people at stage four, who give so generously to a cause that they are rewarded with getting their name on a building, for example. (As you'll see in chapter 23, I'm a huge believer in the impact of the actions of donors who support philanthro-capitalism and other worthwhile causes.) But in my experience, once you become aware of the needs of others and feel the stirrings of compassion in your heart, the pull to take action to help others will continue to grow. The compassion-action connection will become an upward spiral that can transform your DNA and create a new, more powerful, more spiritually-based reality for you and those you are called to help.

Strengthening Your Compassion-to-Action Muscle

Let's be honest: we human beings are pretty self-centered. Being selfish is inherently natural to our DNA. We feel the need to ensure our own survival first, and then to ensure the survival of the "tribe." And even when we get to the point where our compassion is awakened, we need to prod ourselves to take action again and again. You won't strengthen a compassion muscle by serving Thanksgiving dinner at the soup kitchen once a year, for example, or contributing $10 to a friend's GoFundMe campaign. By all means, please continue to take those one-and-done actions. But for *compassion to action* to become a part of your DNA, you need to make the pattern automatic. Just as you had to exercise your risk tolerance regularly to take on bigger and bigger challenges, you need to go to the compassion gym regularly so that those neurological pathways become embedded in your brain and body.

Those actions can be small, like setting up an automatic monthly donation to a charity or cause. Or instead of showing up only on Thanksgiving, you serve food at a soup kitchen once a month, or once a week. Or you make it a practice always to give money or a gift card to McDonalds to a homeless person you encounter at the traffic light or on the sidewalk. Then, as you move up the compassion-to-action spiral, you may find yourself taking much bigger actions when you feel the tap, and experience greater fulfillment as a result. One of the things that I loved most about our many Survival to Thrival trips to Haiti was watching the faces of donors as they left the comfort of their homes and saw in person the impact of the villages their contributions helped to build. But even more important was seeing their hearts opened by the love and joy they felt coming their way from the Haitian children. My hope is that you'll develop the same "addiction" to compassion and action that has enriched my life as well as the lives of our CHPF donors.

It's normal, however, for people to experience lulls in their feelings of compassion for three reasons. First, during stress most people move automatically to a me-first survival mindset. That's completely understandable, yet those are the very times that we must remind ourselves how good it feels to help another person. Even the simplest of actions—like giving a tip to the busboy or helping an elderly person put groceries in their car—can take the focus off ourselves and alleviate the stress or anxiety or depression we may be feeling in the moment.

Second, we get so busy with our lives or professions that taking action on compassion becomes a lower priority. We mean to make that donation for Haiti relief, for example, but we lose the donation envelope or CHPF's number to call. We'd love to volunteer for the school's annual clothing drive, but we have to cancel due to a work deadline or our kid's soccer tournament. When we don't have time to be compassionate, however, that's a sign we need to re-prioritize and recommit to taking at least one small consistent action to help others.

The third thing that can create a decrease in compassion is known as disaster or donor fatigue. Say that you've been tutoring kids at a local shelter. You felt good about volunteering and you saw great results at the

---

... when we get to the point where our compassion is awakened, we need to prod ourselves to take action again and again.

---

start, but now you're frustrated with the constant turnover in students, and you're finding yourself less inspired by the results they're getting. You go on vacation for two weeks and when you come back home, you think, *Maybe I should just make this break permanent and tell the shelter to find someone else.*

To be honest, sometimes I get burnt out on feeling like I must act on my compassionate instincts. But as soon as I do any small thing in service to someone else, the feeling of being burnt out goes away. It's like taking an aspirin for a headache: as soon as I re-engage my compassion, I feel I'm answering my spiritual highest calling again. You have to remind yourself repeatedly of the value of sharing your blessings with others. And once you walk back in the shelter and see a new student sitting there, ready to learn, you'll remember how good it feels to take action on your compassion.

In the 1965 march from Selma to Montgomery, Rabbi Abraham Joshua Heschel walked arm in arm with Martin Luther King, Jr., and other spiritual leaders. When asked, "Did you find time to pray?" Rabbi Heschel answered, "I prayed with my feet."[4] In the Sermon on the Mount, Jesus said, "By your deeds you shall know them" (Matthew 7:16). Saint Francis of Assisi is supposed to have said, "Preach the Gospel at all times—and if necessary, use words." Compassion without walking, without deeds, without some kind of action is a waste of an emotion that I believe comes directly from God. There's a reason compassion has laid itself on your heart, so it's incumbent upon you to act on the feeling. Yes, lulls will happen. Yes, sometimes life intervenes. Yes, sometimes your focus needs to go elsewhere. But anytime you take action in response to compassion, you are building that muscle and strengthening that neurological pathway that will lead you upward. And whenever you act on compassion, you'll feel like you have done what a lot of people say is impossible: you will have altered your DNA *forever.*

~~Consumerism.~~
~~Materialism.~~
Philanthro-Capitalism!

Think of giving not only as a duty
but a privilege.

JOHN H. ROCKEFELLER

Think back to chapter 21 and read about the man who was featured on the front page of a large newspaper for selling that $14 million spec house many years ago. He had the clothes, the cars, the toys, the reputation, the beautiful wife, the hair, the media, the Palm Beach lifestyle . . . and yet he was depressed because his soul was slowly rotting from the inside out. Now contrast that with the man today: happily celebrating his thirty-first wedding anniversary at a Waffle House, living in the same historic (but not opulent) Delray Beach oceanfront house for twenty-five years, and choosing to drive a 1988 Yugo that costs less than the scissors his hairdresser uses to cut his still-classic hair. His idea of fun is to drive from his Canton, North Carolina, mountain home along the Pigeon River to Immaculate Conception church on Sunday, then visit the Ingles grocery store with his wife and walk up and down every single aisle, talking with people and marveling at the bounty on the shelves, especially after what he's seen in Haiti!

Sure, I proudly yet blindly went through a prolonged consumerist/materialist phase when I was a bit younger. Coming to Palm Beach from rural Indiana, I was mesmerized and intoxicated by the "lifestyles of the rich and famous" and the drive to not only keep up with the Joneses but to far outperform them. It's common for many people to be focused only on making money and creating wealth, and to be thrilled when they can finally buy the car or house or jewelry or wardrobe they've dreamed of for years. But with any luck, they quickly discover that consumerism and materialism just don't cut it when it comes to any kind of lasting joy or happiness. In fact, they create a maddening, never-ending cycle.

Think about the last time you bought a new car. You probably dreamed about purchasing it. You couldn't wait to fill your social media accounts with photos of the car, of you posing with the car, of the car parked in front of your house or work or the beach. That moment when you drove the car off the lot you were beside yourself with excitement and happiness. But honestly, how long did those feelings last? For some consumeristic and materialistic addicts, the car's first tank of gas lasts longer than their happiness with the purchase.

The energy and emotion you put into the pursuit of and obtaining of material things are never returned with the same intensity by possessing the thing. That's the problem with consumerism/materialism: too often it's an addiction where every "stick of the needle" of a new purchase gives you bliss for the moment, only to make you immediately crave another "hit." And the more that you feed that addiction of seeking happiness through materialistic things, the worse it can get.

Now, I have no problem with the creation of money and wealth as you pursue your professional highest calling. In fact, I encourage you to create a lot of it. Reaching a certain level of financial abundance can give you both relief from financial pressure and comfort in the form of an abundant lifestyle for you and your family. But if you use the accumulation of money only as a scorecard of your success, you're missing the greatest joy that it can provide, a joy that God intended for you to experience. True fulfillment and joy occur when you use your wealth in the service of others, as a responsible steward for the gifts you have been given. And that means leaving behind the addiction of consumerism and materialism and heeding your soul's call for something more meaningful.

I credit volunteering at the soup kitchen with jump-starting my understanding of how I could use wealth to make a difference in the lives of others. My fascination with consumerism and materialism faded, to be replaced by a focus on what I call *philanthro-capitalism*. It's a philosophy and practice that marries the best of philanthropy—defined as "an active effort to promote human welfare . . . an act or gift done or made for humanitarian purposes,"[1]—with the best of capitalism, which focuses on producing returns on the investment of time, energy, and resources in the service of others. Philanthro-capitalism has one ultimate goal: to uplift people by providing them with the means to realize a generational, self-sustaining existence. And I hope that this chapter will encourage you to adopt it as a method of fulfilling your spiritual highest calling.

Charity, Entitlement, and Philanthro-Capitalism

As someone who has worked hard at his professional highest calling and created wealth as a result, I'm a firm believer in capitalism and free enterprise. In a capitalist system, anyone can start from nothing and create great wealth. I also believe in the ability—in fact, the *responsibility*—of individuals to work to support themselves. At the same time, I know that people are worth more than just the monetary value of their labor, and the playing field does not start out level for all of us when it comes to success. Circumstances of birth, prejudice, lack of education, inadequate access to resources, health issues, bad luck, natural and humanmade disasters, and other factors can push anyone to the bottom of the socio-economic ladder. Those are the times when charity, philanthropy, and philanthro-capitalism can be of help.

As part of our spiritual highest calling, I believe we all have a responsibility to provide care and relief to those who truly need our assistance—in other words, to be charitable. Charity is given in response to immediate need and without expectation of any effort or reciprocation by the recipient. When you hand a homeless person a bottle of water on a hot day, for example, you don't expect him or her to pay for it (or to even thank you for it). And when we were pulling people out of the rubble in Haiti after the earthquake, we didn't expect any kind of payback from either the Haitian government or the people we rescued. We simply went because the need of the Haitian people spoke to our hearts and we sprang into action.

There are many wonderful charities around the world that help those who are not in a position to help themselves. However, the danger lies when people come to expect and/or depend on others' charity—or worse, feel they're *entitled* to it. In both cases (dependence and entitlement), charity *only* serves to exacerbate poverty. It makes it worse and entrenches it in the community and in the mind of the individual. Look at some long-standing efforts in Ethiopia and, some would say, Haiti. "For as long as I can remember nothing ever seems to change there," you say to yourself.

Let me be clear, I have no issue whatsoever with entitlement programs like welfare, food assistance, or disability benefits, because I believe in providing help for those who cannot support themselves and their families. Do yourself a favor and learn about the origins of your favorite entitlement program such as welfare. Although it started in earnest in the U.S. during the Great Depression in 1935, its roots can be traced to the ancient Roman Empire.[2] While I'm not a big fan of homework, all I ask is for you to ask yourself, "Is the system working as it was originally intended?" If it is, great. If not, well then, enter philanthro-capitalism.

My concern is when an entitlement program becomes an entitlement *mentality*. That type of mindset becomes extremely toxic to human advancement outside of government reliance. You see it in kids who feel their parents should buy them the latest sneakers or upgraded mobile phone simply because, they say, all their friends have one. You see the entitlement mentality with some long-running government programs: once someone has received money they have not earned, it can be very difficult to give up that cash stream.

One of the reasons that I love Haiti is that you experience very little entitlement mentality there. Because there's limited expectation of any help or support from the government, the Haitian people are extremely self-reliant. Once Caring House Project Foundation provides the philanthro-capitalistic infrastructure—a safe place to live, a place to go to school and to church, clean water, the means to provide their own renewable food in their village, and some form of free enterprise—then the Haitian residents will work hard to support themselves and to care for their homes and families. That's why the twenty-nine villages we have built in Haiti are *still* thriving. They might not be as pretty as they once were, they might be a little dirty and the paint on the buildings might have worn off, but not a single village has failed or been taken over by the government.

This combination of initial support, free enterprise, and self-sufficiency is at the heart of philanthro-capitalism. As minister William J. H. Boetcker wrote in 1916, "You cannot build character and courage by taking away people's initiative and independence. You cannot help people permanently by doing for them, what they could and should do for themselves."[3] Philanthro-capitalism is founded on the premise that people *want* to support themselves rather than living off of handouts from others, and they take greater pride in their own efforts than they ever would from receiving a government dole, ongoing universal income, or any other perpetual subsidy.

CHPF is run based on the principles of philanthro-capitalism. Even when we undertake charitable activities, like our hurricane disaster relief missions in the U.S. and the Bahamas, and our search and rescue work after the earthquake in Haiti, we quickly go back to our core mission of building or rebuilding communities so the people in those locations can get their lives back on a self-sustaining track. The emphasis is to help others in the short term so they can help themselves in the long term. And twenty-nine successful Haiti villages show the validity of our approach.

From Return on Investment to Return on Donation

Almost every week in Palm Beach County and in your area you'll see a story in the local newspaper about this charity golf or tennis tournament, that luncheon, dinner, cocktail party, or black-tie gala, or some other elaborate event for donors. But CHPF has never held a big, stuffy, fancy event like that to raise money. Instead, a few times a year we flew a large group of donors (who paid for the privilege) to Haiti so they could see firsthand the villages that their donations helped to build. We felt that was a better use of donor dollars than feeding them overpriced chicken dinners while wearing penguin suits or hosting yet another open bar.

Besides the beautiful marrying of the best of philanthropy and capitalism, what separates philanthro-capitalism from generic philanthropy is its focus on responsible stewardship and maximizing the impact of donations. For the most part, every dollar CHPF raises goes directly to support our charitable efforts in Haiti and elsewhere. Our overhead is minuscule, and for a nonprofit with a yearly budget of around a half a million dollars, our impact has been disproportionately significant. That's why the Clinton Foundation (established by former president Bill Clinton in 1997, with revenues of more than $42 million a year as of 2019[4]) contacted us in 2016. They wanted to know how our tiny organization was able to get so much done so efficiently in Haiti. How could we build a single-family home for $4,800? How could we build twenty-nine villages in nineteen years with an average cost per fifty-house village of under $300,000? Those are extraordinary results for such a tiny nonprofit.

Our success is due to a concept that every businessperson knows well, and one that I chose to apply to the work of CHPF. You've heard of ROI, return on investment: it's a measure of how effectively a business is spending its money, by calculating the dollar amount spent on an asset or service versus the amount of return or profit that expense produced. As a businessman, I am quite keen on the ROI for my oceanfront artistry, and I expect a substantial return in the form of financial capital—in other words, a monetary profit. So when I chose to take a business approach to CPHF, I coined the phrase ROD, *return on donation*. It's a measure of how far we can stretch our donors' dollars, with the return measured in how much impact their contributions can produce. Capital is measured in human rather than financial terms, and CHPF's profits are the more than thirteen thousand children we have saved and helped to live healthier, better lives.

One of the reasons CHPF does most of its work in Haiti is due to this concept of ROD. In the U.S., there are plenty of social service programs to help the indigent should they seek assistance. In Haiti, there's no such support available, and it's all too common for families to be struggling and starving even when parents are doing everything they can to earn a living. Not only can we fill an urgent need to lift these enterprising people up, but our donor dollars go twenty-five times further than they would in this

---

Capital is measured in human rather than financial terms . . .

---

country when it comes to providing self-sustaining housing to those that need it. While funding shelter for *one homeless person* costs approximately $15,000 in the U.S., as of this writing, CHPF can build a five-hundred-square-foot, two-room house in Haiti, with a front porch, concrete foundation, rebar in the walls (sturdy enough to withstand earthquakes), a metal roof (that can be replaced for less than $250 if it's blown off in a hurricane), a micro-flush toilet, a cistern, and solar power for just $4,800. That two-room house will provide a home for a family of *eight* that were living in a cardboard or mud shack, with palm fronds for a leaky roof and dirt floors. It works out to be about $600 per person for a beautiful new home—that's a huge return (25x) on donation.

What's more, our donors understand there is a *generational* ROD from our villages. Not only are Haitian families being uplifted today, but the lives of their children and their children's children are also being transformed. Every child who survives because he or she can grow up with clean water and adequate food, in a house safe from the elements, with access to medical care and education and some form of free enterprise, is more likely to become a head of a household and a contributing member of society. That's the result of the business approach we take to CHPF. And, just as the Haitians in our villages are self-sufficient and don't rely on the government or charity to sustain themselves, CHPF doesn't rely on government grants, nor does it provide long-term charity to the villages it builds. Because of Haiti's high unemployment rate (in some of the rural villages we work in it can be as high at eighty percent), we employ only Haitian labor and use only Haitian materials to build the villages. Then we provide the initial resources for the residents to grow or fish for their own food; raise their own chickens, goats, or pigs; sew and sell their own clothes; and so on. That's applying philanthro-capitalism to support the CHPF mission.

Heart, Head, Wallet

A shorthand way to describe the difference found in philanthro-capitalism's approach is three elements: *heart, head,* and *wallet.* You see a need that touches your emotions and you want to help in some way. Then your head speaks up, asking, "What should I do?" or perhaps, "How much can or should I do?" If you make the decision to contribute financially, you pull out your wallet or credit card (or you contribute something other than money—more on that later). It's then the responsibility of the group you support to maximize the impact of your donation.

I've seen the power of appealing to the heart at my keynote speeches. Usually toward the end I'll talk about our Caring House Project's Haiti initiative and show photos of the children whose lives have been saved over the last twenty years. Sometimes I'll ask donors who are in the audience to share their experience of visiting Haiti on one of our trips. One donor, Jordan Guernsey, shared this:

> "It's life-changing. Going there and seeing the impact you had, seeing the smiles on the kids' faces. . . . We get so wrapped up in our day-to-day lives of, 'I gotta make money, I gotta be successful.' It's so nice to go to Haiti and see why we're doing this, to see the house you built and be able to give that kid a hug. And that's all they want. They're not asking for anything. They just want to know that someone cares about them. They just want to

be loved. I'm blown away that I was able to go, and I'm looking forward to going again."

That kind of impact on the heart is why we've been able to build entire villages of fifty houses plus a community center, school, church, clinic, clean drinking water, renewable food, and some form of business venture from the generous response of people touched by what they see and hear at just one keynote. By the way, we recently completed the Jordan Guernsey Family Village in honor of Jordan, who passed away at age thirty from cancer.

But as I've said before, compassion without action is a waste of emotion, so philanthro-capitalism also needs to involve the head. We want donors to understand how their money will be used, and also speak directly to whatever they are interested in supporting. It used to be that the only donation categories listed on the CHPF website were our building projects: "Build a house, or part of a house, in a village in Haiti!" But while some people loved that idea, others were more interested in providing education, or clean water, or medical care, or helping the Haitians grow their own food. So now the CHPF website lists seventy-four different options in eight categories (housing, food, water, orphanages, schools, clinics, community centers and miscellaneous) for people to support: everything from buying one chicken for $4.75, to funding an entire village for $300,000.[5] When I speak to a group, I'll talk about donating $4,800 for a new Haiti house, $2,400 for one-half of a house, $1,200 for one-quarter of a house, $45 for a pregnant goat or providing shelter for a child in an orphanage, $11 a month towards clean drinking water, or $42 a month to provide medical care for one person in the village clinic. Whenever someone opens their wallet and clicks a "Donate" button on the CHPF website, they can feel good for three reasons: 1) everyone can find a project that speaks to their heart, 2) the head knows exactly where their donation is going, and 3) there's a donation level suited to almost everyone's wallet. Go ahead, pause your reading or listening and donate now: visit CHPF.org!

Find (or Create) Your Own
Philanthro-Capitalistic Cause

This chapter is my challenge to you to leave behind the shallow satisfactions of consumerism and materialism and embrace responsible stewardship of your blessings. Yes, follow your professional highest calling, and make use of our capitalistic society to benefit materially from your efforts. In other words, make tons of money! I believe that God wants us to have material as well as spiritual abundance, and there's no shame in attaining financial success. It's no accident that there are 2,350 verses in the Old and New Testaments that deal with money and its use.[6] So, take care of yourself and your family. Don't apologize for being rich and living a comfortable lifestyle, and don't deny yourself the luxuries that you truly enjoy. But if ever you feel that your desire for "more" has morphed into an obsession with, and an addiction to, consumerism and materialism, watch out. The constant pursuit of material things is like salt from the ocean seeping into rebar at an oceanfront property: a slow, cancerous spread that will cause the house of your happiness to crumble.

Remember, human beings are not wired to handle excess in an efficient way: not food, drink, sex, money, or success. That's just human beings being human. What our excess *is* good for is to use for the benefit of others. As Rich DeVos wrote in his foreword to my first bestseller, *Make It Big!*, "Frank believes, as I do, that those of us who enjoy a high or comfortable standard of living must thank God for what we have, and vow daily to be responsible, generous stewards of what we have been given." God wants you to be rich so you can use your wealth to benefit others. So go ahead and spend five dollars on that cup of coffee from Starbucks, but realize that if you can buy the cup of coffee, you also can give a cup of coffee, or its equivalent in the form of a Haitian chicken, to someone who is in need.

At the same time, it's important to remember that feeling guilty about what you have does nothing to benefit the people you can and should be helping. After the first few trips I made to Haiti, I stopped buying anything new. I couldn't even go out to a restaurant in Palm Beach and spend $20 on a glorified hamburger—not when I'd just seen kids eating dirt. Finally, I asked my mentor, Rich DeVos, "How do I get over this feeling?" And he shared with me another quote by clergyman William J. H. Boetcker: "You cannot help the poor by destroying the rich. You cannot strengthen the weak by weakening the strong."[7] It's up to all of us to be as successful as we can so we can bring together our professional and spiritual highest callings and be in service to others.

I hope by now you've made the decision to adopt philanthro-capitalism as a philosophy, and you've committed to take action to make it a part of your life. It's actually very simple to do so.

First, *decide where you want to focus your efforts*. Find a cause or a need that speaks to your heart, then use your head to figure out the best way to be of help. You can establish your own charity or foundation, like I did. Now, that's a lot of work, especially if you want to form a nonprofit registered as a 501(c)(3) so your donors can make tax-deductible contributions to your organization. You'll also need to become comfortable with asking others for money for your cause, which is a challenge for some. As I tell my daughter, Laura, Caring House isn't just about going to Haiti and hugging orphans; it requires consistent effort on my part (and our board of directors) and the willingness to ask for donations over and over again.

If setting up a nonprofit feels like too much work, you can commit to take action by donating to an established organization. Many people use CHPF as a conduit for their charitable contributions because they believe in our mission, feel secure in our long-standing track record, and appreciate our approach of maximizing their donations with our focus on ROD. But whatever organization you choose, make sure you are connected to it with both your heart and head before you open your wallet.

Second, *decide what resources you will contribute: time, talent, and treasure*. When I speak about CHPF, every now and then someone will come up to me and say, "Easy for you to talk about donating, Frank; you're rich. What about us ordinary people who can't just pull out a credit card and pay $4,800 to build a house in Haiti?" Here's the good news: your resource wallet contains much more than just the treasure of your money.

You can choose to donate your *time* or your *talent* as well. After all, the one resource that all of us share in equal measure is time, so where can you give your time to help others? Maybe you could go to the retirement home and visit someone who has no family, or volunteer at the children's hospital or the soup kitchen, like I did. Even one hour a week could make a difference.

You also can donate your talent, either directly or as a means of raising money. For a while I was auctioning off an hour's coaching with me as a fundraiser for CHPF. People would come to the tree house and pick my brain either on real estate, or being an author, or ultrarunning, or on setting up a charitable foundation. But lately I've set aside time on Fridays for mentoring the next generation of philanthro-capitalists, showing them how they can increase their ROD and have a greater impact on those they serve. I honor those requests without expectation of any kind of return because I think it's incumbent upon me to share my insights. In many cases your talent and time could be more valuable to others than your cash donation. (To be clear, at CHPF we don't take volunteers to help build our villages, and we don't import materials from the U.S. If we were to do so, we would be taking jobs away from Haitians who desperately need them.)

Always remember, however, even the smallest amount of *treasure* can be incredibly beneficial when it's used in the right way. On the Yugo Wego Tour I stopped in McKinney, Texas, and met an extraordinary woman named Sharlet and her husband, Ely. In 2017, Sharlet decided she didn't want a big, self-indulgent party for her twenty-seventh birthday; instead, she wanted to do something to help others. A month before her birthday, she committed to saving $1 a day from her modest salary so by the end of thirty days she could buy thirty $1 McDonald's hamburgers and feed thirty homeless people. That simple $30 gesture has grown to be a program where Sharlet and other volunteers feed hundreds of homeless people once a month. She calls her charity "Thirty to Infinity" because she envisions being able to care for multitudes. What if you, too, committed to saving $1 a day to contribute to a cause that speaks to your heart and head? By the way, I will personally deliver a copy of *Aspire!* to Sharlet and Ely on the *Aspire!* book tour.

The third commitment is to *make philanthro-capitalism a regular practice*. The Old and New Testament as well as the Quran say that we should give a portion (in Christianity, a tithe) of what we have to God and to those who need our help. Dāna, the concept of generosity to others, is a key spiritual practice in both Hinduism and Buddhism.[8] And as I said in chapter 22, while there's nothing wrong with a one-and-done donation, turning contribution into a regular practice has the potential to transform your reality while you impact the lives of others.

Keeping time, talent, and treasure in mind also will help you fight what's known as donor fatigue. Maybe you're volunteering your time at the soup kitchen and you get burnt out after a year, or you're so exhausted that you can't even think about coaching you daughter's soccer team this season, or you have a financial setback and can't afford to make that donation you were planning to give to CHPF this year. Switch it up: if you can't spare the time for the soup kitchen this month, maybe you can make a donation to them instead. If you can't coach your daughter's team, maybe you could make some calls from home to help with their fundraising efforts. If you can't give financially to CHPF, perhaps you could offer to promote us on your social media feed. In my experience, the important thing isn't *what* you give, but that you *continue* to give as part of your spiritual highest calling and your commitment to philanthro-capitalism.

God blessed King Solomon with a net worth in today's dollars of $2 trillion (ten times wealthier than Jeff Bezos) because Solomon asked, not for riches or honor, but for "a discerning heart" so he would be a good servant of the people he was to govern (1 Kings 3:9, NIV). My hope is that you return to this chapter again and again, to be reminded that our highest purpose is ultimately to serve and uplift those in need, so they in turn can become benefactors of others. And you will discover that, of all the lessons you've received in this book about how to alter your DNA and create your own reality, the spiritual discipline of sharing your blessings found in a philanthro-capitalistic approach will produce the deepest transformation in every area of your life.

Your Hebrews 13:2 Story

When people think of angels, they think flowing robes and halos. But in the Bible, they also look like ordinary people. Why not today?

JOAN WESTER ANDERSON

There's something special about the book of Hebrews in the New Testament that makes it one of my favorites in the Bible. It has so many commonsense passages and quotes that speak to me with such simplicity and clarity. For instance, not long ago I was talking to someone who was diagnosed with cancer, and I shared with her one of my favorite Bible passages, "Now faith is confidence in what we hope for and assurance about what we do not see" (Hebrews 11:1, NIV), to help her have the faith that she will be healed. To my mind, this definition of faith transcends all religion.

A few years ago when I was reading through Hebrews, another quote struck my heart: "Do not forget to show hospitality to strangers, for by so doing some people have shown hospitality to angels without knowing it" (Hebrews 13:2, NIV). It made me think of times when I have helped a homeless person, or any person for that matter, and had an overwhelming feeling that I was engaging with an angel in disguise. Because of the ethereal aura that person gave off, or the way they looked back at me, it felt like a supremely divine moment, as if Christ himself was present.

Then I came across a story by Muhammad Ali, who in 2004 wrote about an encounter with a panhandler on a street in Harlem. The man asked for a dollar, and Ali pulled out his money clip, gave him some money, and then turned to leave. The man grabbed Ali's hand, shook it, looked him in the eyes and said, "I will bless you."

"Now, I'm not saying that was God Himself," Ali wrote, "But how do we know that it wasn't someone working for him, walking around in disguise, just to see what we would do?"[1]

The Hebrews 13:2 verse was one of the primary reasons I chose to undertake the 6,288-mile odyssey known as the Yugo We-go Tour. When I stopped in Little Rock, Arkansas, I had the chance to discuss the passage with Father David at Christ the King Church. Our talk solidified the meaning of Hebrews 13:2 for me. I believe that angels are earthly people we randomly encounter who deliver or radiate a divine yet everyday presence. They are sent by God to enrich our lives by making us better stewards of the gifts we've been given, whether we are consciously aware of these gifts or not. Angels help us see and ultimately share with the world the treasures that lie hidden inside us. I told Father David that during the trip I knew I would encounter such angels in disguise, and I would find other people with experiences similar to Ali and myself. To discover their stories, I would ask nearly everyone I met to tell me their Hebrews 13:2 story.

At one of my earliest stops on the tour I met Vinnie, who had been a nurse at a large Veterans Administration hospital in New Orleans for more than twenty years. He was just walking out of the hospital and was either too busy or too alarmed to stop to talk to me, so I walked alongside him and struck up a conversation. I noticed that among his many tattoos, Vinnie had one on his arm of three crosses, representing Christ and the two thieves being crucified at Golgotha. "Looks like you're a Christian," I said to Vinnie, trying to break the ice. "Can I ask you about a Bible verse?" Then I recited Hebrews 13:2 to him and asked, "Is there any instance where you feel you've encountered an angel or spiritual being?"

"That happens every day," Vinnie answered, as he kept walking.

"I imagine it does," I said. "But was there a time when you looked in the eyes of someone and you knew that it was more than just an individual, but instead someone sent by God?"

Vinnie finally stopped and thought for a moment. Then he said, "There was this one veteran—he still comes to the hospital for treatment, but this was during the first year I worked here so it would have been more than twenty years ago. We were draining fluid from the area around this man's stomach, and as we worked on him, I got a strong feeling that this was a stigmata. You know, when Jesus was being crucified and he was pierced by a lance, and blood and water flowed from his side, and it made the centurion realize that Jesus was the Son of God? I felt certain that the fluid from this veteran was also holy, and I was helping to care for someone very special. The guy and I have become good friends over the years, and I've never felt anything like that around him since then. But it did feel like we shared a sacred moment all those years ago."

The question, "What's your Hebrews 13:2 story?" became a regular feature in all twenty-two cities of the Yugo We-go Tour. I would explain the passage and then ask people if they had ever had such an encounter. Some were reluctant to share their experiences, as they felt the incidents were a little too "out there" or sacred for our very practical world. But once we chatted a little and they understood my intentions were pure, amazing stories came pouring out. I then put the request to others I had met through the years, to share the moments when they felt the touch of something angelic. You'll read some examples of these experiences to follow in what is really a chapter written by those who have shown compassion to strangers who turned out to be angels.

To tell the truth, I'm more excited about the chance to share these encounters with you than any other chapter in this book, and honestly, I could have written an *entire* book from the hundreds of life-changing accounts that were shared with me—and maybe someday I will. Some stories are from those who gave hospitality; others tell of the impact an angel had in someone's life. Regardless, I hope the experiences of angels just like you will inspire you to look a little deeper into the eyes of the people you meet and to treat everyone as angels in disguise, appearing to you unawares and offering you the chance to show hospitality to these messengers from God.

Kevin: Angel in a Rust-Bucket Buick

The year 2008 was nothing short of a nightmare. I lost my career, real estate investments, retirement, marriage, and ultimately time spent with my children. It was devastating; I beat myself up a lot that year. I ended up moving from Flint, Michigan, to Knoxville, Tennessee, for work. I was often alone, depressed, and miserable. I felt that my life was useless, excruciatingly painful, and I was borderline suicidal.

Because I was living alone, I often went to Cracker Barrel at the end of the day. Every evening, after eating their grilled chicken with three sides of mac-n-cheese, I'd sit in a front porch rocker with my ear buds in, listening to Pearl Jam and trying to motivate myself and/or question God as to why all this had happened to me.

In the middle of one of these rocking chair "therapy sessions," I watched a junky, old, tan, rust-bucket Buick LeSabre pull into the parking lot about fifteen feet away. A scraggly, unkempt, middle-aged man smoking a cigarette got out and started walking toward me, saying something that I couldn't hear as my music was turned up so loud.

He walked right up to me and politely waited for me to ask what I could do for him. Annoyed at the smell of cigarette smoke and the thought that he was just going to ask for money or directions, I jerked out one ear bud and asked, "Can I help you with something?"

He looked me straight in the eyes and said, "God wanted me to tell you to just commit and that everything will be all right."

He smiled a toothy smile as if he knew I'd been judging him from the moment I laid eyes on him. Then he turned around, walked back to his LeSabre, semi-slammed the creaky car door, started the engine, backed out, and in a cloud of smoky fumes noisily drove away.

I was stunned. I sat there with one ear bud in and the other one dangling, music aimlessly blasting, for what seemed an eternity. I literally had been begging God for answers and wondering what to do next with my life, or even if I should keep it, and He had sent the most unlikely angel imaginable.

God uses angels who come in forms we least expect to not only deliver messages for us but about us, and our opportunities for growth. I will never again judge myself or others by either their books or their covers, but rather by how God sees me, and how He sees those who have made mistakes and who may be hurting.

Tatiana: The Eyes of Christ

What I'm about to share I've never told anyone, and it happened to me when I was seven years old. I'm thirty-four now.

I grew up in Nantua, France, and was raised in a very religious family, going to church every Sunday. One day I was on my way to the supermarket with my mother and siblings. When I got out of the car, as we started walking toward the store, I noticed a man, dressed in shabby clothes with a scruffy grey beard, leaning against the side of the building. While I had always been very afraid of strangers, and my mom warned me to stay away from them, for some reason I was drawn to this man.

My mom noticed my reaction and said it was okay for me to go and talk to him, and if I wanted, I could give him something. She gave me one franc (less than twenty-five cents), and I mustered up the courage to walk over there alone. My knees were shaking as I approached him. As I came around from behind him and peered into his deep blue eyes, I became mesmerized. I was drowning in a feeling of love, one that I never experienced in any church before or since. I had held this image of what I thought Christ looked like in my mind, and there, standing before me, was that image. The man had a kind and gentle soul, different from any other I had ever experienced in the short time I'd been alive. He took my hand, smiled and softly said, "Merci beaucoup" as he walked away.

This angelic encounter will stay with me for as long as I live. And by the way, Frank, meeting you at the locked gates of the Church of the Holy Cross in Sedona, Arizona, where you gave me your book *The Tap* and asked me to share my Hebrews 13:2 story, was another divine moment for me. I'm glad we met that day.

Jennifer: The Power of a Smile

Since I was a teenager, it was put on my heart to acknowledge people, to look at them and smile no matter how you may be feeling, as you never know what someone else is dealing with. This particular day, I was walking down the street, and I noticed this young girl about my age heading towards me from the opposite direction. Her demeanor was sluggish, she walked with her head down, and she wore a hoodie that covered most of her face. I remember thinking, *I MUST smile at her.* It was almost like a game, but I wasn't sure how I'd get her to look at me.

As she got closer I thought it wasn't going to happen. But just as we were about to pass, she looked up, and our eyes met. I smiled so big because I did it—I got her to look up! She responded with a half-crooked smile, and we both walked on.

A couple of weeks later, the same girl walked up to me on that same street. She told me how on that day, at that very moment, she was on her way to end her life: she had tons of pills in her pocket that she intended on taking. She said she felt invisible to this world, and that no one would even know she was gone. But when we made eye contact and I smiled at her, she realized that she *wasn't* invisible—and she chose to live.

Angelo: Cheetos and a Clothespin

This moment still seems like yesterday even though it happened thirty-two years ago. On Thanksgiving I was helping at a soup kitchen at a church on the New Haven Green at Yale University. I was scooping soup from large buckets into bowls, to serve to the homeless people who lined up that evening. That's when an elderly gentleman's bag caught my eye. It was a satchel with everything he owned on his back, and sticking out of the top was a bag of Cheetos® held shut with a clothespin.

I was marveling how I had never seen a clothespin used in that manner when the gentleman caught me looking at him. I believe he thought that I was eying his bag of Cheetos. What happened next was astonishing: even though it was one of only about ten belongings he owned, he offered me his bag of Cheetos!

I was sincerely moved by this act of kindness and generosity. Here I was helping others at a soup kitchen when this stranger helped inspire me to be a better person and focus on serving others before being served. This way of living hasn't left me since that moment thirty-two years ago.

Linda: The Holy Spirit Told Me to Stop

In 2014, I saw a man in the bushes beside the road. I assumed he was sleeping off a night of drinking. But then the Holy Spirit told me to stop. *What???* I thought. I proceeded to the grocery store and, anxiously tapping on my steering wheel, I stewed in the parking lot for a few minutes and then decided to drive back to check on the man. It turned out he was stuck and couldn't get himself up. He was recently released from the hospital and was very frail.

Two strangers saw me trying to help him up and came over to assist. I had already watched three people pass him by earlier. (Hmm . . . where have I read that before?) We managed to get him on his feet, and I got back in my car. But the Holy Spirit said, "You are not done yet," so I went to Starbucks and got him some water, coffee, and food.

I learned a profound lesson that day: don't judge the condition of others. And remember that Jesus says: whatever we do for others, it is as if we did it for Him. #humbled.

Debbie: Make a Point to Say Good Morning

I was grocery shopping one morning before work when I saw a young lady sitting in front of the store. She had several different colors of hair and rings in her eyebrow and nose. I noticed how people just passed her and never even acknowledged her.

At one time I was that girl, so I decided not to ignore her but to talk to her and see if there was something I could do to help. She said she was hungry, so I said, "Let's go inside and get you something to eat." As we walked through the store I knew people were looking at us, so I made a point to say good morning to them.

The young lady was so nice and appreciated the food. I never saw her again but I know she helped me remember not to ignore people just because they are different but instead to say good morning and take a walk with them.

James: Be an Angel of Generosity

On a long-distance bicycling trip throughout the U.S., I was inside a bike shop in Springfield, Missouri, when a homeless person came in. He was a veteran with no legs, confined to a wheelchair, and he started to bother one of the employees over a lost debit card. He was going on about how it held access to all the money he had—about $300, he said. He was somewhat out of it, but it was clear he was really upset.

As I was leaving the store I walked by and slipped $500 in cash into his wheelchair, then I just walked out and pedaled off. The guy in the wheelchair didn't notice me do it, which made it all that more fun. My hope was he would spend the next few days trying to figure out where it came from!

Another time I took my sick dog to the emergency vet to get checked out. There was a couple there who were talking about putting their dog to sleep. I overheard the whole conversation and asked the doctor why they wanted such a young beautiful dog put down. He said that they couldn't afford the medical treatment. When I asked him how much it was, he said $1,400. I pulled out my AmEx card and paid the bill.

One of my favorite Hebrews 13:2 moments happened during a food drive at a local TV station. They were looking for donations but weren't getting much cash in, so I thought I'd put them over the top. I showed up at the station, filthy dirty, riding my bicycle, and handed the reporter a check for $10,000. The coolest thing was the surprised look he had when I pedaled off!

Awin: An Anonymous Gift Saves a Marriage

Thirteen years ago I was doing a summer internship at the court near Zurich during my law studies, and I met a young couple with a newborn baby during a court session prior to their official divorce verdict. They said their problems had started when the husband lost the family savings in a bad investment, causing massive financial problems that had triggered even bigger problems in their relationship. I don't know why, but I had an overwhelming feeling that this couple was not supposed to split up. The whole evening at home I thought about coming up with a way I could help this family stay together.

The next day I went to work earlier than usual. Before the first court session started, I looked in the couple's file to see if I could provide something that could possibly help them rethink their decision. But the only information I could find in the file was an address and the schedule of the hearing for their final divorce decree. That date was very soon, so I had to act quickly.

I decided to withdraw from my bank account some of the money I had saved for an upcoming summer session of law school. Something guided me to put it in an envelope and drive to the address I had found in their file. I wore big sunglasses and dressed differently so they wouldn't recognize me in case I happened to see them. A woman opened the door of their building and said the couple wasn't at home. I handed her the envelope and said, "This is a document for Sarina (the newborn baby)." And before the woman could ask any questions, I left.

On the way back home, although I had no clue whether the money would help change their decision or even make it to the couple, something inside told me I did the right thing. A week later we received a letter from the couple's lawyer with an official request to cancel the divorce hearing. I smiled in silence and felt my heart smile as well. I was grateful to have been able to help a young poor family whom I didn't even know. And they'll never know who brought that envelope to their door.

A few years later I decided to look up the family on social media and was delighted to see a picture of all three of them around the Christmas tree. I thought how sometimes minor moves can make major impacts. In such moments it is God who puts us to the test and gives us the means to offer a helping hand to strangers.

One Final Story from Me

Not all people who are homeless have a shelter, yet some provide emotional shelter for others living on the street, and it's truly angelic to witness. At the start of this section you heard a little about Stevie, the twenty-eight-year-old transsexual autistic savant who is the self-designated caregiver for a group of homeless people living in a park by a stream in Manitou Springs, Colorado. I met Stevie on my first night in Manitou Springs on the Yugo We-go Tour. When I decided to get a pizza and eat it in the park, I saw a group of people by the stream and thought that I'd like to give them the rest of my pizza. So I put six $5 bills in the box and walked over to the group. Someone popped up from sitting cross-legged in the dirt and cheerfully approached me as I was walking over. This person introduced themself as "Indigo," who later told me their real name, Stevie. Stevie thanked me, took the pizza box—and promptly divided up the pizza and money equally and shared it with the others sitting by the stream.

For two more nights I bought a pizza and delivered it to my new friends in the park. Each time Stevie would make sure the other homeless people living there got a piece of pizza and an equal share of the money. Stevie never took anything for Stevie.

On my final night in town, as I was on my way to buy the last pizza, Stevie saw me walking along and cheerfully called out, "Hi Frank, how are you? Hope you had a good day on your tour for your new book." I couldn't see Stevie; I could only hear the voice. I later returned with the pizza and spent time with my new friends by the stream in the park before saying goodbye.

The way that Stevie called my name across the parking lot—just a voice coming from the woods—brought me to tears. Stevie has a soul that radiates love like few people I've encountered. Not only was Stevie an angel to me, but Stevie was also an angel for that small group of people in their care, making sure everybody else had the pizza and a share of the money I put in the pizza box. Stevie's example touches me whenever I remember sitting on the banks of that stream in Colorado, surrounded by people with whom Jesus would have felt right at home. I still can feel the love radiating from Stevie, and it inspires me to look for more opportunities to give to the invisible, unexpected angels that God puts in my path.

Go find your angel, your Stevie—today, this week, this life.

If you'd like to share your Hebrews 13:2 story, visit TheAspireBook.com and you can do so right there! I'm sure others and I would love to read of your encounter.

With Aspiration YOU Will Change the World

25

Our aspirations are our possibilities.

SAMUEL JOHNSON

ongratulations! You've made it to the final chapter, and I want to acknowledge you. For me, writing this book has been an epic odyssey of exploration, a journey to the pinnacle of the aspiration cosmos, and I hope you have had even a taste of the same experience reading it. I also hope you already have started to adopt some of the practices described in these pages to help you lead a more fulfilling, joyful, and aspirational life.

Let's do a quick recap of the primary lessons of this book.

- YOU EAGERLY STARTED OUT IN THE VERY FIRST SECTION understanding that motivation washes off like soap that goes down the drain, inspiration wears off in a few days like a bad sunburn, but aspiration (an almost otherworldly desire to achieve something high or great) will alter your DNA and allow you to create your own reality, forever changing your life and the lives of those you love.

  You answered three key questions that will help you define who you want to become: 1) *What do you aspire to accomplish that's beyond your current ability to comprehend?* 2) *Who do you aspire to emulate?* and 3) *What legacy do you aspire to leave behind?* You also learned the critical importance of being an executioner, getting the mind right and the money will follow, and being willing to reinvent and renew at any point in your life.

- **IN SECTION 2** you discovered that fear is simply a signal you are facing a risk associated with a big change or challenge in your life, and the only way to grow is to exercise your risk tolerance like a muscle on a regular basis. You also came to know that risk Requires Intense Self-Knowledge (R.I.S.K.) and you must apply relentless forward motion on a daily basis. Most important, you understood that you don't have to change even the "worst" personal characteristic—you simply can redirect your energies into more positive aspirations.

- **SECTION 3** focused on one of my favorite topics, personal branding: the art of amplifying your essence to the point where your customers (current or future) become subliminally intoxicated with you first, then your product or service. You discovered that creating a powerful, dynamic, authentic personal brand allows you to live more of your inside on the outside. Then you learned how to take an artist's approach to your life and your work, become comfortable with exhibiting a healthy sense of ego, and let your creativity and ingenuity out to play.

- **SECTION 4**, on relationships, isn't really an area of my expertise, but my relationship with Nilsa for more than thirty-four years has enriched my life beyond measure while teaching me more valuable lessons than any other aspiration I've pursued. In this section you heard about choosing your significant other and the joys of finding a guardian angel who will help uplift you when you fall. You understood how to use the inevitable pressure in a relationship to make it as strong as a diamond rather than tearing it apart. You also discovered ways to increase your personal "magnetic-ism" to attract the people and situations you desire in your life, and how to turn up the heat in the bedroom by giving mind-blowing sex to your partner.

- **FINALLY, IN SECTION 5,** which is the core of the book, you learned how to create true fulfillment by connecting to something bigger than yourself and becoming a responsible steward of your riches by using them in service of others. You understood the importance of identifying and following both your professional and spiritual highest callings, and why it's critical not only to feel compassion for others but to act on it consistently. You left behind the seductions of consumerism and materialism for the practice of philanthro-capitalism: using your time, talent, and treasure to uplift others by providing them with the means to create a generational, self-sustaining existence. Finally, you recognized the presence of angels in our midst, there to enrich our lives by making us better stewards of the gifts we've been given.

Assuming you've done (or are in the process of doing) even a tenth of what's described in this book, you should have made progress toward accomplishing the aspirations and creating the legacy you designed for yourself in section 1. You also should have discovered a *purpose* that will continue to drive you until you achieve those aspirations. In personal development, people talk about passion all the time, telling you to "follow your passion" if you want to be fulfilled. Well, even though I'm a passionate guy, I feel that's bad advice. Passion is like motivation or inspiration: great in the moment but lasting only a day or two at most. Instead, get to the *why*, your purpose, the big reason you're here on earth. Purpose, fueled by the energy of your aspirations, will draw you to pursue what's most important to you in life and will exponentially increase your impact.

I hope that I've touched a nerve—your aspiration nerve—and caused you to aspire to leave a lasting legacy that you and your family and their families will be proud of. In my life, I've aspired to only five big things:

#1: *Be a bestselling author.*

#2: *Finish Badwater.*

#3: *Be a real estate artist.*

#4. *Run a charity in the poorest country in the Western Hemisphere.*

#5: *Family.*

While some of my aspirations have taken a quarter-century to accomplish (or are still a work in progress), I'm proud to say that I've done what I set out to do. I've written seven bestselling books in six different categories. I've run Badwater twelve times and finished seven. (Five times more people have summited Everest than have finished Badwater, and only twenty-two people have finished the race more than I have.) I've created more than forty magnificent oceanfront masterpieces that set records for price and luxury. With the generosity of its donors, CHPF has built twenty-nine self-sustaining villages in Haiti that support over thirteen thousand children and their families. And my relationships with my wife and daughter provide enormous fulfillment and happiness to all three of us.

That's a lot to celebrate. At the same time, for the past year or more I've been asking a question—one that you too should consider as part of our final chapter together.

What's next?

Time to Reinvent

Remember the quote from *Rocketman:* "You gotta kill the person you were born to be in order to become the person you want to be." Ultimately, this book is all about *reinvention*. It's about never settling for who you are "supposed" to be, or even what you think you're capable of, and instead breaking free of that limited mindset to, yes, alter your DNA and create a new reality on your terms. But the most important time to reinvent is not restricted to when you're unhappy with your life and want a change: it's key to do the same when you're coming off of the high of accomplishing exactly what you set out to do. This approach is counter to most thinking, yet it provides the greatest opportunity for lasting, and dare I say, explosive transformation.

When I announced that 3492 South Ocean would be my final oceanfront masterpiece, a lot of people asked me, "Why are you retiring? You're still so young, and that's the best house you ever built." My answer was this: "A Renaissance man shifts passion at the peak of his or her endeavor. I've never loved what I do more or been better at it than at this very moment, but that tells me it's time to redirect my passion and purpose into a new, exciting direction." You don't want to be that man or woman in corporate America, walking into a conference room to hear, "Congratulations on your thirty years, here's your cake and a fake Rolex." And you don't want to come to the end of an endeavor only to struggle to find a new aspiration. It's in those moments of elevation, when you're at the top of your game, that you need to envision what your next great pursuit will be. Then, if

---

Ultimately, this book is all about *reinvention*.

---

you have the courage, you can walk away at the pinnacle and shift your aspirations into something new. That "something new" is found as you, the visionary, boldly peer into your crystal ball and clearly see the future, with the image becoming more accurate as you gain experience.

I'm not saying that you shouldn't celebrate your accomplishments before you move forward. As you read in chapter 3, you should not only enjoy the extraordinarily golden moments when you reach a goal but also relish the process of attaining it. But don't try to hang onto a moment once it's done. *Savor everything. Cling to nothing.* I've seen too many people take newspaper articles about their victories or achievements, frame them, and hang them on their walls, trying to keep alive those glory days. I choose a different approach: whenever an article comes out about me, one of my oceanfront properties, a daredevil stunt, a Badwater race, or our latest village in Haiti, I read it once, slowly, enjoying the acknowledgment, and then I put it away so Laura and her kids can read about the small scar their grandfather left on the world. I appreciate the moment and then move on. I want to keep my focus on the new reality that I'm creating today.

I'm not saying that it's easy to walk away from an aspiration that you've poured your heart and soul into for years. In the introduction to this book, I described looking in the rearview mirror as I drove away from Florida at the start of the Yugo We-go Tour: I felt that I was driving away from what had given me purpose for thirty years. And I'll be honest, there are still times that it's been tough to give up that identity. Occasionally I'll still get calls from realtors who want advice on big transactions, or offer me tempting oceanfront opportunities, and it feels really good to engage that part of my brain and emotions again. I'm not ruling out a comeback in my real estate career at some point in my life, and if there is one, I assure you it will look totally different from what I've done before. But for the most part, I've dissociated myself from the identity of a real estate artist who builds oceanfront masterpieces in Florida, because I know I'll create better things ahead—if I maintain the courage to turn my face to the future.

That's one of the reasons that Nilsa and I are spending most of our time in the small mountain town of Canton, North Carolina. It reminds me of Delray Beach thirty years ago, with its much slower pace. It's the perfect place for us to get away from the "lifestyles of the rich and famous" vibe of Palm Beach County. We won't give up our house in Delray Beach—yet. But Nilsa and I are ready for something new.

I'll admit that leaving behind the aspirations that fed my adrenaline addiction can be a process. It's not something you can just yank out of the vein in your arm, so to speak, not without some significant withdrawal pains. And I'm probably going to pursue ways to get a little adrenaline drip every now and then, even in the mountains of North Carolina. But what's the old saying: "The only thing that stays the same is reinvention"? (Since I don't believe in change, that's my version of it.) Life can be grand if you are willing at any point to kill the person you are in order to become someone new. You don't have to do a 180 like I've done, and go from building multimillion-dollar oceanfront mansions to living in a town with a population of a little over four thousand and more churches per square mile than grocery stores. But you do have to seek out a new purpose to drive your passion and be willing to leave behind the routines and patterns that have created success for you in the past.

As all professional athletes know, sometimes you are forced to reinvent yourself. In 2021 I didn't qualify to run the Badwater 135 Ultramarathon, the first year since 2005 that I failed to make the cut. So I decided that I would run fifty-eight miles of the Badwater course for my birthday, one mile for each year of my life. No other participants, no crew other than Nilsa, no t-shirt, no finisher's belt buckle, no fanfare at all. I would begin at the race's starting line in Death Valley at minus-282 feet, below sea level, on Sunday, June 27; I'd run through the night and finish on Monday (my birthday), fifty-eight miles later, at the top of Towne Pass, 4,956 feet above sea level. At that time of year, temperatures in Death Valley average between 110 and 120 degrees during the day, but since I've run Badwater twelve times before, I knew what to expect. Or so I thought.

When Nilsa and I arrived at the starting line in Death Valley, the temperature was already 109 degrees. (To give you some context, when the temperature exceeds 110, the National Park Service can suspend the Badwater race.) As I started to run, temperatures quickly rose to 125 degrees. Even though I backed my pace waaay down, by mile 26 I had to stop due to heat exhaustion bordering on heat stroke. We drove back to

The mind is willful and forgetful, and the body, not so much.

the hotel, where Nilsa eventually was able to lower my body temperature with cold towels. We waited until nightfall, then drove back to mile 26 so I could run the remaining thirty-two miles of my race. However, my undertrained body—and Death Valley—had other ideas. That night the temperature never dropped below 109. I ran/power-walked all the way to Stovepipe Wells, mile 42, which is the second checkpoint during the actual race, but at that point I had nothing left, and we called my birthday "race." I was disappointed, but I decided to focus on the miles I had run successfully and declared I was celebrating my forty-second birthday all over again.

That solo run in 2021 was an opportunity to re-evaluate my aspiration to run the Badwater 135 Ultramarathon. While I'm proud that only twenty-two people have finished the race more times than I have, I don't know if I'll ever finish it again, much less get to the top tier of the record books by finishing the race ten times. With the twelve times that I've qualified to enter Badwater, I've proved that I can push my body and mind to extraordinary levels. But at this point, it might be time to appreciate what I have accomplished and then reinvent, renew, and refresh this particular aspiration. I say that with the crystal-clear understanding that hope and belief can be a blessing and a curse. The mind is willful and forgetful, and the body, not so much. Never say never, but it may be time to look to the future and find new races to run. (It's just so damn hard to type that . . .)

As you look at your own aspirations and the areas of your life that you need to reinvent, here are a few more questions you should consider.

What are you doing all this for?

Are your aspirations and your purpose big enough?

Are you pursuing goals that are worthy of you and that you are capable of accomplishing?

And what if you knew that by following your aspirations you could *change the world*?

Yes, You Can Change the World

Everything you have learned in this book has one simple goal: to help you live your aspirations, alter your life at the level of your DNA, and ultimately to create a new reality for you and the people you love. But in this final chapter, I'm going to come clean: that's not my sole purpose in writing this book. Yes, I want you to aspire to accomplish things that are beyond your current ability to comprehend. I hope you will take what you've learned, put it into practice, and as a result, change reality—but not just for yourself, not just for your family, and not just for the people you do business with or mentor. **I want to enroll you in a mission to change the world.**

Remember the core message of section 5: lasting happiness (which is the emotion we are all seeking) comes not just from fulfilling our aspirations but from helping others as part of those aspirations. Running Badwater, writing books, and creating oceanfront masterpieces mean so much more when I use those aspirations to raise money for Caring House Project

Foundation. And as I said in the introduction to this section, I'm happy with the knowledge that my legacy won't be the multimillion-dollar houses that I built or the records I set in selling them. Instead, my greatest legacy will be the thousands of children—and their children, and their children's children—who grow up healthier and happier in our Haitian villages.

But I will admit that for many years, whenever I drove to the airport in Haiti after a ribbon-cutting for one of those villages, I would get incredibly depressed. With all due respect and love for the Haitian people, for two solid hours outside of the car windows I'd see the same terrible poverty, the same blight, the same slums; I'd see naked children on the streets begging for food as we drove by. I'd think, *Oh, my God, no matter how much I do, I'm not making any difference whatsoever.* Then one day it came to me: I needed to change my definition of what "making a difference" means. It doesn't take eliminating malaria, or curing cancer, or fixing climate change (although those are all admirable goals for governments and big foundations). **Every time you change the world for one person, you are changing the entire world.**

Let me explain. As of 2021 there were 7.9 billion people on the planet. (Check the world population clock for the latest figures.[1]) Every one of those 7.9 billion individuals perceives the world through their own eyes. In essence, every one of us creates our world every single moment we are alive. Your world is *the* world, perceived through the eyes of the beholder. Your world is *the* world because it's the only world you live in. Therefore, whenever you uplift a life—with a smile, a bottle of water, a dollar given away, a village built, or a helping hand of any kind—you have changed the *entire* world with your gesture.

This realization was a huge breakthrough for me. It broadened my joy, and I no longer felt that my efforts to make a difference in Haiti and elsewhere were futile, minimalized, or in vain. Each of us has the capability in any moment to change the world, and that's a beautiful, powerful thing. When you ask a homeless person their name and to share a little bit about themselves, you are changing *the* world. When you share what you have with others, like Sharlet with her McDonald's hamburgers and

Stevie who gave pizza and money to everyone else instead of keeping it, you are changing *the* world. When you donate a chicken or a pregnant goat or a whole house to a family in Haiti, you are changing *the* world. You don't have to be Bill Gates or Oprah Winfrey or some huge foundation to make a difference. Whenever you act on your compassion, or contribute to someone as a philanthro-capitalist, you have changed *the* world through the eyes of that individual. You don't have to affect all 7.9 billion people in the world; you just need to change it for one person at a time.

I'm not alone in understanding how helping one person changes the entire world. Mother Teresa's Order of the Missionaries of Charity has always focused its mission on helping individuals in their most difficult moments. Mother Teresa said, "Never worry about numbers. Help one person at a time and always start with the person nearest you." I thought about Mother Teresa when I read an article recently about a gentleman in Nanjing, China, who has spent his weekends for thirteen years patrolling a Yangtze River bridge that is the most popular spot in the world for committing suicide. He's not a professional social worker or psychologist; he simply starts conversations with people who look despondent or lonely or who are just loitering on the busy bridge, and helps them to make a different decision that potentially fateful day. Over the years he has managed to save more than three hundred lives.[2] Talk about the ultimate in changing *the* world!

Whenever you change the perception of one person, you don't know what the effects of that are going to be. Think back over your life. Who changed the world for *you* with one gesture, one word, or one action that made a huge difference? Maybe it was a teacher, coach, or clergyman who encouraged you to believe in yourself. Maybe it was a relative or good friend who stopped you from doing something stupid and got you back on track. Maybe it was your spouse, partner, or child who changed your world with their love. Or (as you read in chapter 24) it was someone on the street who smiled at you at the moment you needed it most. What were the instances that changed the direction of your life for good? Well, it's time for you to do the same for others.

This entire book has never been just about you. The only way to move from rich to enriched, to live a life of purpose and passion, and to ensure that at the end of your life you can look back on a legacy that will make you and your loved ones proud and happy, is to serve others, especially those who need your help the most. As Jesus said in the Sermon on the Mount, "Whatever you did for one of the least of these brothers and sisters of mine, you did for me" (Matthew 25:40, NIV). The only way to change the world as a whole is to change it for one person at a time.

A Few Final Words

At many stops along the Yugo We-go Tour I would find a Catholic church and go to mass in the morning before I hit the road. In Aspen I stuck around after mass to talk with the priest, Father Derek Lear. In the course of our conversation we struck up a friendship, and I decided that I felt comfortable enough to ask Father Lear to hear my confession face to face. In the Catholic church you're supposed to go to confession regularly, but it had been about a year since I had gone, and as you might imagine, it took a while.

At the end of confession, the priest gives you a penance to help you atone for the sins you've committed. Well, Father Lear was very creative. I had told him about the rosary I carry with me everywhere: I had received it from Pope (now Saint) John Paul II in a private audience in 2004, and to me it's a sacred relic. A rosary has five sections, or "decades," with ten beads per decade upon which you say ten Hail Mary's, and one bead at the end of each decade where you say one Our Father. As my penance, Father Lear told me to say the rosary, and each time I held a bead, to focus on something I was grateful for.

I'd never had a priest tell me to do something like that, but I went back to a pew in the church, knelt down, and began what was to be fifty-five moments of gratitude. For the first few beads I wasn't really feeling anything. By the third or fourth one in, however, I found myself looking at my life in a new way. I'll spare you all fifty-five thankful thoughts, but

I reflected on Nilsa and Laura and thanked God for having them in my life. I remembered how sick I had been earlier in the year and thanked God for bringing me back from a life-threatening illness. I thanked God for the children in Haiti whom I'd been privileged to help out of poverty. I thanked Him for all the incredible people I had met on the road as part of the tour, for the people who had supported me through the years, and for those who supported our charity in Haiti. I thanked God for being able to pursue my professional and spiritual callings, for the gift of my real estate artistry, for allowing me to write my seven books, and for my twelve Badwater experiences. I thanked Him for the naysayers and doubters, and those who had told me I'd never amount to anything. I thanked Him for the cops who'd arrested me, the judges who jailed me, the school officials who had expelled me, and anyone who had done their best to save me from my own negative tendencies. Most of all, I thanked God for my life, and the circuitous, bumpy, self-inflicted-wounds-filled path that He had given me to live. If there was ever a poster child for the power of the grace of God and aspiration to transform a life, it's Frank McKinney. I'm truly grateful for the path that led me to write this book for you and to share my ideas and insights as honestly as I can. I hope you'll revisit and reread this book as you follow your aspirations throughout your life.

Winston Churchill once wrote, "You create your own universe as you go along." No one is given a sentence at birth, be it a good sentence, a privileged sentence, or a death sentence. Every day you have an opportunity to rewrite your DNA by choosing to reinvent yourself and redirect your life. At any point in time you can listen to the whispers inside that say, "You're greater than this. You're more than this. You were born to fulfill greater aspirations and to leave a bigger legacy. When are you going to be brave enough to live the life you truly desire?" You can discover your purpose, the reason you are here, and let the energy it produces lead you to accomplish what many people think is impossible. Most of all, as Theodore Roosevelt described it, your place will be with those who strive valiantly, dare greatly, and while they may experience setback and failure, they come to the end of their lives knowing they have sought to accomplish what was beyond the ability of others to comprehend.[3]

While I've done a tour for each of the six books I've written, and I'll do the same with the "Frank McKinney's *Aspire!* Book Tour," my tours are a little different. I don't just go to TV stations, radio stations, and bookstores. Instead, I visit homeless shelters, soup kitchens, food pantries, juvenile detention centers, jails, veterans' facilities, abused women's shelters, and so on. During one tour I swapped places with homeless people in twenty-three cities, putting them up in hotels while I slept under bridges and on the streets. Between those tours and all the outreach Caring House Project

When are you going to be brave enough to live the life you truly desire?

Foundation has done, I calculate that I have met ten thousand homeless people face to face, and I always make a point to look each person in the eye, shake their hand, and say, "What's your name? Tell me a little bit about yourself and where you're from." I'm inevitably humbled in those moments by the dignity and humanity of these souls whom most of us look past when we encounter them on the street. They have taught me a profound lesson: human beings live for purpose and appreciation. We need purpose to give our days and lives meaning, and we want to feel appreciated, both for what we do and, more important, for who we are.

I think the simplest definition of a successful life is feeling that we are living our purpose and being appreciated for who we are. For that, you don't need to fulfill huge aspirations. You don't need to launch yourself into space, or cure malaria, or make a billion dollars, or lift thousands of people out of poverty. All you need to do is to change the world, one person at a time.

Creating the kind of reality that brings you joy and fulfillment is a process, not a result. The chances you discover this new reality and alter your DNA are in direct proportion to the amount of truth you can take without running away. I've provided quite a bit of truth in *Aspire!* How much are you ready to take? How much of everything that you've held dear are you ready to have shattered without running away, back to the safety of the old reality, the old DNA, the old you?

You don't fear the unknown: you can't fear something you don't know. What you fear is leaving the known. So, get back into the gym of sharing your blessings and taking action consistently. Yes, you'll get fatigued. You'll need to remind yourself again and again why you are working so hard, even when it may seem your efforts are not making any difference. But remember, God will not lay any call upon your heart without giving you the means of answering it and making it a reality. When your heart and mind devise an aspiration, even one that's beyond your current ability to comprehend, much less accomplish, you have the ability to make it happen—even when that aspiration is to change the world. And yes, the end result is a new reality, a new DNA, and a new life.

Acknowledgments

Writing a book is very much like an ultramarathon. In fact, it's far longer and more grueling. From writing the first word to holding the first book off the press, the process can take well over a year. To succeed at running an ultramarathon, with success defined for me as seeing the finish line, you need an all-star crew to help get you there. In the case of the world renowned 135-mile Badwater Ultramarathon, there is no mile five, let alone breaking the finishing tape at mile 135, without that stellar crew. With *Aspire!* being my seventh book, and also having finished seven Badwater ultramarathons, I know a good crew when I experience one (or seven!).

Who made this book possible? Who inspired me to *Aspire!?*

I must begin with my crew chief, Victoria St. George of Just Write. Vicki collaborated with me on all 111,111 words you've read. It was really special to work with the person who collaborated with me twenty years ago on my first bestseller, *Make it BIG!* She gets me and is one of the few who are able to capture my essence. I think it shows in what you experienced reading this book.

Deciding to leave my beloved publisher of four of my six prior bestsellers and create the publishing entity Caring House Books for *Aspire!* was a huge undertaking. We chose to publish both a hardback and paperback version on the same date, with the Audible version to follow quickly. If it weren't for the publishing guidance and expertise of Karen Risch Mott (who also collaborated on my books *The Tap* and *Burst This! Frank McKinney's Bubble-Proof Real Estate Strategies),* you would not be holding the book you are today.

I did something with *Aspire!* that I didn't do with my other six books: I embarked on a 6,288-mile pre-release book tour to interview dozens of people for the book. I stopped in twenty-two cities over a month-long span to gather data, gauge sentiment, and collect content feedback on much of what you read. You read about people like Stevie, Tatiana, Vinnie, Debbie, Darnell, Robert, and many more, and saw how they applied elements found in this book to lead very aspirational lives. Thank you to all these angels of aspiration for your contribution.

I'm a very visual person, and although I've created some of the most beautiful oceanfront mansions in the world, I can barely read a set of blueprints. I need three dimensions. I need color. I not only dream in color; I make reality colorful. Just look at the book cover you're holding! I want to thank Erik Hollander for creating this Monet-besting work of art. Erik also created the cover art for *The Other Thief; Dead Fred, Flying Lunchboxes and the Good Luck Circle;* and *The Tap*.

A book is a business in itself, one that doesn't sell itself. You've got to be the adamant advocate, the carnival barker, the megaphone. Much of the graphic art that was created for the promotional pieces for *Aspire!* were done by Brian Kay, who I've worked with for a decade.

I not only dream in color; I make reality colorful.

Coming from a guy who has folded the end of the toilet paper in each bathroom of his oceanfront masterpieces to a perfect diamond-tip point and lined up the screwheads in each of his electrical cover plates to flawlessly align north-south, rest assured I am hyper-sensitive to the minutest of details. The font styles, sizes, spacing, color gradient, section starts, chapter starts, interior images layout, endnotes, and, yes, even that Library of Congress and copyright page that *nobody* reads but me are the product of the mastery of Robert Mott, the angel who took the devil out of the details.

I added someone new to the crew for the creation of an NFT that was distributed to 111 lucky people who attended "Frank McKinney's Aspire

Book Launch Experience" on 11.11.21. The supremely talented James Sommerville was responsible for the revitalization of the brand identities for Coke, Virgin, Adidas, and Heineken, to name a few. I know James will do the same for *Aspire!*

Speaking of the book launch, that circus-like sensory assault on the senses would not have been possible without Sarah Martin and the team at Experience Epic. Sarah has worked on many of my grand unveilings, launches, and reveals.

Shortly after the book launch, I will leave for "Frank McKinney's *Aspire!* Book Tour." As of the writing of these acknowledgments, I don't know what this epic odyssey will entail, yet it's planned to span more than ten thousand miles and thirty cities. That tour won't be possible without Juan Restrepo, a Caring House Project Foundation Board of Directors member, who has driven the tour buses and provided the digital media for my book tours dating back to *The Tap* over a decade ago. Imagine being cooped up with me for that many miles!

I want to sincerely thank Dennis Moran, who is also a Caring House Project Foundation Board member, and Leslie Barrett with PR by the Book, for scheduling all stops on the *Aspire!* Book Tour that we made at homeless shelters, soup kitchens, food pantries, veterans facilities, abused women's shelters, juvenile detention centers, schools, hospitals, TV stations, radio stations, podcasts, and bookstores. What an impact they made!

Mom gets her own paragraph. I want to acknowledge my mom, Katie (who I have saved in my phone as "Abraham Lincoln"), for giving birth to me and much of the wisdom I think I have (hence the contact name in my phone). I love you, Mom!

When writing a book, the thesis and message begins to stir in the deep recesses of the mind far before the first word is written, oftentimes for years or decades. While you read about the people who I aspired to emulate in the very first chapter, if it weren't for my wife, Nilsa, and daughter, Laura, who encouraged me to pursue then live out my aspirations, there would be no *Aspire!* book. And, dare I say, I'm not sure I'd be around to be able to write it, or any book, for that matter. Yes, you read about my guardian angel, and our little angel, and how to find yours. I found mine, and I ask that you keep them in the forefront of your mind as you continue on in your own life!

P.S. Notice a recurring trend, a theme? All the people on my crew, the people who made *Aspire!* possible, have been with me for a *very* long time (with the exception of James). Find your crew, who, when you compose your story, you'll know it wouldn't have been possible without them.

Thank you to my all-star crew!

About Frank McKinney

FRANK MCKINNEY is a true modern-day Renaissance man who has pushed the limits of success in his every endeavor. His early years were not very promising, however: upon attending his fourth high school in four years (he was asked to leave the first three), he earned his high school diploma with a 1.8 GPA. (It would have been lower, but he received an A in creative writing.) So, with $50 in his pocket and without the benefit of further education, he left his native Indiana for Florida in search of his life's highest calling.

Today, Frank's life is a testament to the power of aspiration to create a completely new reality. As a real estate artist, he has created and sold forty-four oceanfront mansions on spec, with an average price of $14 million. As a philanthro-capitalist, he has built twenty-nine self-sustaining villages over the last nineteen years in Haiti, providing more than thirteen thousand children and their families with homes, renewable food and clean water, and means to support themselves. A bestselling author, actor, and keynote speaker, he has written seven books in six genres, starred in two movies, and keynoted before audiences of ten to ten thousand around the world. Physically, Frank has pushed the limit of his body by racing in the Badwater 135-mile Ultramarathon twelve times in the scorching summer in Death Valley, California, a race referred to by *National Geographic* as "the world's toughest footrace."

As with all of his books, Frank wrote *Aspire!* in his Delray Beach, Florida, oceanfront treehouse office that has spectacular views and includes a bamboo desk, shower, bathroom, sink, air conditioning, hardwood floors, cedar walls, a loft with a king-size bed, and a suspension bridge to the master bedroom in the main house—that's Frank's commute to and from work! Today Frank and his wife, Nilsa, split their time between Delray Beach and their "glass cottage" in the mountains of Canton, North Carolina. They enjoy visiting their twenty-three-year-old daughter, Laura, in New York City, where she started and runs StrataBrand, a brand strategy firm.

Share the Profound Message of

Give copies of *Aspire!* to family, friends and co-workers . . .

Hardcover and paperback book (Caring House Books, 2021) • Available at TheAspireBook.com • $29.95 and $19.95

Other Exciting Offerings from Frank McKinney

The Other Thief is a controversial, heart-wrenching story of deception, pride, and lust, along with mercy, grace, forgiveness, and—above all—love. Frank McKinney boldly enters the Christian romance genre with this seductively spiritual novel. *The Other Thief* will arouse readers and their faith, leaving them wondering which side of the cross they would choose.

Hardcover book (HCI, 2018) • Available at TheOtherThief.com • $20

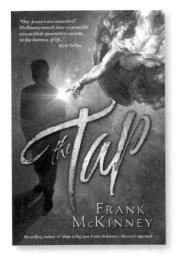

Bestselling author Frank McKinney introduces *The Tap,* a profound spiritual practice leading to success in the business of life. Your prayers for more are answered! *The Tap* shows how to sensitize yourself to feel and then act on life's great "Tap Moments," embracing the rewards and responsibilities of a blessed life. Feel it, follow it and find your highest calling. This book is about accepting the responsibility, and it gives you confidence in your ability to handle your "more," whether it's more wealth, health, happiness, or relationships.

Hardcover book (HCI, 2009) • Available at The-Tap.com • $25

Burst This! Frank McKinney's Bubble-Proof Real Estate Strategies continues Frank McKinney's international bestselling tradition of delivering paradoxical perspectives and strategies for generational success in real estate. Tired of all the "bubble" talk, all the doom and gloom? Here comes McKinney in his unassailable fear-removal gear and hip boots to help you wash away the worry—the anxiety that financial theorists and misguided media constantly dump into the real estate marketplace. During his 30-year career, this "maverick daredevil real estate artist" has not only survived but thrived through all economic conditions by taking the contrarian position and making his own markets.

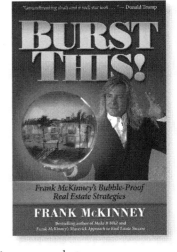

Hardcover book (HCI, 2009) • Available at Burst-This.com • $30

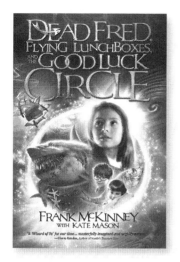

With *Dead Fred, Flying Lunchboxes, and the Good Luck Circle,* Frank McKinney boldly enters young reader fiction in this fantasy novel charged with fairy tale wonder, enthralling magic, page-turning suspense, and the deep creativity he's known for. It will both race and gladden the hearts of readers of all ages. This classic was inspired by real-life Laura McKinney's 1,652 walks to school with her friends and her father, Frank McKinney.

Hardcover book (HCI, 2009) • Available at Dead-Fred.com • $25

Frank McKinney's Maverick Approach to Real Estate Success takes the reader on a fascinating real estate odyssey that began more than two decades ago with a $50,000 fixer-upper and culminates in a $100-million mansion. Includes strategies and insights from a true real estate "artist," visionary, and market maker.

Paperback book (John Wiley & Sons, 2006) • Available at Frank-McKinney.com • $25

Make It BIG! 49 Secrets for Building a Life of Extreme Success consists of forty-nine short, dynamic chapters that share how to live a balanced life, with real estate stories and "deal points" sprinkled throughout.

Hardcover book (John Wiley & Sons, 2002) • Available at Frank-McKinney.com • $30

The Frank McKinney Experience, Public Speaking, Appearances and Personal Success Coaching
One-on-one or group events
Prices and schedule available through Frank-McKinney.com

Please visit Frank-McKinney.com to peruse our entire online store and take advantage of savings with assorted product packages. It's important to note that proceeds benefit Frank McKinney's nonprofit Caring House Project Foundation (CHPF.org).

Caring House

End Notes

SECTION ONE: The DNA Difference Between Motivation, Inspiration, and Aspiration

1. Thomas W. Mcdade et al. "Social and Physical Environments Early in Development Predict DNA Methylation of Inflammatory Genes in Young Adulthood," *PNAS* 114, no. 29 (2017): 7611-7616; https://doi.org/10.1073/pnas.1620661114

2. Linda E. Carlson et al., "Mindfulness-Based Cancer Recovery and Supportive-Expressive Therapy Maintain Telomere Length Relative to Controls in Distressed Breast Cancer Survivors," *Cancer* 121, no. 3 (2015): 476-484; https://doi.org/10.1002/cncr.29063

3. David S. Black and George M. Slavich, "Mindfulness Meditation and the Immune System: A Systematic Review of Randomized Controlled Trials," *Annals of the New York Academy of Sciences* 1373, no. 1 (2016): 13-24; https://www.ncbi.nlm.nih.gov/pmc/articles/PMC4940234/

Chapter 1: Emulation Is the Sincerest Form of Aspiration

1. Lisa Trei, "New Study Yields Instructive Results on How Mindset Affects Learning," *Stanford Report*, Stanford University, February 7, 2007, https://news.stanford.edu/news/2007/february7/dweck-020707.html

2. Sopan Deb, "A Look Back at Evel Knievel: A Daredevil Unafraid to Fail," *The New York Times*, June 29, 2018, https://www.nytimes.com/2018/06/29/arts/television/evel-knievel-travis-pastrana.html

Chapter 2: What Legacy Do You Aspire to Leave Behind?

1. Martin Luther King, Jr., "I've Been to the Mountaintop," transcript of speech delivered at Mason Temple (Church of God in Christ Headquarters), Memphis, Tennessee, April 3, 1968, https://www.americanrhetoric.com/speeches/mlkivebeentothemountaintop.htm

Chapter 3: Be an Executioner

1. P. Lorenz-Spreen et al., "Accelerating Dynamics of Collective Attention," *Nature Communications* 10, article 1759 (2019), https://doi.org/10.1038/s41467-019-09311-w

2. "Novelty Speeds Up Learning Thanks to Dopamine Activation," ScienceDaily.com, February 5, 2020, https://www.sciencedaily.com/releases/2020/02/200205132255.htm

3. "48 Famous Failures Who Will Inspire You to Achieve," WanderlustWorker. com, accessed August 4, 2021, https://www.wanderlustworker.com/48-famous-failures-who-will-inspire-you-to-achieve/

4. Ari Herstand, "22 Musicians Who Made It After 30," Aristake.com, October 22, 2019, https://aristake.com/older-musicians

5. Damon Lavrinc, "After 10 Years in the Business, Tesla Finally Turns a Profit," Wired.com, May 8, 2013, https://www.wired.com/2013/05/tesla-profit-q1-2013/

6. Geoff Weiss, "How a 10-Minute Spot on QVC Turned This Woman Into a $100 Million Cosmetics Mogul," Entrepreneur.com, accessed August 4, 2021, https://www.entrepreneur.com/article/237379

7. Chloe Sorvino, "How Jamie Kern Lima Built IT Cosmetics Into A $1.2 Billion Business," Forbes.com, May 17, 2017, https://www.forbes.com/sites/chloesorvino/2017/05/17/jamie-kern-lima-loreal-beauty-it-cosmetics/?sh=22edaa853b4f

Chapter 4: Get the Mind Right and the Money Will Follow

1. Elizabeth W. Dunn et al., "Spending Money on Others Promotes Happiness," *Science* 319, issue 5870 (2008): 1687-8, DOI:10.1126/science.1150952

2. Andrew T. Jebb et al., "Happiness, Income Satiation and Turning Points around the World," *Nature Human Behavior* 2 (2018): 33–38, https://doi.org/10.1038/s41562-017-0277-0

3. Jamie Ducharme, "This Is the Amount of Money You Need to Be Happy, According to Research," Money.com, February 14, 2018, https://money.com/ideal-income-study/

4. Tania Lombrozo, "The Truth about the Left Brain/Right Brain Relationship," NPR.org, December 2, 2013, https://www.npr.org/sections/13.7/2013/12/02/248089436/the-truth-about-the-left-brain-right-brain-relationship

5. Carl Sherman, "Right Brain, Left Brain: A Misnomer," Dana.org, August 2, 2019, https://www.dana.org/article/right-brain-left-brain-really/

Chapter 5: Re-Invent and Re-Create

1. "Elton John Biography," Encyclopedia of World Biography, accessed August 4, 2021, https://www.notablebiographies.com/Ho-Jo/John-Elton.html

2. "Biography," Freddiemercury.com, accessed August 4, 2021, http://www.freddiemercury.com/en/biography

3. D. Lawrence Tarazano, "People Feared Being Buried Alive So Much They Invented These Special Safety Coffins," *Smithsonian Magazine,* October 26, 2018, https://www.smithsonianmag.com/sponsored/people-feared-being-buried-alive-so-much-they-invented-these-special-safety-coffins-180970627/

4.   Bill Hutchinson, "Details Emerge After Woman Found Alive in Body Bag at Funeral Home," ABC News, August 26, 2020, https://abcnews.go.com/US/details-emerge-woman-found-alive-body-bag-funeral/story?id=72600258

5.   Ashlee Vance, *Elon Musk: Tesla, SpaceX, and the Quest for a Fantastic Future* (New York: HarperCollins, 2015).

SECTION TWO: Risk = Fear = Big Change or Challenge

1.   https://www.merriam-webster.com/dictionary/fear

Chapter 6: The Differentiator

1.   Taylor Locke, "Mark Cuban: This Is How You Get Through Your Lowest Point," Make It: CNBC.com, February 5, 2020, https://www.cnbc.com/2020/02/05/mark-cuban-how-to-get-through-the-hard-times.html

2.   Kiara Williams, "How Mary Kay Ash Translated Her Failure Into a $3.6 Billion Dollar Personal Brand," BetterMarketing.pub, September 3, 2020, https://bettermarketing.pub/how-mary-kay-ash-translated-her-failure-into-a-3-6-billion-dollar-personal-brand-199ae196567e

3.   Allison Linn, "What Steve Jobs Taught Us: It's OK to Fail," NBCNews.com, October 5, 2011, https://www.nbcnews.com/id/wbna44278117

4.   Melanie Curtin, "Billionaire CEO Sara Blakely Says These 7 Words Are the Best Career Advice She Ever Got," INC.com, Sep 29, 2017, https://www.inc.com/melanie-curtin/billionaire-ceo-sara-blakely-says-these-7-words-are-best-career-advice-she-ever-got.html

5.   Jon Nordheimer, "Knievel Safe as Rocket Falls Into Snake Canyon," *The New York Times*, September 9, 1974, https://www.nytimes.com/1974/09/09/archives/knievel-safe-as-rocket-falls-into-snake-canyon-knievel-safe-as-he.html

Chapter 7: What Were You Thinking!

1.   B. J. Casey, "Beyond Simple Models of Self-Control to Circuit-Based Accounts of Adolescent Behavior," *Annual Review of Psychology* 66 (January 2015): 295-319, https://doi.org/10.1146/annurev-psych-010814-015156

2.   Bart Larsen et al., "Developmental Changes in the Integration of Affective and Cognitive Corticostriatal Pathways are Associated with Reward-Driven Behavior," *Cerebral Cortex* 28, Issue 8 (2018): 2834–2845, https://doi.org/10.1093/cercor/bhx162

3.   Adriana Galvan et al., "Risk-taking and the Adolescent Brain: Who Is at Risk?" *Developmental Science* 10, Issue 2 (2007): F8-F14, https://doi.org/10.1111/j.1467-7687.2006.00579.x

4.   Michele Chandler, "Tony Hsieh: Happiness Leads to Profits," *Insights by Stanford Business*, Stanford Graduate School of Business, October 01, 2010, https://www.gsb.stanford.edu/insights/tony-hsieh-happiness-leads-profits

Chapter 8: R.I.S.K. = Requires Intense Self-Knowledge

1.   "Biography of Nelson Mandela," Nelson Mandela Foundation, accessed August 4, 2021, https://www.nelsonmandela.org/content/page/biography

2.   Kevin and Jackie Freiberg, "Madiba Leadership: 5 Lessons Nelson Mandela Taught The World About Change," Forbes.com, July 19, 2018, https://www.forbes.com/sites/kevinandjackiefreiberg/2018/07/19/madiba-leadership-5-lessons-nelson-mandela-taught-the-world-about-change/?sh=7530990641bg

3.   "Mother Teresa of Calcutta: Biography," MotherTeresa.org, accessed August 4, 2021, https://www.motherteresa.org/biography.html

4.   James Martin, S.J., "In My Soul: The Long Dark Night of Mother Teresa," AmericaMagazine.org, September 24, 2007, https://www.americamagazine.org/faith/2007/09/24/my-soul-long-dark-night-mother-teresa

5.   Susan Cain, *Quiet: The Power of Introverts in a World that Can't Stop Talking* (New York: Crown Publishers, 2012), https://www.thepowerofintroverts.com/about-the-book/

6.   Sanidhya Samyak, "Your Introversion Is Your Super Power," Medium.com, November 8, 2020, https://medium.com/illumination/your-introversion-is-your-super-power-4e49f218b3ad

7.   Richard Karlsson Linnér et al., "Genome-wide Association Analyses of Risk Tolerance and Risky Behaviors in Over 1 Million Individuals Identify Hundreds of Loci and Shared Genetic Influences," *Nature Genetics* 51 (2019): 245–257, https://doi.org/10.1038/s41588-018-0309-3

8.   Andra Picincu, "The Physical Difference Between Long Distance Runners & Sprinters," Livestrong.com, April 6, 2020, https://www.livestrong.com/article/550102-the-physical-difference-between-long-distance-runners-sprinters/

9.   "Narcissistic Personality Disorder," Mayoclinic.org, accessed August 4, 2021, https://www.mayoclinic.org/diseases-conditions/narcissistic-personality-disorder/symptoms-causes/syc-20366662

10. "10 Narcissistic Leadership Characteristics," YScouts.com, accessed August 4, 2021, https://yscouts.com/10-narcissistic-leadership-characteristics/

11. Nancy L. Segal et al., "Genetic and Experiential Influences on Behavior: Twins Reunited at Seventy-Eight Years," *Personality and Individual Differences* 73 (2015): 110-117, doi: 10.1016/j.paid.2014.09.017

12. Kristen Jacobson, "Considering Interactions between Genes, Environments, Biology, and Social Context," *Psychological Science Agenda*, American Psychological Association, April 2009, https://www.apa.org/science/about/psa/2009/04/sci-brief

Chapter 9: Don't Change: Redirect

1.   Kendra Cherry, "Freud's Psychosexual Stages of Development," Verywellmind.

com, November 19, 2020, https://www.verywellmind.com/freuds-stages-of-psychosexual-development-2795962

2.   Christopher S. Nave et al., "On the Contextual Independence of Personality: Teachers' Assessments Predict Directly Observed Behavior after Four Decades," *Social Psychological and Personality Science* 3, no. 1 (2010): 1–9, https://www.ncbi.nlm.nih.gov/pmc/articles/PMC2947027/

3.   Avshalom Caspi et al., "Personality Differences Predict Health-Risk Behaviors in Young Adulthood: Evidence from a Longitudinal Study," *Journal of Personality and Social Psychology* 73, no. 5 (1997): 1052–1063, https://doi.org/10.1037/0022-3514.73.5.1052

4.   Avshalom Caspi and Terrie E. Moffitt, "When Do Individual Differences Matter? A Paradoxical Theory of Personality Coherence," *Psychological Inquiry* 4, no. 4 (1993): 247-2, http://www.jstor.org/stable/1449633

5.   Zoya Gervis, "Average American Abandons their New Year's Resolution on this Date," Swnsdigital.com, January 28, 2020, https://swnsdigital.com/2020/01/the-average-american-abandons-their-new-years-resolution-this-many-days-into-the-year/

6.   Richard Branson, "Dyslexia and Imagination," *Richard Branson's Blog*, October 3, 2019, https://www.virgin.com/branson-family/richard-branson-blog/dyslexia-and-imagination

7.   "Richard Branson," Dyslexiahelp. umich.edu, University of Michigan, accessed August 4, 2021, http://dyslexiahelp.umich.edu/success-stories/richard-branson

8.   Richard Branson, "Why You Shouldn't Judge Me on My Spelling," *Richard Branson's Blog*, July 23, 2019, https://www.virgin.com/branson-family/richard-branson-blog/why-you-shouldnt-judge-me-my-spelling

9.   Zahavit Paz, "Famous People With Dyslexia: Sir Richard Branson Dyslexia Coping Tips," Ldrfa.org, accessed August 4, 2021, https://www.ldrfa.org/famous-people-with-dyslexia-sir-richard-branson-dyslexia-coping-tips/

SECTION THREE: The Art of Personal Branding

1.   Zia Muhammad, "Research Indicates that Attention Spans Are Shortening," Digitalinformationworld.com, February 27, 2020, https://www.digitalinformationworld.com/2020/02/report-shows-that-attention-spans-are-shortening.html

2.   Jason Miller, "The Great Goldfish Attention Span Myth—And Why It's Killing Content Marketing," *LinkedIn Marketing Solutions Blog*, November 25, 2016, https://business.linkedin.com/marketing-solutions/blog/best-practices--content-marketing/2016/the-great-goldfish-attention-span-myth--and-why-its-killing-cont

3.   Sam Carr, "How Many Ads Do We See A Day In 2021?" PPCProtect.com, February 15, 2021, https://ppcprotect.com/how-many-ads-do-we-see-a-day/

4.   Mallory, "Conformity: Standing up means standing out," Socialpsyq.com,

December 20, 2016, https://socialpsyq.com/2016/12/20/conformity-standing-up-means-standing-out/

5.   N.T. Feather, "Attitudes Towards the High Achiever: The Fall of the Tall Poppy," *Australian Journal of Psychology* 41, no. 3 (1989): 239-267, https://www.tandfonline.com/doi/abs/10.1080/00049538908260088

6.   Birga Mareen Schumpe and Hans-Peter Erb, "Humans and Uniqueness," *Science Progress* 98, no. 1 (2015): 1-11, https://www.jstor.org/stable/26406272

7.   Kaitlyn Frey, IT Cosmetics Founder Jamie Kern Lima on Business, Beauty and Breaking Boundaries," People.com/Style, October 23, 2019, https://people.com/style/it-cosmetics-founder-jamie-kern-lima-interview/

8.   Hal Hodson, "Pitch Drop Caught on Camera After 69-Year Wait," Physics/New Scientist.com, July 18, 2013, https://www.newscientist.com/article/dn23896-pitch-drop-caught-on-camera-after-69-year-wait/

9.   Priscilla Blossom, "Rachel Hollis Compared Herself to Harriet Tubman and Malala Yousafzai," Yahoo.com/Life, April 6, 2021, https://www.yahoo.com/lifestyle/rachel-hollis-backlash-explained-011125933.html

10.   "Rachel Hollis Issues Apology After Privilege Video Backlash," Yahoo.com/Entertainment, April 6, 2021, https://www.yahoo.com/entertainment/rachel-hollis-issues-apology-privilege-221300299.html?fr=sycsrp_catchall

Chapter 13: Live Your Inside on Your Outside

1.   Elisa Bergagna and Stefano Tartaglia, "Self-Esteem, Social Comparison, and Facebook Use," *Europe's Journal of Psychology* 14, no. 4: 831-845, https://doi.org/10.5964/ejop.v14i4.1592

Chapter 14: Healthy Ego

1.   Kendra Cherry, "Freud's Id, Ego, and Superego," Verywellmind.com, September 28, 2019, https://www.verywellmind.com/the-id-ego-and-superego-2795951

2.   "Ego," APA Dictionary of Psychology, accessed August 4, 2021, https://dictionary.apa.org/ego

3.   Roy F. Baumeister et al., "Does High Self-Esteem Cause Better Performance, Interpersonal Success, Happiness, or Healthier Lifestyles?" *Psychological Science in the Public Interest* 4, no. 1 (2003): 1-44, https://pubmed.ncbi.nlm.nih.gov/26151640/

4.   Harriet Brown, "The Boom and Bust Ego," *Psychology Today*, January 1, 2012, https://www.psychologytoday.com/us/articles/201201/the-boom-and-bust-ego

5.   Dorothy Neufeld, "The Richest People in the World in 2021," Visualcapitalist.com, March 9, 2021, https://www.visualcapitalist.com/richest-people-in-the-world-2021/

6.   "Narcissistic Personality Disorder," Mayoclinic.org, accessed August 4, 2021, https://www.mayoclinic.org/diseases-conditions/narcissistic-personality-disorder/symptoms-causes/syc-20366662

7.   "Prizes," NI Memorial house of Mother Teresa, accessed August 4, 2021, https://memorialhouseofmotherteresa.com/mother-teresa/prizes/

Chapter 15: Creativity and Ingenuity Are Rewarded

1.   "How Many Books Are Published Daily?" JDandJ.com blog, January 19, 2019, https://www.jdandj.com/book-design--publishing-blog/how-many-books-are-published-daily

2.   Simeon Djankov and Eva Zhang, "Startups Boom in the United States during COVID-19," *Realtime Economic Issues Watch blog,* Peterson Institute for International Economics, February 17, 2021, https://www.piie.com/blogs/realtime-economic-issues-watch/startups-boom-united-states-during-covid-19

3.   Magdalena M.H.E. van den Berg et al., "Autonomic Nervous System Responses to Viewing Green and Built Settings: Differentiating Between Sympathetic and Parasympathetic Activity," *International Journal of Environmental Research and Public Health* 12, no. 12 (2015): 15860–15874, https://www.ncbi.nlm.nih.gov/pmc/articles/PMC4690962/

4.   May Wong, "Stanford Study Finds Walking Improves Creativity," *Stanford News,* Stanford University, April 24, 2014, https://news.stanford.edu/2014/04/24/walking-vs-sitting-042414/

5.   Ruth Ann Atchley et al., "Creativity in the Wild: Improving Creative Reasoning through Immersion in Natural Settings," *PLOS One,* December 12, 2012, https://doi.org/10.1371/journal.pone.0051474

SECTION FOUR: Love Life. Love-Life.

1.   Kirsten Weir, "Life-saving Relationships," *Monitor on Psychology* 49, no. 3 (2018): 46, https://www.apa.org/monitor/2018/03/life-saving-relationships

2.   Jessica Kansky, "What's Love Got to Do with It? Romantic Relationships and Well-Being," in *Handbook of Well-Being,* eds. E. Diener et al. (Salt Lake City, UT, DEF Publishers, 2018), 1-24.

3.   Brooke C Feeney and Nancy L. Collins, "A New Look at Social Support: A Theoretical Perspective on Thriving Through Relationships," *Personality and Social Psychology Review* 19, no. 2 (2105):113-47, https://doi.org/10.1177/1088868314544222

4.   "Highlights from the NAR Member Profile," NAR.realtor website, accessed August 4, 2021, https://www.nar.realtor/research-and-statistics/research-reports/highlights-from-the-nar-member-profile Unfortunately, women are still underrepresented in commercial real estate, as well as in real estate development and investing. As of 2019, only 30 percent of commercial real estate brokers, 31 percent of

people in real estate development, and 30 percent of real estate investors are women. Sources: Sarah Paynter, "Most Residential Brokers May Be Women, But Inequality Is Still Prevalent in the Real Estate Industry," Yahoo Entertainment, March 27, 2020, https://www.yahoo.com/entertainment/most-residential-realtors-may-be-women-but-inequality-is-still-prevalent-in-the-real-estate-industry-143341098.html; "Real Estate Developer Demographics and Statistics In The US," Zippia.com, accessed August 4, 2021, https://www.zippia.com/real-estate-developer-jobs/demographics/; Whitney Hutten, "Why We Really, Really Need More Women Investors in the Real Estate Industry," Biggerpockets.com, November 8, 2019, https://www.biggerpockets.com/blog/women-investors-real-estate-industry

5.   " . . . higher share-price performance": "Gender Diversity Is Good for Business," Credit Suisse, October 10, 2019, https://www.credit-suisse.com/about-us-news/en/articles/news-and-expertise/cs-gender-3000-report-2019-201910.html;" . . . better corporate profitability growth": Meggin Thwing Eastman, "Women On Boards: One Piece of a Bigger Puzzle," ESG Research, *MSCI Blog,* March 6, 2018, https://www.msci.com/www/blog-posts/women-on-boards-one-piece-of-a/0872932779; " . . . fewer long-term governance issues": Alexandre Di Miceli and Angela Donaggio, *Women in Business Leadership Boost ESG Performance: Existing Body of Evidence Makes Compelling Case,* IFC Corporate Governance Knowledge Publication 42 (Washington, DC: International Finance Corporation, 2018): 7-9, IFC + PSO_Women_Business_Leadership_web.pdf.

Chapter 16: The Significance of a Significant Other

1.   "The State of Relationships, Marriages, and Living Alone in the US," USAfacts. org, February 14, 2020, https://usafacts.org/articles/state-relationships-marriages-and-living-alone-us/

2.   "Married people tend to live longer": Robert M. Kaplan and Richard G. Kronick, "Marital Status and Longevity in the United States Population," *Journal of Epidemiology and Community Health* 60, no. 9 (2006): 760–765, https://www.ncbi.nlm.nih.gov/pmc/articles/PMC2566023/

3.   "Couples in happy, stable relationships have lower risk of heart disease": Timothy W. Smith and Brian R.W. Baucom, "Intimate Relationships, Individual Adjustment, and Coronary Heart Disease: Implications of Overlapping Associations in Psychosocial Risk," *American Psychologist* 72, no. 6 (2017): 578–589, https://doi.org/10.1037/amp0000123; " . . . lower blood pressure, less stress, less depression": Julianne Holt-Lunstad et al., "Is There Something Unique about Marriage? The Relative Impact of Marital Status, Relationship Quality, and Network Social Support on Ambulatory Blood Pressure and Mental Health," *Annals of Behavioral Medicine* 35, no. 2 (2008): 239–244, https://doi.org/10.1007/s12160-008-9018-y; " . . . better outcomes for cancer and surgery": Janice K. Kiecolt-Glaser and Stephanie J. Wilson, "Lovesick: How Couples' Relationships Influence Health," *Annual Review of Clinical Psychology* 13 (2017): 421-443, https://www.ncbi.nlm.nih.gov/pmc/articles/PMC5549103/#R1

4.   Bert N. Uchino and Baldwin M. Way, "Integrative Pathways Linking Close Family Ties to Health: A Neurochemical Perspective," *American Psychologist* 72, no. 6 (2017): 590–600, https://doi.org/10.1037/amp0000049

5.   ". . . physical activity and fast-food consumption": Brea Perry et al., "Partner Influence in Diet and Exercise Behaviors: Testing Behavior Modeling, Social Control, and Normative Body Size," *PLOS One,* December 29, 2016, https://doi.org/10.1371/journal.pone.0169193; ". . . likelihood that you're obese": Kirsten P. Smith and Nicholas A. Christakis, "Social Networks and Health," *Annual Review of Sociology* 34 (2008): 405-429, https://doi.org/10.1146/annurev.soc.34.040507.134601

6.   Kiecolt-Glaser et al., "Lovesick."

7.   ". . . physical pain": Ethan Kross et al., "Social Rejection Shares Somatosensory Representations with Physical Pain," *Proceedings of the National Academy of Sciences of the United States of America* (PNAS) 108 no. 15 (2011): 6270-6275, https://doi.org/10.1073/pnas.1102693108. ". . . withdrawal symptoms": Helen E. Fisher et al., "Reward, Addiction, and Emotion Regulation Systems Associated With Rejection in Love," *Journal of Neurophysiology* 104 no. 1 (2010): 51-60, https://doi.org/10.1152/jn.00784.2009

8.   Claire M. Kamp Dush and Paul R. Amato, "Consequences of Relationship Status and Quality for Subjective Well-Being," *Journal of Social and Personal Relationships* 22, no. 5 (2005): 607-627, https://doi.org/10.1177/0265407505056438

9.   "Being in love can elevate dopamine": Bianca P. Acevedo et al., "Neural Correlates of Long-term Intense Romantic Love," *Social Cognitive and Affective Neuroscience* 7, no. 2 (2012): 145–159, https://doi.org/10.1093/scan/nsq092; ". . . oxytocin, the 'love' chemical": Katherine Wu, "Love, Actually: The science Behind Lust, Attraction, and Companionship," *Science in the News blog,* Harvard University Graduate School of Arts and Sciences, February 14, 2017, https://sitn.hms.harvard.edu/flash/2017/love-actually-science-behind-lust-attraction-companionship/?web=1&wdLOR=c91AB35A4-754D-D141-997C-ED6BE3A0FA22

10.   Acevedo et al., "Neural Correlates of Long-term Intense Romantic Love."

11.   Daniel N. Hawkins and Alan Booth, "Unhappily Ever After: Effects of Long-Term, Low-Quality Marriages on Well-Being," *Social Forces* 84, no. 1 (2005): 451–471, https://doi.org/10.1353/sof.2005.0103

12.   K. Daniel O'Leary et al., "A Closer Look at the Link Between Marital Discord and Depressive Symptomatology," *Journal of Social and Clinical Psychology* 13, no. 1 (2011): 33-41, https://doi.org/10.1521/jscp.1994.13.1.33

13.   Arne Mastekaasa, "Marital Dissolution and Subjective Distress: Panel Evidence," *European Sociological Review* 11, no. 2 (1995): 173–185, https://doi.org/10.1093/oxfordjournals.esr.a036355

14.   "What is Secure Attachment?" Attachmentproject.com, July 2, 2020, https://www.attachmentproject.com/blog/secure-attachment/

15. Harry T. Reiss et al., "Toward Understanding Understanding: The Importance of Feeling Understood in Relationships," *Social and Personality Psychology Compass* 11, no. 3 (2017): e12308, https://doi.org/10.1111/spc3.12308

Chapter 17: Marry Your Guardian Angel

1. "Angels in the Life of the Church," *Catechism Of The Catholic Church*, 2nd ed., Part One, Section Two, Chapter One, Article I, Paragraph 5, I. The Angels, #336. http://www.scborromeo.org/ccc/p1s2c1p5.htm

Chapter 18: Relationship Pressure Creates Diamonds

1. "Divorce Statistics: Over 115 Studies, Facts and Rates for 2020," Wilkinson & Finkbeiner Family Law Attorneys, accessed August 4, 2021, https://www.wf-lawyers.com/divorce-statistics-and-facts/

2. "Diamonds are formed 90 miles": Hobart M. King, "How Do Diamonds Form?" Geology.com, accessed August 4, 2021, https://geology.com/articles/diamonds-from-coal/

3. "Divorce Statistics."

4. Bob Pisani, "The Billion Dollar Business of Diamonds, From Mining to Retail," CNBC.com, August 27 2012, https://www.cnbc.com/2012/08/27/the-billion-dollar-business-of-diamonds-from-mining-to-retail.html

5. Matthew D. Johnson et al., Temporality of Couple Conflict and Relationship Perceptions," *Journal of Family Psychology* 32, no. 4 (2018): 445–455, https://doi.org/10.1037/fam0000398

6. Christine A. Johnson et al., *Marriage in Oklahoma: 2001 Baseline Statewide Survey on Marriage and Divorce* (Stillwater, OK: OSU Bureau for Social Research, Oklahoma State University, 2002): 15, https://app.box.com/s/uoew21bvb9ertq3gqonozx0euq3laq4j

7. Korin Miller, "What Your Fight-or-Flight Argument Style Says About You, Whether You Cry, Clam up, or See Red," Wellandgood.com, April 25, 2019, https://www.wellandgood.com/how-to-argue-effectively/

8. Julie Petersen and Benjamin Le, "Psychological Distress, Attachment, and Conflict Resolution in Romantic Relationships," *Modern Psychological Studies* 23, no. 1 (2017): 1-26, https://scholar.utc.edu/mps/vol23/iss1/3/

9. Miller, "What Your Fight-or-Flight Argument Style Says About You."

10. John M. Gottman, Amber Tabares, "The Effects of Briefly Interrupting Marital Conflict," *Journal of Marital and Family Therapy* 44, no. 1 (2017): 61-72, https://doi.org/10.1111/jmft.12243

11. Petersen, "Psychological Distress."

Chapter 19: Magnetic-ism

1. "Magnetism," National Geographic Resource Library Encyclopedic Entry, accessed August 4, 2021, https://www.nationalgeographic.org/encyclopedia/magnetism/

2. "Electromagnetism and magnetism," BBC Bitesize, accessed August 4, 2021, https://www.bbc.co.uk/bitesize/guides/z3g8d2p/revision/2

3. "Ism," Merriam-Webster Dictionary definition, accessed August 4, 2021, https://www.merriam-webster.com/dictionary/ism

4. "Charisma," U.S. Dictionary/Oxford English and Spanish Dictionary, accessed August 4, 2021, https://www.lexico.com/en/definition/charisma

Chapter 20: Oh, and Give Mind-Blowing Sex

1. Susan Sprecher and Rodney M. Cate, "Sexual Satisfaction and Sexual Expression as Predictors of Relationship Satisfaction and Stability," in *The Handbook of Sexuality in Close Relationships*, J. H. Harvey, A. Wenzel, & S. Sprecher, eds., (Mahwah, NJ: Lawrence Erlbaum Associates Publishers, 2004), 235–256, https://psycnet.apa.org/record/2004-13774-010

2. Sinikka Elliott and Debra Umberson, "The Performance of Desire: Gender and Sexual Negotiation in Long-Term Marriages," *Journal of Marriage and Family* 70, no. 2 (2008): 391-406, https://onlinelibrary.wiley.com/doi/abs/10.1111/j.1741-3737.2008.00489.x

3. Daniel Kahneman et al., "Toward National Well-Being Accounts," Papers and Proceedings of the One Hundred Sixteenth Annual Meeting of the American Economic Association, *American Economic Review* 94, no. 2 (2004): 429-434, https://www.jstor.org/stable/3592923

4. David G. Blanchflower and Andrew J. Oswald, "Money, Sex and Happiness: An Empirical Study," *The Scandinavian Journal of Economics* 106, no. 3 (2004): 393-415, https://www.jstor.org/stable/3441116

5. Anthony Smith et al., "Sexual and Relationship Satisfaction Among Heterosexual Men and Women: The Importance of Desired Frequency of Sex," *Journal of Sex & Marital Therapy* 37, no. 2 (2011): 104-115, https://doi.org/10.1080/0092623X.2011.560531

6. Blanchflower, "Money, Sex and Happiness."

7. David A. Frederick et al., "What Keeps Passion Alive? Sexual Satisfaction Is Associated With Sexual Communication, Mood Setting, Sexual Variety, Oral Sex, Orgasm, and Sex Frequency in a National U.S. Study," *The Journal of Sex Research* 54, no. 2 (2016): 186-201, https://doi.org/10.1080/00224499.2015.1137854

8. Elliott, "The Performance of Desire."

9. Ann Gold Buscho, "Why Do People Divorce?" A Better Divorce blog,

Psychologytoday.com, February 22, 2020, https://www.psychologytoday.com/us/blog/better-divorce/202002/why-do-people-divorce

10. Jacqui Gabb, "The Relationship Work of Sexual Intimacy in Long-Term Heterosexual and LGBTQ Partnerships," *Current Sociology,* International Sociology Association, March 11, 2019, https://doi.org/10.1177/0011392119826619

11. Uzma S. Rehman et al., "Understanding Barriers to Sexual Communication," *Journal of Social and Personal Relationships* 36, no. 9 (2019): 2605-2623, https://doi.org/10.1177/0265407518794900

12. Sprecher, "Sexual Satisfaction."

13. Marcel D. Waldinger et al., "A Multinational Population Survey of Intravaginal Ejaculation Latency Time," *Journal of Sexual Medicine* 2, no. 4 (2005): 492-497, DOI: 10.1111/j.1743-6109.2005.00070.x

14. David L. Rowland et al., "Orgasmic Latency and Related Parameters in Women During Partnered and Masturbatory Sex," Orgasm Original Research, *The Journal of Sexual Medicine* 15, no. 10 (2018): 1463-1471, DOI: https://doi.org/10.1016/j.jsxm.2018.08.003

15. Waldinger, "A Multinational Population Survey."

16. Gabb, "The Relationship Work of Sexual Intimacy."

17. Esther Perel, *Mating in Captivity: Reconciling the Erotic and the Domestic* (New York: HarperCollins, 2006): 35-37.

18. Brien Ashdown et al., "In and Out of the Bedroom: Sexual Satisfaction in the Marital Relationship," *Journal of Integrated Social Sciences* 2, no. 1 (2011): 40-57, https://www.researchgate.net/publication/228470046_In_and_out_of_the_bedroom_Sexual_satisfaction_in_the_marital_relationship

19. Esther Perel quoted in Barb DePree, "Wanting What You Have: The Love/Desire Paradox," Middlesex MD blog, May 08, 2013, https://middlesexmd.com/blogs/drbarb/46969539-wanting-what-you-have-the-love-desire-paradox

Chapter 21: Your Highest Calling

1. "Malala Yousafzai: Facts," The Nobel Peace Prize 2014, NobelPrize.org, accessed August 4, 2021, https://www.nobelprize.org/prizes/peace/2014/yousafzai/facts/

Chapter 22: Compassion Without Action Is a Waste of Emotion

1. Kathryn Reid, "2010 Haiti Earthquake: Facts, FAQs, and How to Help," Worldvision.org, updated November 25, 2019, https://www.worldvision.org/disaster-relief-news-stories/2010-haiti-earthquake-facts

2. "Compassion," Merriam-Webster.com, accessed August 4, 2021, https://www.merriam-webster.com/dictionary/compassion

3. "A Commitment to Philanthropy," Givingpledge.org, accessed August 4, 2021, https://givingpledge.org/Pledger.aspx?id=177

4. "Pray With Your Feet," General News/Repairing the World, Centralsynagogue. org, January 12, 2014, https://www.centralsynagogue.org/news/pray-with-your-feet

Chapter 22: ~~Consumerism~~. ~~Materialism~~. Philanthro-Capitalism!

1. "Philanthropy," Merriam-Webster.com, accessed August 4, 2021, https://www. merriam-webster.com/dictionary/philanthropy

2. Kabira Namit, "What Have the Romans Ever Done For Us? A Brief Examination of the Roman Welfare State," Econ+ Blog, June 14, 2016, https://econplus. wordpress.com/2016/06/14/what-have-the-romans-ever-done-for-us-a-brief-examination-of-the-roman-welfare-state/

3. William J. H. Boetcker, *Inside Maxims: Gold Nuggets Taken from the Boetcker Lectures* (Wilkinsburg, Pa., Inside Publishing Company, 1916). Quote appears in "Fact check: William J. H. Boetcker Quote Misattributed to Abraham Lincoln," Everything News, Reuters.com, August 25, 2020, https://www.reuters.com/article/uk-factcheck-lincoln-quote-boetcker/fact-checkwilliam-j-h-boetckerquote-misattributedto-abraham-lincoln-idUSKBN25L1NF

4. Amounts according to "Clinton Foundation," CharityNavigator.org, accessed August 4, 2021, https://www.charitynavigator.org/ein/311580204

5. https://www.frank-mckinney.com/caring-house-project/donate/

6. Brandon Park, "2,350 Bible Verses on Money," Churchleaders.com, November 30, 2017, https://churchleaders.com/outreach-missions/outreach-missions-articles/314227-2350-bible-verses-money.html

7. Boetcker, Inside Maxims.

8. Bhikkhu Bodhi, "Dāna: The Practice of Giving," Accesstoinsight.org (Kandy, Sri Lanka: Buddhist Publication Society, 1995), https://www.accesstoinsight.org/lib/authors/various/wheel367.html

Chapter 24: Your Hebrews 13:2 Story

1. Muhammad Ali and Hana Yasmeen Ali, *The Soul of a Butterfly: Reflections on Life's Journey* (New York: Simon and Schuster, 2004): 103.

Chapter 25: With Aspiration YOU Will Change the World

1. https://www.worldometers.info/world-population/

2. Rebecca Wojno, "How One Compassionate Man Saved the Lives of Over 300 People," Goodnet.org, February 15, 2019, https://www.goodnet.org/articles/how-one-compassionate-man-saved-lives-over-300-people

3. https://www.mentalfloss.com/article/63389/roosevelts-man-arena

Aspire! Index Goes Digital

Some people (like me) love being able to use a book's index to find references to particular topics or search for stories that we loved. Well, now you can find the topics and references you're searching for in an instant—with *Aspire!*'s unique online, digital index!

You can access it in one of two easy ways:

#1: Go to https://www.frank-mckinney.com/the-aspire-book/index/

#2: Use your mobile device to scan the QR code below:

When you access the complete Digital Index for *Aspire!* from your computer or mobile device, you can search for any word or phrase in the book and instantly be referred to the page numbers that address that topic. You'll also see snippets of text that appear around the term to provide a little context and make the reference clear.

We hope you will agree this is a better and easier experience (and saves paper too) that will allow you to dive even deeper into *Aspire!* Happy searching!

Made in the USA
Middletown, DE
07 March 2023

26332715R00217